PRIORITIZING FAITH

Prioritizing Faith

*International Religious Freedom
and U.S. Foreign Policy*

Ashlyn W. Hand

NEW YORK UNIVERSITY PRESS
New York

NEW YORK UNIVERSITY PRESS
New York
www.nyupress.org

Library of Congress Cataloging-in-Publication Data
Names: Hand, Ashlyn W., author.
Title: Prioritizing faith : international religious freedom and U.S. foreign policy /
Ashlyn W. Hand.
Description: New York : New York University Press, [2025] | Revision of the author's thesis
(PhD, University of Texas at Austin, 2021) under the same title. | Includes bibliographical
references and index.
Identifiers: LCCN 2024060053 (print) | LCCN 2024060054 (ebook) |
ISBN 9781479838691 (hardback) | ISBN 9781479838721 (ebook) |
ISBN 9781479838714 (ebook other)
Subjects: LCSH: United States. International Religious Freedom Act of 1998. |
United States—Foreign relations—Law and legislation. | Religion and international
relations—United States. | Freedom of religion (International law) | Freedom of
religion—China. | Freedom of religion—Vietnam. | Freedom of religion—Saudi Arabia. |
International law and human rights.
Classification: LCC KF4650.A3281998 H36 2025 (print) | LCC KF4650.A3281998 (ebook) |
DDC 342.7308/52—dc23/eng/20250113
LC record available at https://lccn.loc.gov/2024060053
LC ebook record available at https://lccn.loc.gov/2024060054

This book is printed on acid-free paper, and its binding materials are chosen for strength
and durability. We strive to use environmentally responsible suppliers and materials to the
greatest extent possible in publishing our books.

The manufacturer's authorized representative in the EU for product safety is Mare Nostrum
Group B.V., Mauritskade 21D, 1091 GC Amsterdam, The Netherlands. Email: gpsr@mare-
nostrum.co.uk.

Manufactured in the United States of America

10 9 8 7 6 5 4 3 2 1

Also available as an ebook

For my mom,
and in loving memory of my dad.

But denunciatory rhetoric is so much easier and cheaper than good works, and proves a popular temptation. Yet is it far better to light the candle than to curse the darkness.
—William Lonsdale Watkinson, 1907

CONTENTS

ABBREVIATIONS

IRF   International Religious Freedom

IRFA   International Religious Freedom Act

NAE   National Association of Evangelicals

NRB   National Religious Broadcasters

RFRA   Religious Freedom Restoration Act

USCIRF   U.S. Commission on International Religious Freedom

UNHRC   U.N. Human Rights Commission

RGA   Religion and Global Affairs Office

DRL   Bureau of Human Rights, Democracy, and Labor

MFN   Most Favored Nation

WTO   World Trade Organization

NATO   North Atlantic Treaty Organization

CPC   Country of Particular Concern

CCP   Chinese Communist Party

SARA   State Administration for Religious Affairs (China)

CPVPV   Committee for the Promotion of Virtue and Prevention of Vice (Saudi Arabia)

CPV   Communist Party of Vietnam

BTA   Bilateral Trade Agreement

Introduction

This is a book about belief.

It is a story of competing beliefs about the relationship between religion and politics and about the nature of religion itself. Beliefs surrounding the United States' own unique religious history and its role in the world. Beliefs about U.S. foreign policy, the power of the executive branch, and the responsibility—if any—America has to religious believers worldwide.

It is also a story about beliefs of a supernatural order, ones that extend beyond space and time. Beliefs people die to protect. It considers the plight of Uyghur Muslims in China, evangelicals in Vietnam, agnostics in Saudi Arabia, and the millions of people the world over who dare to remain true to their deepest convictions, even in the face of persecution and death.

The Tipping Point

The story begins at the historic Mayflower Hotel, blocks from the White House. In January 1996, hundreds of evangelical heavyweights came together to protest one of the most pressing human rights crises of the time: worsening religious persecution, especially against Christians, across the globe. Within the small confines of DC proper, these types of gatherings and summits are manifold, often perfunctory, and without consequence. However, this meeting set off a cascading ripple effect, one the White House could not ignore.

The National Association of Evangelicals (NAE) had long lamented the pain of their fellow Christians persecuted around the world. But in the 1990s they demanded action—not only from their congregations and constituents, but also from the U.S. government. In the Statement of Conscience released after the meeting, the NAE stated plainly: "We know that the United States government has within its power and discretion the capacity to adopt policies that would be dramatically effective in curbing such reigns of terror and protecting the rights of all religious dissidents." They understood that the foreign policy establishment was hesitant to wade into questions of belief, but they believed the U.S. government could and should do more to protect those rights.

Meanwhile, in Congress, the struggle of religious minorities gripped the consciences of a few congressional members and their staff. Images of the torture of Tibetan monks in China, religiously motivated genocide in Sudan, and brutal attacks against the Coptic Christians in Egypt flashed across television screens nationwide and demanded a response.[1] Representative Frank Wolf, who would go on to spearhead initial congressional efforts on international religious freedom, argued that "religious freedom, often referred to as the first freedom, is of central import to the American experiment. As such, it should feature prominently in U.S. foreign policy."[2]

After an arduous process, these legislative efforts were successful, and Congress passed the International Religious Freedom Act (IRFA) in 1998. The legislation formally enshrined international religious freedom promotion as a "foreign policy and national security priority." President Clinton—somewhat reluctantly—signed it into law.

The IRFA was at once sweeping and limited. Its mandate required the executive branch to monitor and respond to religious freedom violations across the globe and to promote religious freedom instead. But its primary vehicle for taking on this ambitious goal was a tiny, ill-resourced office in the State Department—a State Department whose very leader referred to religion within diplomatic affairs as "treacherous." As the pages that follow detail, Secretary of State Madeleine Albright's fears were well placed. Engaging religion, specifically religious freedom violations, did "invite trouble." It still does. From the drafting of the legislation to its erratic implementation, the IRFA has been marked by difficulty across administrations. Why?

Because, in this story, as in most, beliefs prove to be resilient. Just as religious believers held tightly to their convictions, policymakers held tightly to their views about how America should conduct its foreign policy. And so the advocates and policymakers tasked with implementing the IRFA struggled to work within existing bureaucratic structures, mostly unable to persuade their leaders to believe that they should, as the law demanded, prioritize faith.

Favorable Conditions: Evangelical Advocacy and the Human Rights Movement

Though they reached a tipping point in the 1990s, efforts to combat religious freedom abroad did not begin during the Clinton administration. Evangelical advocacy and the broader human rights movement developed in parallel, creating fertile soil for the international religious freedom movement of the 1990s to flourish. Evangelicals founded powerful organizations like the NAE and the National Religious Broadcasters Association (NRB), both of which aimed at pushing back against the preeminence of Mainline Protestant influence and asserting traditional values domestically. But they also set their sights on engaging foreign policy, specifically to protect and extend missionary efforts that made worldwide evangelism possible. International religious freedom and the embedded rights to share and change your faith were central to the evangelical mission.

As evangelicals mobilized and amassed political power in the United States, another movement was gaining momentum: the push for international human rights. In the wake of the atrocities of World War II, the newly formed U.N. Human Rights Commission (UNCHR) worked quickly to draft the Universal Declaration of Human Rights (UDHR)—managing competing views of human rights in the process.

In the middle of the declaration is Article 18, which explicitly covers religious freedom protections. During the drafting process, the UNCHR went through multiple iterations—expansions and reductions—as it sought to define religious freedom. In the end, it read: "Everyone has the right to freedom of thought, conscience, and religion. This right includes freedom to change his religion or belief, and freedom, either alone or in community with others and in public or private, to manifest his religion or belief in teaching, practice, worship, and observance."

The most contentious part of the article was the "freedom to change his religion or belief." Some believed that the inclusion of this phrase, which would be incompatible with some of the world's religions, encapsulated a specifically American vision of religious freedom. Despite the controversy, the right to evangelize and change one's religious beliefs was incorporated into the final document. Along with the International Covenant on Civil and Political Rights, the Helsinki Accords, and the Declaration on the Elimination of All Forms of Intolerance and Discrimination Based on Religion or Belief, the UDHR set the legal foundation for the development of the IRFA.[3]

It is within this context the international religious freedom movement found its moment. Advocacy organizations like Voice of the Martyrs, Open Doors, International Christian Concern, and Christian Solidarity Worldwide gained significant traction. Prominent *New York Times* writer Abe Rosenthal repeatedly called for "an awakening" to the realities of Christian persecution and the gross inadequacies of the U.S. response.[4] For many Christians, once they turned their attention toward their suffering brethren overseas, they could not look away.

Lamenting perceived inaction from the executive branch, Congress took notice. Efforts of congressional leaders like Tony Hall (D-OH), Tom Lantos (D-CA), Nancy Pelosi (D-CA), Joe Pitts (R-PA), John Edward Porter (R-IL), Chris Smith (R-NJ), and Frank Wolf (R-VA) in the House, and Sam Brownback (R-KS), Dan Coats (R-IN), Joseph Lieberman (D-CT), Richard Lugar (R-IN), Don Nickles (R-OK), Sam Nunn (D-GA), and Arlen Specter (R-PA) in the Senate, and their committed staffers, would prove consequential. Many of these congressional leaders witnessed the effects of persecution firsthand and believed that this was the moment for U.S. action.[5]

What began as an effort to help persecuted Christians was met with pushback from the broader human rights community, which insisted that the legislation be expanded to aid religious believers of all types. After months of tense negotiations, Congress passed the IRFA. It created a new Office of International Religious Freedom at the State Department to be led by the ambassador-at-large for international religious freedom. It also created a mechanism for monitoring religious freedom conditions abroad and a process to designate countries with egregious violations as Countries of Particular Concern (CPC). The CPC designation triggered mandatory action from the executive branch, though these ranged from significant sanctions to public denouncement.

As the next chapter will describe in detail, though the final vote to pass the IRFA was unanimous, it was preceded by bitter internal fights. Several scholars note the existence of external bureaucratic tensions like regional desk officers who feared human rights concerns would derail their diplomatic efforts or human rights activists who resented religious freedom's elevation as a special concern. But *Prioritizing Faith* surfaces another key challenge in IRFA's passage and implementation: a clear internal tension within the international religious freedom community. This book identifies two competing groups—the IRF Purists and the IRF Pragmatists. Allen Hertzke describes the group that came together to lobby for the IRFA's passage as an "unlikely alliance."[6] But the "unlikely alliance" was never perfectly aligned. This framing provides a useful tool in understanding the tense, and sometimes personal, fights that took place during the drafting of the legislation and later, during the first two decades of its implementation.

Defying Predictions: Religion's Resurgence

That this "alliance," however divided, existed at all is surprising, given the widespread belief in the later twentieth century that religion would lessen in importance and fade as a major driver of international relations. During the mid-twentieth century, the primary theoretical frame describing religion and international affairs was secularization theory. Secularization theory found its roots in some of the most preeminent intellectuals of the nineteenth century. Scholars like Émile Durkheim, Max Weber, and Sigmund Freud all believed that, as the world industrialized, the role of religion in governing society would lessen and eventually shrink into obsolescence. Durkheim understood religion as another metaphor for understanding social order.[7] Weber predicted, with some regret, that scientific progress and the "iron cage" of rationality might render religiosity and other premodern worldviews outdated.[8] Freud considered religion an infantile quest and thus welcomed secularization as a necessary step toward greater human maturity.[9] For their different reasons, these scholars believed that religion's influence was on the decline. As C. Wright Mills explained: "Once the world was filled with the sacred—in thought, practice, and institutional form. After the Reformation and the Renaissance, the forces of modernization swept across the globe, and secularization, a corollary historical process, loosened the dominance of the sacred. In due course, the sacred shall disappear altogether except, possibly, in the private realm."[10] This hypothesis set the foundation for sociological inquiry for decades.

Popularized by sociologist Peter Berger, secularization theory contended that as societies modernized, religious activity would recede.[11] Secularization theory also posited that religious freedom would increase with modernity because religion's role in society would be less important.[12] In 1968, Berger predicted that by "the 21st century, religious believers are likely to be found only in small sects, huddled together to resist a worldwide secular culture."[13] This reductive attitude seeped into the U.S. diplomatic corps, too. After all, if religion was not a meaningful lever in shaping world affairs, then what was the incentive for "inviting trouble"?[14]

Despite the theory's popularity and academia's almost dogmatic assent to its premises, over time, history disproved its claims. Religiosity expanded in most regions of the world, even while those regions modernized. In the 1980s and 1990s, titles like "Secularization, R.I.P." and "Toward Desacralizing Secularization Theory" flooded sociological journals.[15] The data confounded conventional wisdom, and, as the world welcomed the twenty-first century, religious believers were hardly huddled together in small sects. They were more numerous and more powerful than ever. Indeed, scholars Monica Duffy-Toft, Daniel Philpott, and Timothy Shah forcefully argued in *God's Century* that religiosity and its associated political power have been on the rise over the last several decades, representing a reversal in trends that undergirded secularization theory. The implications here are difficult to overstate as religion is, and will likely remain, "a vital—and sometimes furious—shaper of war, peace, terrorism, democracy, authoritarianism, national identities, economic growth and development, productivity, the fate of human rights, the United Nations, the rise and contractions of populations, and cultural mores regarding sexuality, marriage, the family, the role of women, loyalty to nation and regime, and the character of education."[16]

It is difficult to deny this religious resurgence. Even in the late 1980s and 1990s, global rates of religious belief increased to 73 percent. By 2000, the number jumped to 79 percent.[17] In 2017, as PEW released its latest report on the "Changing Global Religious Landscape," 84 percent of the world's population believed in God.[18] Even more, this same report predicts that by 2060, this rate will rise to a staggering 87.5 percent. Potential reasons behind this resurgence vary widely. Political scientist Gilles Kepel offers several potential factors, including societal confusion, postindustrialization, exponential population growth, and increased literacy rates.[19] Others highlighted the spread of democracy for religion's ascent, noting that many prophetic political movements "will emerge from democratic processes more organized, more popular, and more legitimate than before—but quite possibly no less violent. Democracy is giving world's peoples their voice, and they want to talk about God."[20]

What do these developments mean for international relations? And what do they mean for international religious freedom? Many scholars have noted the dual effects of religion in society, simultaneously causing division and unity. As religion rises as an increasingly salient factor in world politics, so too do its associated challenges and opportunities. On the one hand, history shows a brutal record of violence and terrorism, often in the name of God. But religion can also promote reconciliation, inspire generosity and care for the most vulnerable, and promote human dignity.

In most places throughout the world, the relationship between governments and religious actors is tense, if not hostile. As governments recognize religion's growing influence, efforts to control and repress religion have also increased. In 2018, PEW reported that some 28 percent of countries within its "Global Restrictions on Religion" study (56 of 198), had "high" or "very high" rates of religious restriction. For moderate levels of restrictions, the numbers jump much higher. A growing literature on religious persecution chronicles the reverberations of repression.

In his pioneering work *Why Men Rebel*, published in 1970, Ted Gurr argues that minority discrimination produces grievances against the state. The shared experience of discrimination creates new linkages of solidarity. Combined, these factors make minority groups more likely to turn to violence and can lead to religion-related civil wars.[21] More recently, Nilay Saiya conducted a global quantitative study, affirming that when minority groups feel constrained by the state, they commit more acts of terror. In Saiya's research, he terms religious freedom a "weapon of peace."[22] Even as scholars and advocates shifted toward caring more about religion and its role in international affairs, specifically the problem of religious repression, questions on what that should mean for U.S. foreign policy remained contested.

But advocates were ready to highlight one of the most pervasive policy challenges of the day: religious persecution across the globe. It is an enduring problem with effects ranging from minor inconveniences to genocide. At the individual level, victims experience imprisonment, displacement, and death. However, the consequences also reverberate outward, causing refugee crises, regional instability, and, thus, large-scale violent conflict.[23] During its 105th session in 1997–98, Congress considered numerous pieces of legislation related to persecution, focusing on Christians in Pakistan,[24] Assyrians in the Near East,[25] and Christian minorities in China, among others.[26] In that same year, Congress lamented the treatment of Tibetan Buddhists[27] and Baha'i in Iran.[28] But the most substantial legislative effort surrounded international religious freedom around the world.

Defining Foreign Policy in a Post–Cold War World

The passage of the IRFA cannot be separated from its unique historical moment. At the end of the Cold War, existing paradigms governing U.S. foreign policy required reconsideration. The mission of U.S. foreign policy shifted, as Susan Woodward writes, "from defender of the free world and its principles to an unlimited guardian of global order and morality." The implications of this mission shift are difficult to exaggerate. Woodward continues, it left "the United States with no criteria for intervention, no ideology to define national interest, no clear basis for making choices, amongst the many occasions calling for external action."[29] How should the United States handle governments that are committing grievous assaults against the human rights of their people? What diplomatic response from the U.S. government will give it leverage to make a difference in these places? Should it even be trying to influence foreign governments? Or is it outside the bounds of a pragmatic foreign policy strategy?

By the time Congress passed the IRFA, human rights promotion was already identified as a formal foreign policy aim.[30] Congressional and executive branch efforts in the 1970s and 1980s solidified the linkage between human rights and trade and military assistance. Strategically, this linkage implied a critical connection between human rights and U.S. national security. The question at the crux of the debate shifted from

"Should the U.S. prioritize human rights concerns abroad or U.S. security?" to the more meaningful, and arguably more challenging question "What is the relationship between human rights priorities and U.S. security?" This is an important and often ignored distinction; indeed, the international religious freedom community grapples with it today. To what degree is U.S. national security predicated on religious freedom conditions abroad? And, even without a pressing security threat, do we have a moral obligation to aid the persecuted?

To be clear, this book does not offer complete answers to these questions. It does, however, emphasize the role of geopolitics in determining presidential decision-making on international religious freedom. Critics often reductively paint presidents' decisions about international religious freedom as either a result of their being for or against international religious freedom, and, as one journalist quipped, "like motherhood and apple pie, religious freedom is one of those things that's awful hard for a politician to seem to oppose."[31] But IRF's successes and failures must be placed within their larger foreign policy contexts. Somewhat ironically, one of the major criticisms from international religious freedom advocates concerns the lack of integration of the issue within the broader foreign policy calculus. The United States should not compartmentalize international religious freedom, they argue. But, when writing on the subject, they often fail to consider the geopolitical contexts involved.

Attention, Priorities, and Constraints

Prioritizing Faith focuses on the first two decades of IRFA's implementation, looking at the Clinton, Bush, and Obama administrations. Each administration under study occupied a unique moment in U.S. foreign relations. For Clinton, it was a unipolar moment. For Bush, the moment was defined by the attacks of 9/11 and the War on Terror, and, for Obama, the return of great power politics.

It is easy to inflate the attention given to a policy area when it is the only subject under study. But an honest account places international religious freedom relatively low on the agenda, across the three administrations.[32] Presidential attention is limited. Sometimes presidents can establish their own priorities but often the agenda is usurped by outside events, problems that are inherited from a previous administration and persist over time, and in response to constituent demand.[33]

Across the three presidencies under study, the number of issues vying for attention was overwhelming. Without the simple frame that the struggle against communism provided, the Clinton administration grappled with the question of how to define American interests and the role of American leadership in global affairs. Despite Clinton's campaign promises to focus on domestic issues and economic growth, intensifying human rights crises in Somalia, Rwanda, and the Balkans captured attention, as did China's trade status and the expansion of the North Atlantic Treaty Organization (NATO). Regarding international religious freedom, the Clinton administration represents the final hold-out of a previous paradigm that avoided intertwining religion and diplomacy. But it was also a turning point. By the end of his term, Clinton signed the IRFA. Importantly, it was during this period that the U.S. National Security Strategy articulated international religious freedom as a foreign policy priority.

George W. Bush was more vocal with his support for international religious freedom and more directly involved in its promotion, meeting with dissidents and issuing public statements. After the terror attack of 9/11, the War on Terror dominated President Bush's agenda. By the beginning of his second term, Bush articulated the Freedom Agenda and directly connected U.S. security to human freedom around the globe. President Obama's foreign policy approach, and his approach to international religious freedom, represented a fundamental departure from the Bush administration's efforts. Obama's tenure marked the return of great power politics. Regarding international religious freedom, Obama focused on religious engagement, creating a new organization at the State Department, and prioritized international efforts over unilateral action.

The bureaucratic mechanisms evolved too. Most of the analysis in this book centers on the two bureaucratic agencies created by the IRFA: the IRF office at the State Department and the U.S. Commission for International Religious Freedom (USCIRF). An analysis of the IRF office is really an analysis of several organizations, as it changed significantly and grew tremendously through the years. What began as a small office expanded rapidly, and the bureaucratic challenges it faced at the beginning dissipated over time. This chapter necessarily considers other adjacent bureaucratic mechanisms. This is particularly true for the Obama administration, which created the Office of Religion and Global Affairs as part of the Community and Faith-Based Initiatives Program.

Throughout the period under study, the IRF office's positionality within the State Department limited its efficacy, particularly in the first decade of IRFA's implementation. Lodged within the Bureau of Human Rights, Democracy, and Labor (DRL), the IRF office had little clout. Given the bureaucratic structure at the State Department, the regional bureaus retained most of the decision-making power, and regional bureaus often resented what they perceived as an overreach of functional bureaus. But for the IRF office, the tension was even worse. It was a niche bureau within an already ostracized functional bureau. These tensions took considerable time, mental space, and emotional energy to navigate. As expected, these compounding effects limited the IRF office's ability to make a change on the ground.

But, within these constraints, policy entrepreneurs were able to leverage uncertainty, amass power, and create change. In the absence of such policy entrepreneurs, however, the issue fell off the agenda.

Plan of the Book

The first half of this book begins with a deeper look at the driving factors that allowed for IRFA's passage in the first place. It is an interesting historical account in its own right, but those interested in modern-day policy will find the blueprint for many of IRFA's implementation challenges today. It then considers the foreign policy strategies of each administration and how international religious freedom was prioritized—or not. Finally, part 1 shows how strategy at the top levels of government interacted with the bureaucratic mechanisms present during each administration.

Part 2 of the book considers the effectiveness of IRF policy on the ground in three countries: China, Saudi Arabia, and Vietnam. Each of these cases involves a country with severe restrictions on religious freedom but explores diverse dynamics. They were selected after initial exploratory interviews and with the aim of showcasing diverse human rights challenges and varying degrees of policy leverage afforded to the IRF office, given the U.S. strategic interests involved. Each of the governments under study restrict religion for particular reasons and in specific ways. In China, persecution involves multiple faith communities, allowing for greater insight into how the United States handled governments that are generally opposed to religion rather than states that only discriminate against individuals in the minority religion(s). The case of China also highlights the complications involved in balancing human rights concerns involving another major world power. As such, the China case provides an opportunity to analyzes foreign policymaking when other priorities—like economic prosperity, regional stability, and national security—are also involved.

The Vietnam case considers another communist regime, one whose treatment of religion mirrors the Chinese system. However, this case shows the difference in IRF policy when the U.S. operated from a position of clear leverage. It was also a unique time when the IRF office creatively used the IRFA to create meaningful change on the ground.

Finally, the case of Saudi Arabia was selected, in part, because of the reasons for religious persecution within the country. It provides an opportunity to explore the challenges of promoting international religious freedom within a theocratic regime. The Saudi government views itself as the guardian of the faith, rigorously adhering to its strict interpretation of Wahhabism and opposing anything that might undermine its fidelity. The case underscores the delicate balance between advocating for religious freedom and addressing religious extremism. And it provides an opportunity to consider how religious freedom promotion can help protect nonbelievers. Moreover, like the China case, it provides another example of how religious freedom concerns were balanced against other foreign policy priorities and strategic interests.

Prioritizing Faith considers the effects of religious repression on individuals and systems. Successful efforts protect individuals from the effects of religious discrimination or persecution and promote systematic change with greater respect for religious freedom. Determining success in these scenarios is difficult for several reasons. First, it is often the case that the most repressive regimes are also the most secretive, limiting communications and squashing dissent. Thus, finding reliable data sources that accurately measure conditions on the ground is a challenge. Even more, progress in this policy space can be difficult to quantify. For example, the threat of arrest or punishment in a hostile regime may keep individuals from practicing their faith at all. Thus, typical quantifiable measures—how many individuals were imprisoned for their beliefs? How many churches were destroyed?—may fail to capture the reality for believers on the ground. As one former IRF staffer noted about competing with economic priorities at the State Department, "You're pitting something that's really tangible against something that's very amorphous and nebulous." Another challenge here is that defining success requires a balancing of short-term goals with longer-term societal change. As one senior State Department official put it, "The true goal involves generational change, with more people believing that inclusion matters and more people understanding that pluralism is a value instead of a threat."[34]

On the individual level, this book does take into consideration efforts to advocate on behalf of religious prisoners. This approach is profoundly important. It quite literally saves lives. In so doing, it also restores families, renews hope for progress, and strengthens communities that have been negatively impacted by repression. The pages that follow include powerful stories of individuals who, with the help of the IRF office's advocacy, were freed. At times, the IRF office secured large-scale amnesty programs whereby dozens of prisoners were released, as occurred in Vietnam during both the Clinton and Bush administrations. Also, at the microlevel, this book considers IRF efforts to help specific religious groups and houses of worship. These actions took many forms such as helping a church register, preventing a mosque's destruction, and advocating for the education and placement of clergy.

But again, these microlevel efforts are only one avenue for progress. Exclusively focusing on individual cases leaves the IRFA apparatus in a grim whack-a-mole game. Elliott Abrams put it bluntly: "They can jail them faster than we can get them out."[35] Advancing religious freedom necessitates a systemic approach that addresses the root causes of persecution.[36] As such, *Prioritizing Faith* also considers systematic change usually by noting significant shifts in the legal code and new government programs. It appraises Saudi Arabia's efforts to reform its religious police and Vietnam's overhauling of its religious registration process. Importantly, part 2 of this book analyzes implementation of such changes. As IRF Ambassador John Hanford noted, "Implementation is where the rubber meets the road."[37]

PART ONE

1

Sustained Advocacy and the International Religious Freedom Act

Writing for *The American Mercury* in 1954, prominent evangelical Billy Graham warned with apocalyptic urgency, "Either communism must die, or Christianity must die."[1] Graham's warning resonated with the American people, especially evangelicals who understood the Cold War as an age-old battle between good and evil, between providential liberty and godless totalitarianism. With the triumph of democracy fundamentally linked to the preservation of the Christian faith, the stakes were high. Against this bleak backdrop and new tensions dividing Protestants in America, evangelicals ascended as a formidable advocacy force. Simultaneously, the international human rights movement gained momentum, and, in 1948, countries around the world came together to draft the Universal Declaration of Human Rights. In the wake of the Cold War, Jewish activists emerged as another key group fighting for human rights, particularly religious freedom. Also, in the latter half of the twentieth century, new questions about the rightful scope of American foreign policy emerged. Each of these parallel developments combined to create fertile soil for the movements of the 1990s to flourish, culminating in the passage of the International Religious Freedom Act (IRFA).

This chapter summarizes the contours of these dynamics, considering the foundational efforts of congressional leaders, advocacy organizations, the human rights community, and the evangelical lobby. It contextualizes the IRFA and situates its passage as a policy success that resulted from years of sustained effort and widespread mobilization. Furthermore, it identifies the primary debates in human rights advocacy during this period and analyzes the predominant criticisms of the legislation. And, since current debates mimic the debates 1990s, this chapter offers more than a historical account; it also provides a frame for understanding why the issue remains so contentious today.

The final section of this chapter considers two types of criticisms levied against the IRFA. The first type, which criticized IRFA's purpose, largely came from outside the IRF community. However, the second line of criticism, which considered IRFA's scope and effectiveness, highlighted divisions among supporters of international religious freedom efforts. Allen Hertzke describes the group that came together to lobby for the IRFA's passage as an "unlikely alliance."[2] But, again, the "unlikely alliance" was never perfectly aligned. Instead, two competing groups emerged: the IRF Purists and the IRF Pragmatists. This framing provides a valuable tool for understanding the tense and sometimes bitter fights that took place during the drafting of the legislation and, later, during the first two decades of its implementation.

Early Evangelical Advocacy

After two decades of relative inaction, in the 1940s, the evangelical movement sought to assert itself more forcefully in American political life.[3] In 1942, just months after the attack at Pearl Harbor, prominent pastor Harold J. Ockenga gave an impassioned speech entitled "The Unvoiced Multitudes," whereby he lamented the position of evangelicals in the United States. Likening evangelicals to small nations threatened by Japan and Germany, Ockenga called for sustained and united evangelical action.[4] Ockenga's friendship with J. Elwin Wright, the leader of a small Pentecostal network in New Hampshire called the New England Fellowship, motivated the creation of the National Association of Evangelicals (NAE). These leaders formed the new organization to represent a growing number of evangelicals in the United States who no longer aligned with the Mainline Protestant advocacy organization, the Federal Council of Churches.[5] Similarly, two years later, in 1944, evangelical broadcasters founded the National Religious Broadcasters Association (NRB) in response to growing concerns that the Mainline Protestant churches were attempting to censor their communications by lobbying the major networks and generating unfair regulatory practices that required approval from traditional denominations, to which most evangelicals did not belong. During the 1940s and 1950s, Christian organizations like Catholic World Relief and World Vision, founded in 1943 and 1950, respectively, built extensive networks overseas and advocated for humanitarian relief.

Activism intensified over the next two decades, especially in the 1960s, as evangelicals pushed back against the burgeoning progressive counterculture. Instead, they reasserted their commitment to traditional family values, universal morality, and, faced with growing secularism, the necessity of evangelism. Evangelicals did not constrain their commitment to evangelism to the domestic sphere. In her book *To Bring the Good News to All Nations*, historian Lauren Turek chronicles the revival of evangelical missionary activity, which coincided with the increasing political influence of the Christian right and public attention to international human rights concerns in the mid-1970s.[6] Many evangelicals could not draw neat boundaries between sacred commitments and secular responsibilities. Nor did they believe they should try. Writing about missionary activity in the late 1940s and early 1950s in China, historian William Inboden notes, "Some missionary organizations . . . saw their work as an extension of American foreign policy—and saw American foreign policy as an extension of their work."[7] Similarly, undergirding evangelical foreign policy lobbying in the 1960s and 1970s was a sincere commitment to fulfill the Great Commission, the biblical mandate encapsulated in Matthew 28, where Jesus calls his followers to "go and make disciples of all nations, baptizing them in the name of the Father and of the Son and of the Holy Spirit."[8]

In the summer of 1974, the International Congress on World Evangelization (ICOWE) convened in Lausanne, Switzerland, to discuss a unified, international approach to spreading Christianity across the globe. By this point, Christianity in the Global South was already expanding rapidly. Evangelicals found commonality with many growing religious communities in Africa and Latin America, partly because of their conservative theological convictions. ICOWE provided an avenue to capitalize on these newly formed relationships.[9] The resulting agreement, the Lausanne Covenant, quickly became one of the most formative documents in American evangelical history. The covenant mentions international religious freedom specifically in its Article 13. Here, it calls upon governments "to guarantee freedom of thought and conscience, and freedom to practice and propagate religion in accordance with the will of God."[10] This focus on the right to propagate one's religion, instead of only the right to believe, was intentional. Faced with increased pushback and ongoing allegations of religious imperialism, many Protestant churches shifted their focus from evangelism toward social justice initiatives. This tension and criticism reappeared throughout advocacy efforts to pass the IRFA and, later, in the early days of its implementation. Aimed first at providing relief for religious adherents living in repressive regimes, the commitment to religious freedom, as laid out in Article 13 of the Lausanne Covenant, also protected evangelicals' most sacred purpose: to spread the Gospel. As Turek notes, "Evangelicalism requires evangelism."[11]

The Push for Universal Human Rights

As evangelicals mobilized and amassed political power in the United States, another movement was gaining momentum—the push for international human rights. The United Nations (U.N.) was founded in October 1945, weeks after the official end of World War II. With the U.S.-Soviet alliance deteriorating, the newly created U.N. Human Rights Commission (UNCHR) quickly drafted what would become the Universal Declaration of Human Rights (UDHR). In her seminal work *A World Made New: Eleanor Roosevelt and the Universal Declaration of Human Rights*, Mary Ann Glendon notes that the Declaration's drafters "had to surmount linguistic, cultural, and political differences and overcome personal animosities as they strove to articulate a clear set of principles with worldwide applicability."[12] These delegates included Eleanor Roosevelt from the United States, Peng Chun Chang of China, René Cassin of France, and Charles Malik of Lebanon.

For the most part, delegates from Western Europe and North America wanted to focus on first-generation rights, which encompassed an individual's civil and political liberties. This class of rights protected an individual's physical security, thus prohibiting torture or slavery, and guaranteed a person's right to free expression and political participation. Second-generation rights, which socialist governments often touted as preeminent, focused on equality. These included rights to basic human needs like healthcare and nutrition. Balancing the often competing values of liberty and equality proved a formidable challenge for the drafters of the Declaration, but, after vigorous debate, the UDHR was signed in December 1948. In the end, it covered both first-

Figure 1.1. Eleanor Roosevelt addresses the U.N. General
Assembly at the United Nations, July 1947. Source: Franklin D.
Roosevelt Presidential Library and Museum.

and second-generation rights. The final version included thirty articles
ranging from basic principles of human dignity and equality, guarantees of freedom of movement and prohibitions against slavery and torture. Other articles promised economic, social, and cultural rights.

In the middle of the Declaration is Article 18, which explicitly covers
protections for religious freedom. Charles Malik played an outsized role
in developing the final article. Malik, a Lebanese scholar and diplomat,
argued vehemently for the universality of human rights, and scholars
note that his contributions "allowed human rights at the U.N. to transcend their European genealogy."[13]

As human rights scholar Linde Lindkvist describes in his book *Religious Freedom and the Universal Declaration of Human Rights*, in some

ways Article 18 diverged from previous international documents from the early twentieth century because it distinguished between the internal commitments one makes (freedom of conscience) and the external expressions of one's faith.[14] As they considered religious freedom, contentious debates emerged among the committee members. How should the committee handle communist understandings of human rights, which subordinate the individual rights to the health of the community?[15] Was the term "conscience" sufficiently expansive and inclusive? Should Article 18 specifically mention God or the sacred? In the end, Article 18 read: "Everyone has the right to freedom of thought, conscience, and religion. This right includes freedom to change his religion or belief, and freedom, either alone or in community with others and in public or private, to manifest his religion or belief in teaching, practice, worship, and observance."[16]

Expectedly, the most contentious part of the article was the phrase "freedom to change his religion or belief"—an amendment added into later drafts of the Declaration, at Malik's pleading. At the time, Malik was moved to fight for the change after witnessing many victims of religious persecution flee to Lebanon.[17] While the amendment was adopted, it caused significant controversy, particularly among majority Muslim countries that were deeply resentful of Christian missionary activity and feared that the amendment might encourage apostasy.[18]

Indeed, this phrase was largely the cause of Saudi Arabia's notable abstention from signing the UDHR.[19] Because of its strict interpretation of the Qur'an and the regime's insistence that only Muslims could be citizens, Saudi officials argued that Article 18 was incompatible with Islam.[20] Within Sharia law, committing apostasy or speaking against Islam is illegal. (Chapter 6, which covers international religious freedom efforts in Saudi Arabia, explores these complex legal dynamics in greater detail.)

International agreements from the latter half of the twentieth century set the foundation for the development of the IRFA. It explicitly mentioned the UDHR, the International Covenant on Civil and Political Rights, the Helsinki Accords, the Declaration on the Elimination of All Forms of Intolerance and Discrimination Based on Religion or Belief, the U.N. Charter, and the European Convention for the Protection of Human Rights and Fundamental Freedoms.[21]

Human Rights and the Struggle Against Communism

The rise in prominence of evangelical advocacy and the growth of the international human rights movement occurred as new questions concerning the proper role of U.S. foreign policy emerged. Should the United States get involved when other governments repress religion? Under what conditions and for what purposes?

These questions stemmed from diplomatic relations between the United States and the Soviet Union, and one issue, in particular, garnered ongoing attention: the Kremlin's systematic harassment and persecution of Soviet Jews. The Soviet Union prevented Soviet Jews from emigrating by enforcing prohibitive costs associated with renunciation of Soviet citizenship and, separately, for applying for exit visas. After applying for permission to leave, the government targeted Soviet Jews, often resulting in the loss of employment and the confiscation of property. Sustained advocacy for Soviet Jews began in the 1950s and gained momentum in 1964 as Leonid Brezhnev assumed power and cracked down on dissidents. For many Soviet Jews, the Six-Day War inspired renewed pride in their Jewish identity and a desire to emigrate to Israel. The lobbying efforts surrounding Jewish refuseniks were extensive, well coordinated, and ongoing. Cases like Andrei Amalrik and Natan Sharansky gripped the nation's attention. Groups like the American Jewish Conference on Soviet Jewry (AJCSJ), the Moscow Human Rights Committee (MHRC), Wives for Soviet Jewry, and the Academic Committee on Soviet Jewry, among many others, campaigned to increase U.S. and international involvement and to pressure the Soviet Union to change.

Then, in 1972, Senator Henry Jackson (D-WA) and Representative Charles Vanik (D-OH) introduced what would become the Jackson–Vanik Amendment, an amendment to the Trade Act connecting U.S. trade relations with human rights expectations. In so doing, it made the extension of Most Favored Nation (MFN) status to nonmarket economies incumbent on freedom to emigrate. President Nixon and Secretary of State Henry Kissinger opposed the Jackson–Vanik Amendment, believing instead that improving trade relations with the Soviet Union would make détente more tenable. On March 7, 1974, Kissinger testified in front of the Senate Committee on Finance, "Let us remember that we seek détente with the Soviet Union for one overwhelming reason: Both countries have the capability to destroy each other—and most of the rest of the world in the process. Thus, both of us have an overriding obligation to do all in our power to prevent such a catastrophe."[22]

President Nixon argued that the nuclear age predetermined the aims of foreign policy "not by our choice, but by our capability."[23] In private, Nixon's and Kissinger's words were more chilling. "The emigration of Jews from the Soviet Union is not an objective of American foreign policy," Mr. Kissinger said. "And if they put Jews into gas chambers in the Soviet Union, it is not an American concern. Maybe a humanitarian concern."[24] The release of these conversations in 2010 led to revived outrage. In a column in *The San Diego Union-Tribune*, Michael Gerson lamented the "sad limits of realism . . . discounting American ideological advantages in global ideological struggles."[25] After recognizing the offensiveness of this comment and issuing an apology, Kissinger pushed back against what he deemed a reductionist reconstruction of past events: "Gerson presents the issue of Jewish emigration from the Soviet Union in the 1970s as if it had been an abstract debate between those who relied on a relaxation of tensions and advocates of ideological confrontation, in which the realists were willing to sacrifice Jewish emigration on the altar of détente. The opposite is true. That emigration existed at all was due to the actions of 'realists' in the White House."[26]

Combined, Kissinger's comments crystallized his view and the views of many in the traditional realist camp of international relations during the Cold War era: The United States should be careful not to allow humanitarian concerns to define the American interest or dictate its foreign policy strategy. Indeed, in this view, progress made on the humanitarian front would be because of the realist approach, not despite it. Congress disagreed. In a watershed moment for the human rights community, Congress unanimously adopted the Jackson–Vanik Amendment, and then-President Gerald Ford signed the Trade Act into law in January 1975. The Soviet Jewry movement exemplified how a concerted group could mobilize and alter foreign policy. Evangelicals took notice and expanded their focus. Instead of focusing only on Soviet Jewry and the rights of emigration, evangelicals lobbied on behalf of Christians in the Soviet bloc, particularly unregistered Baptists and Pentecostals.[27] Organizations like Voice of the Martyrs (VOM),[28] founded by Richard

Wurmbrand, and Open Doors, founded by Andrew van der Bijl, proved effective in mobilizing support for Christians behind the Iron Curtain.[29]

In the years to come, the movement to protect Soviet Jewry and the passage of the Jackson–Vanik Amendment proved to be an essential model for international religious freedom advocacy two decades later. It demonstrated that Congress could take meaningful steps to advance human rights, with or without executive branch backing. In the shadow of the Watergate scandal and the painful turmoil of the Vietnam War, the American public resented what they saw as executive branch over-reach and welcomed congressional action to promote human rights.[30] The events of the 1970s foreshadowed what was to come almost twenty years later when President Clinton grappled with his own scandal, and the American people, led by a concerted group of advocates, pushed for congressional action to promote religious freedom.

In the wake of Nixon's resignation, Ford continued the policies of his predecessor, preferring to focus on international order rather than human rights. Of his Cold War strategy, President Ford argued, "What is more moral than peace, and the United States is at peace in the world."[31] But human rights activism in the international community was on the rise. In 1975, the Conference on Security and Cooperation in Europe (CSCE) met in Helsinki, Finland, leading to the signing of the Helsinki Final Act, a critical juncture in embedding human rights protections in international norms. Signed by the United States, the Soviet Union, Canada, and thirty-two European nations, the Helsinki Final Act contained three "baskets" of priorities. Besides political, military, and economic considerations, the act included specific provisions for human rights, cultural cooperation, and freedom of the press. Activists criticized Ford for not holding the Soviet Union accountable for its commitments at Helsinki.[32] But, soon after its passage, the international community's monitoring groups like the Moscow Helsinki Watch Group and the Helsinki Commission emerged, further institutionalizing human rights and religious freedom.

In the presidential race of 1976, President Ford and Democratic nominee Jimmy Carter went head-to-head on a myriad of divisive issues. The threat of communism loomed large. The recent Supreme Court decision *Roe v. Wade* incensed traditionalists. American anger over U.S. involvement in Vietnam raged. The Equal Rights Amendment (ERA) caused divisions to surface. The shame of Watergate left many votes disaffected. The magnitude of the issues on the table led historian Daniel K. Williams to say of the election: "Whether they fully realized it or not, their campaigns were not only about who should be the nation's chief executive but also about what the ideological identities of the parties should be."[33] Newsweek also termed 1976 "The Year of the Evangelical," and evangelical heavyweights like Jerry Falwell and Billy Graham urged Christians to exert their voice in politics with vigor. Initiatives like "I Love America" laid the groundwork for founding the Moral Majority three years later.[34] In addition to budding domestic efforts, international organizations like Christian Solidarity International were formed to promote religious liberty and provide aid to victims of religious repression.

With the evangelical vote split between candidates, President Jimmy Carter, a devout man and self-described born-again Christian, confounded the evangelical community. On the one hand, he was one of their own, with an unassailable commitment to his faith and the Southern Baptist denomination. But he followed a strict separationalist approach with matters of church and state. Carter opposed prayer in schools and expanding tax credits for church property beyond formal houses of worship. He vocally supported the ERA, a cause that vexed many evangelicals. Still, with his faith, open criticism of Kissinger-style détente, and commitment to human rights, the evangelicals hoped for progress in U.S. foreign policy and religious freedom concerns abroad. In the words of political scientist Clair Apodaca, in the Carter era "human rights would redefine the identity of America and act as a salve to overcome the Nixon legacy."[35]

In October 1977, the State Department established the Bureau of Human Rights and Humanitarian Affairs.[36] The following year, Carter issued Presidential Directive 30, which identified human rights promotion as a formal foreign policy aim.[37] PD-30 included dual purposes: 1) reducing violations of the integrity of persons and 2) enhancing civil and political liberties. Violations of the integrity of persons include blatant harm like torture, arbitrary imprisonment, and other forms of inhumane treatment. In the religious freedom context, these efforts included negotiating a religious prisoner's release or securing religious dissidents' rights to flee a persecuting country. Carter's administration succeeded at many points, using quiet diplomacy to negotiate with governments on specific cases, like securing the release of Soviet Baptist pastor Georgi Vins in 1979. However, many saw this type of casework as insufficient, requiring too much government attention without long-term changes.[38] To many, Carter seemed less inclined to act on the second aim of PD-30, the promotion of civil and political liberties. Many criticized Carter's human rights policy as being soft on communism, attacking right-wing dictators far more than left-wing ones.[39] These tensions fractured the Democratic Party, and many neoconservatives joined the Republican ranks.[40] Carter's perceived inaction also frustrated evangelicals, a reality made clear in the next presidential election.

In 1980, Republican presidential nominee Ronald Reagan's platform pledged unapologetic support for conservative social issues and a firm commitment to economic improvement at home. His foreign policy agenda focused on defeating communism. He secured the evangelical vote and won the election in an unexpected landslide. Historian Andrew Preston argues that the most remarkable feat was "his own idealistic synthesis, successfully blending the militant nationalism of the religious conservatives with the peaceful aspirations of religious liberals."[41] Preston also notes Reagan's reliance on Judeo-Christian values as a tool to unite forces against secularism. This tactic was not new. Reagan resurrected it from the Truman and Eisenhower eras and redeployed it in the 1980s. Years earlier, President Eisenhower minimized theological differences to rally Protestants, Jews, and Catholics together under the inclusive banner of "God and country."[42] This language resonated with evangelicals in the eighties, who understood the Cold War in stark terms as a war against atheistic evil.

Soon after Reagan's election, a new conception of human rights solidified in direct opposition to the liberal understandings of human rights espoused by the Carter administration. Historian Barbara Keys attributes this divergence from opposing reactions to the horrors of the Vietnam War.[43] Liberals grieved America's responsibility for the violence, while conservatives lamented communism's victory. When articulating human rights policy, "liberals aimed to abandon what they saw as an outmoded fixation on anti-communism . . . though concerned with Soviet repression, they felt it was most important to battle repression where there was an element of American culpability."[44] Conservatives rejected this "false guilt." In their view, this misplaced regret led the Carter administration to ignore human rights abuses in communist countries, which subsequently contributed to the fall of the shah in Iran and the Somoza regime in Nicaragua. In response to the perceived failure of the Carter administration, Reagan's conception of human rights delineated between totalitarian and autocratic regimes and defended its preferential treatment of the latter. As Reagan's ambassador to the United Nations, Jeane Kirkpatrick, stated: "It is not a betrayal of the democratic idea to imply that some dictatorships are better than others."[45] In addition, Reagan's policy centered international terrorism as a primary human rights concern.

Historian Rasmus Sinding Søndergaard attributes Reagan's newfound commitment to human rights—at least as his administration so defined it—to mounting congressional pressure for executive branch action.[46] In particular, he identifies several congressional leaders, such as Representative John Porter (R-IL) and Representative Tom Lantos (D-CA), as foreign policy entrepreneurs who wielded outsized political power because of the coalitions they formed.[47] These two formed the Congressional Human Rights Caucus (CHRC) in 1983. The bipartisan caucus included hundreds of members, and its efforts were vital in securing widespread support for U.S. human rights activism and efforts to promote religious freedom. Tom Lantos was a victim of the Holocaust in Hungary, which contributed to his firm commitment to protecting religious minorities around the globe. An active Baha'i community within his constituency in Illinois prompted John Porter to devote considerable attention to the plight of Baha'i in Iran. The work of the CHRC brought attention to persecuted groups across the world by bringing together victims with congressional leaders through programs like the Religious Prisoners Adoption Program and the Soviet Christian Adoption Program.[48] These programs institutionalized efforts promoted by evangelicals and the activist community throughout the 1970s.

The position of assistant secretary of state for human rights remained vacant for almost a year after Reagan took office. His first pick, Ernie Lefever, withdrew his nomination, knowing he lacked Senate support. Elliott Abrams took the job in December 1981 after he put forth what he termed "a summary of neocon foreign policy" with the Kennedy–Clark memorandum. Abrams found a welcomed supporter in Secretary of State George Shultz, who lent credence to the Human Rights Bureau, elevating its status within the U.S. State Department. These efforts led to the establishment of the National Endowment for Democracy (NED).

In the years that followed, Reagan enjoyed consistent support from evangelicals. By this time, the political aims of the NAE were overt. In 1986, the NAE established the Peace, Freedom, and Security Studies Program (PFSS). In direct contrast to Mainline Protestant initiatives that focused only on arms control, PFSS focused on confronting totalitarianism in addition to nuclear proliferation.[49] After finding a leader in Reagan, NGOs focused on religious persecution, like Voice of the Martyrs, grew during this period.[50]

Grappling with Post–Cold War Confusion

President George H. W. Bush took office in January 1989. Later that year, the world witnessed the fall of the Berlin Wall. As the Soviet Union dissolved, existing U.S. foreign policy paradigms required reconsideration. James Baker, who served as Bush's secretary of state, described the uncertainty of the moment: "We are in a period without precedent. We no longer have a clearly defined adversary. We no longer have a clearly defined objective."[51]

One of the most obvious cases vying for attention was China. In May 1989, the Chinese Communist Party (CCP) declared martial law as demonstrators coalesced in Beijing. Inspired by the death of prominent reformer, Hu Yaobang, the demonstrators, many of them students, pushed for democratization. They advocated for a free press and the freedom of conscience. They demanded political autonomy. The CCP sensed the power undergirding the movement. Subsequently, it met the peaceful protest with fury. On June 4, 1989, the tension reached a breaking point as troops moved into Tiananmen Square, firing indiscriminately into the crowd. Death tolls from the massacre vary widely, ranging from several hundred to several thousand lives lost.

Many criticized the Bush administration for its response—or, rather, for its lack of response. What President Bush considered "reasoned, careful action" considering "long-term interests and recognition of a complex internal situation in China," many Americans saw as inadequate.[52] Some interpreted the administration's restrained reaction as apathy. While President Bush was intentionally unemotional on the subject, many Americans sought an impassioned and immediate castigation of the CCP. Bush's nuanced approach to U.S.-China relations, undoubtedly influenced by his former role as U.S. chief liaison to Beijing in 1974–75, proved challenging to communicate to the American people. These complexities and "countervailing priorities" could be read as political weakness rather than astute political strategy.[53] These criticisms were early indicators of a growing movement in the United States—a movement that would demand U.S. action to confront human rights abuse in China. Writing for *Christianity Today* in 1989, prominent evangelical Chuck Colson argued emphatically, "What a tragedy if, at the very moment the oppressed masses of the East reach for the torch of democracy, the West disintegrates, morally unable to sustain the spirit by which democracy must be fueled."[54]

In the 1992 presidential campaign, then-Governor Clinton capitalized on this critique, lamenting that "when China cracked down on pro-democracy demonstrators, exported weapons to radical regimes, and suppressed Tibet, Mr. Bush failed to stand up for our values. Instead, he sent secret emissaries to China, signaling that we would do business as usual with those who murdered freedom in Tiananmen Square."[55] As it would turn out, Clinton's tough stance on China's human rights record proved too difficult to maintain, and the early 1990s brought with it many new foreign policy challenges. (These dynamics are discussed in detail in chapter 4.)

After the Cold War, the evangelical foreign policy agenda also expanded.[56] Besides causes like fighting the AIDS epidemic ravaging Africa and confronting human trafficking, evangelicals marshaled support for international religious freedom. The 1990s also provided new opportunities for alliances to form in the struggle for human rights. Political scientist Allen Hertzke writes: "The end of the Cold War also meant that the quest for human rights would no longer be submerged within superpower rivalry. The endless and often debilitating debate between liberals and conservatives about the relative evil of superpower clients—of right-wing versus left-wing dictatorships—was rendered moot. As these ideological veils were lifted, new alliances for the cause became possible."[57]

International Religious Freedom Finds Its Moment

Amid the confusion of post–Cold War foreign policy, congressional leaders, advocates, and religious leaders were beginning to act. A group of legislators from both parties joined to develop strategies and eventual legislation that would focus on human rights and, specifically, religious freedom. These developments occurred when the U.S. foreign policy apparatus often avoided religion and while the academic community argued that religion would continue to fade into irrelevance as a factor in international relations.[58] Congressional leaders Tony Hall (D-OH), Tom Lantos (D-CA), Nancy Pelosi (D-CA), Joe Pitts (R-PA), John Edward Porter (R-IL), Chris Smith (R-NJ), and Frank Wolf (R-VA) in the House, and Sam Brownback (R-KS), Dan Coats (R-IN), Joseph Lieberman (D-CT), Richard Lugar (R-IN), Don Nickles (R-OK), Sam Nunn (D-GA), and Arlen Specter (R-PA) led the way to highlight religious freedom abroad. By the mid-1990s, these efforts would coalesce into large-scale action impossible to ignore.[59]

Outside the halls of Congress, mobilization efforts among activists and religious groups were also gaining momentum. Research organizations like the Center for Religious Freedom at Freedom House and advocacy organizations such as Voice of the Martyrs and Open Doors at home and International Christian Concern and Christian Solidarity Worldwide, abroad, gained significant traction.[60] Books like *Their Blood Cries Out* by Paul Marshall and Lela Gilbert and *In the Lion's Den* by Nina Shea, both published in 1997, chronicled the plight of persecuted Christians around the globe and served as another catalyst for action.

With the evangelical machinery firmly established, leaders like Don Argue, Richard Cizik, Chuck Colson, and Richard Land ardently supported nascent efforts to protect religious freedom, focusing on Christians suffering persecution. Drawn together by Michael Horowitz, a former official in the Reagan Administration, the NAE met in Washington, DC, in January 1996 for a summit focused on persecution around the world. The summit resulted in a Statement of Conscience, which called for action:

Religious liberty is not a privilege to be granted or denied by an all-powerful State, but a God-given human right. Indeed, religious liberty is the bedrock principle that animates our republic and defines us as a people. We must share our love of religious liberty with other peoples, who in the eyes of God are our neighbors. Hence, it is our responsibility, and that of the government that represents us, to do everything we can to secure the blessings of religious liberty to all those suffering from religious persecution.[61]

Over a hundred influential evangelical leaders attended the summit which garnered national attention. Drawn to the cause in part by his Jewish heritage, Michael Horowitz heavily influenced the forthcoming legislative efforts. Known for his rather bold way of speaking, Horowitz made plain his motivation: "Evangelicals were with us on Soviet Jewry, and it was time to pay them back. . . . You're only allowed to sit out one Holocaust each lifetime."[62] Recognizing the work of evangelicals who advocated for Soviet Jews and passed the Jackson–Vanik Amendment years earlier, Horowitz took the lead on championing the rights of persecuted Christians. Overtly political, the Statement of Conscience took aim at the State Department, calling for "more carefully researched, more fully documented and less politically edited reports."[63]

The message from the summit in Washington resonated. Churches mobilized, and the movement expanded. Under the leadership of the World Evangelical Fellowship, the evangelical community declared the last Sunday of September an International Day of Prayer for the Persecuted Church. This event brought together over one hundred thousand congregations in the United States and religious groups from eighty-two other countries.[64] This event also marked the beginning of new coalitions as Pentecostals, Catholics, and other denominations joined traditional evangelical churches to pray for persecuted Christians. This growing movement of activists, religious leaders, and congressional leaders dialed up the pressure on the executive branch to act with urgency.

When Secretary of State Warren Christopher announced the creation of the 1996 Advisory Committee on Religious Freedom Abroad, he attempted to appease a now formidable movement without compromising presidential authority. Assistant Secretary of State for Human Rights, Democracy, and Labor John Shattuck convened the committee early in 1997. There, he laid the foundation for the committee's work: to increase awareness of religious persecution abroad and to "amplify U.S. concern and action about religious freedom."[65] In his remarks, he poignantly described the dual nature of religiosity. He acknowledged that "religious differences have been manipulated to instigate bloody and sometimes genocidal conflicts" but recognized that "religion is often a key factor in the resolution of those conflicts." Preempting the now common criticism of insufficient action, Shattuck continued, "The establishment of the Advisory Committee on Religious Freedom Abroad is one indication of U.S. Government recognition that more can and should be done to address the issue."[66]

Secretary of State Madeleine Albright joined the committee's initial meeting and stated: "Religious freedom belongs squarely in any comprehensive discussions that we should be having and are having about American foreign policy."[67] She stressed the importance of increasing monitoring and accountability surrounding religious freedom, noting with "better information about when persecution begins and if we have thought more creatively about how to bridge differences and build tolerance."[68] In addition, Secretary Albright maintained that increased understanding in this area would allow the State Department to better support religious leaders in restricted countries, hoping to encourage reconciliation.[69] NSC staffer Matthew Lorin hoped a well-organized meeting, well-attended by major political players like Shattuck and Albright, would increase the amount of serious coverage the issue received instead of "the religious politics that have plagued this initiative since its inception."[70]

Albright's remarks set the stage for the development and organization of the Advisory Committee. They divided their work into two parallel goals. First, they would report on the state of religious freedom abroad, paying particular attention to the status of minority groups. Second, they would focus on encouraging interreligious cooperation to facilitate reconciliation.[71] These two goals encompassed a wide range of efforts, from understanding the grievances of persecuted groups, easing democratic transitions, and finding alternative ways to leverage community religious leaders.[72]

Political tensions surrounded the creation of the committee. In an email to senior leadership, Lorin defended the timing of the announcement of the committee, arguing that the administration had "been promising to announce this committee since April and have been fully prepared for two weeks. However, certain key members, who are under considerable pressure from their constituencies not to participate, re-quested that we postpone until after the elections." Lorin explained the necessity of working around John Shattuck's tough schedule because, "without him, we are concerned that it may appear that we are seriously low-balling—a criticism that has already been launched at us for choos-ing to establish this committee at State as opposed to a Special Advisor to the President."[73] In June 1998, President Clinton appointed Robert Seiple as the State Department senior advisor for international religious free-dom. While imminently qualified, with years of leadership experience serving as president of World Vision, the Clinton administration also chose Seiple to satisfy evangelicals calling for more definitive action. The administration hoped that if evangelicals perceived adequate executive branch action, they might back off their lobbying efforts in Congress.

Congressional Activism and Legislation

The Wolf–Specter Act

Despite the budding efforts at the executive branch to consider religious freedom in foreign policy, congressional leaders continued to push to elevate the issue further, resulting in several congressional hearings where advocates and victims of persecution shared their stories. During the 105th Session (1997–98), Congress considered numerous pieces of legislation related to persecution in Pakistan, the Near East, and China.[74] That same year, Congress lamented the treatment of Tibetan Buddhists and Baha'i in Iran.[75] In a congressional hearing in 1997, Sam Brownback denounced the perceived inaction of the U.S. government, noting: "Because of many diplomatic reasons and sometimes, unfortunately, just sheer indifference, our government and others in our country have not chosen to speak out in some cases. The press is always hyper-sensitive to the observation of civil and human rights but finds the idea sometimes of religious freedom less interesting. Our silence has only emboldened the persecutors."[76]

Less than a month after Brownback's remarks, Representative Frank Wolf introduced H.R. 1685, the Freedom from Religious Persecution Act. Senator Arlen Specter (D-PA) sponsored a concurrent bill in the Senate (S. 772), and the legislation became known as the Wolf–Specter Act. Wolf–Specter focused on preventing egregious persecution. It per-tained to the "widespread and ongoing persecution of persons because of their membership in or affiliation with a religion or religious denomination, whether officially recognized or otherwise, when such persecution includes abduction, enslavement, killing, imprisonment, forced mass resettlement, rape, or crucifixion or other forms of torture."[77]

The act mandated the creation of the Office of Persecution Monitoring in the executive branch and required the imposition of sanctions. With few exceptions, Wolf–Specter limited exports and terminated U.S. assistance to offending governments. The act showed that the United States would actively work against multilateral efforts to secure nonhumanitarian aid or development assistance. Initial versions of the legislation included a section about Sudan, where ongoing persecution against Christians and moderate Muslims was brutal. Activism for the Sudanese case represented "a global moment in faith-based advocacy and humanitarianism."[78] While sponsors eventually dropped this section from the bill, the outrage over the atrocities in Sudan motivated congressional activism on international religious freedom during this period.

The Wolf–Specter Act garnered support from a variety of actors. As expected, prominent evangelicals like Chuck Colson and James Dobson mobilized their followers to advocate for the legislation. Organizations like the NAE, the Southern Baptist Convention, the National Religious Broadcasters, the Christian Coalition, and the Family Research Council lent their support. Outside of the evangelical community, the U.S. Conference of Catholic Bishops joined the efforts. Rabbi David Saperstein, a prominent Jewish activist and ardent supporter of religious freedom, initially criticized the bill for being unbalanced. Saperstein worked with the Catholic Conference to offer recommended changes, many of which Representative Wolf included in updated versions of the legislation.[79] Saperstein and other representatives from non-Christian faith communities called for more inclusive language in the findings section of the bill, resulting in specific mentions of Tibetan Buddhists, Muslim Uyghurs, and Baha'i in Iran. With devoted lobbying efforts and a more inclusive strategy, diverse groups like the International Campaign for Tibet, the Anti-Defamation League, and the National Jewish Council signaled official support for the legislation.

With the Wolf–Specter Act, the Clinton administration found itself on shaky ground. While praising the bill's intent with sensitivity, the administration challenged "the blunt instrument," arguing that it ran "the

risk of harming vital bilateral relations," created "a confusing bureaucratic structure," and established "a de facto hierarchy of human rights
violations."[80] Fearing repercussions for trade, many in the business community also fiercely opposed the act, including the National Foreign
Trade Council. The debates surrounding Wolf–Specter revealed a growing tension within the Republican Party between religious conservatives
and business interest groups. A controversial set of memos, leaked by
progressive news magazine *Mother Jones*, detailed the happenings of a
high-level meeting of USA*Engage, an anti-sanction lobbying group, as
they strategized how to respond to the Wolf–Specter Act.[81] The memo,
written by Haliburton lobbyist Don Deline, reported that two State Department officials suggested they find religious leaders who would publicly oppose the bill. Deline narrowed in on Billy Graham and Drew
Christiansen as potential targets, both of whom eventually opposed the
bill.[82] The National Council of Churches, the ecumenical partnership of
Mainline churches, also opposed it. While the Wolf–Specter Act easily
passed the House, it faced many obstacles in the Senate. As criticism
mounted, other congressional members and their devoted staffs worked
on a new piece of legislation with a more flexible strategy. Eventually, it
would become the Wolf–Specter Act's Senate alternative.

The International Religious Freedom Act of 1998

The new legislation, which would become known as the International
Religious Freedom Act of 1998, served as a compromise. It was more
flexible. However, it did not pass without controversy. As Wolf–Specter
did not have enough support to get through the Senate, alternative
approaches surfaced. The Wolf–Specter Act ignited a sense of urgency;
after decades of activism, it galvanized diverse groups and put international religious freedom at the center of the foreign policy debates of
the 105th Congress. With the policy window finally opened, advocates
were hard-pressed to let it close without concrete legislation. Senator
James Inhofe (R-OK) put forth one novel approach. His was limited in
scope and focused only on persecution occurring in Sudan and China.
Lamenting the reduction in breadth and the expected loss of allies,
Horowitz and others vigorously opposed the initiative, and eventually,
Inhofe abandoned his efforts.[83]

The IRFA took an opposite approach, with an expanded scope. Introduced by Senator Don Nickles, it resulted from a bipartisan effort including Senator Richard Lugar (R-IN), Representative Bob Clement (D-TN), and Representative Tom DeLay (R-TX) and committed staff members like John Hanford, Laura Bryant, and William Inboden, respectively. Senator Joe Lieberman's (D-CT) staff helped fine-tune the legislation, and eventually, Lieberman added his name as a cosponsor. The Nickles–Lieberman Act did not focus on severe persecution alone but approached violations of religious freedom more broadly. Its explicit purpose was to "condemn violations of religious freedom, and to promote, and to assist other governments in the promotion of, the fundamental right to freedom of religion." This legislation took an incremental approach with various potential responses to violations, which was met with mixed reactions. "The goal," as Bryant stated, "is changing behavior. It's not punishment."[84] Still, Horowitz and many leaders who spent their capital promoting the Wolf–Specter Act believed the new legislation to be unnecessarily divisive. They viewed it as a threat to the international religious freedom movement. Many found the flexibility of the bill more workable, while others claimed it did not handle religious persecution with the seriousness it deserved. After a bitter and often unnecessarily personal battle, the legislation passed unanimously. While the Clinton administration still opposed encroachment on executive branch privilege, it recognized the IRFA as a compromise.

Elements of the Law

In contrast to the Wolf–Specter Act, the IRFA was broad.[85] It considered religious freedom conditions in each country instead of focusing only on the most egregious cases of persecution. The legislation itself found its foundation in international agreements.[86] In the legislation, the definition of religious freedom violation offered more specificity. Besides explicit persecution where people are targeted, imprisoned, or tortured because of their religious beliefs, the IRFA identified violations as including any "arbitrary prohibitions on, restrictions of, or punishment for" religious assembly and practice, expressing one's faith and educating one's children in the faith, changing religions, and possessing and distributing religious materials and texts.

The IRFA included seven subchapters: Subchapter I denoted activities at the State Department; Subchapter II established and directed the U.S. Commission for International Religious Freedom; Subchapter III concerned the National Security Council; Subchapter IV denoted presidential actions; Subchapter V considered religious freedom promotion and international efforts; Subchapter VI involved refugee and asylum policies; and the final section, Subchapter VII included miscellaneous provisions.

At the State Department, the IRFA established the Office on International Religious Freedom (IRF). The IRFA also established a new ambassadorship—the ambassador-at-large for international religious freedom, a position appointed by the president, confirmed by the Senate, who would report directly to the secretary of state. It tasked the office with compiling the Annual Report on International Religious Freedom to supplement preexisting Human Rights Reports.[87] By May 1st of each year, the IRFA required a detailed report for each country in the world, including 1) the status of religious freedom; 2) violations of religious freedom, if any; 3) U.S. policies and actions to promote religious freedom; 4) international agreements in effect; and 5) training of government personnel. The IRF office was then to deliver this report to Congress. This report identified Countries of Particular Concern, or CPCs, where persecution and limitations on religious freedom are severe. To qualify as a CPC, there must be: "Systematic, ongoing, egregious violations of religious freedom, including violations such as—(A) torture or cruel, inhumane, or degrading treatment or punishment; (B) prolonged detention without charges; (C) causing the disappearance of persons by the abduction or clandestine detention of those persons; or (D) other flagrant denial of the right to life, liberty, or the security of persons."

According to the IRFA, a CPC designation required government action. First, it indicated that with the help of human rights organizations, the U.S. government would draft policy possibilities to discuss in formal meetings with the offending government. Then, it required that the offending government enter a binding agreement whereby both nations agreed on a scheduled plan to stop religious freedom violations. If, for whatever reason, the binding agreement was untenable, then the U.S. government was required to respond punitively. The IRFA stipulated that all of these activities be reported to Congress.

The IRFA also established the U.S. Commission on International Religious Freedom, or USCIRF, an independent watchdog organization of nine commissioners tasked with making policy recommendations to the president, the secretary of state, and Congress on religious freedom violations and progress. To keep USCIRF bipartisan, the IRFA indicated that the president should appoint three commissioners, the president pro tempore of the Senate appoint three commissioners (two must be of the opposing party than the president), and the speaker of the House appoint three commissioners (again, two must be of the opposing party than the president). The Commission was formed, in part, to prevent international religious freedom from becoming lodged in the bureaucracy at the State Department.

The IRFA required that any CPC designations trigger mandatory presidential action unless an "important national interest of the United States" was at stake, and the executive branch called for a waiver. It stipulated a range of potential government actions, including public condemnations, cancellation of scientific or cultural exchanges, denial of state visits, withdrawal of U.S. development or security assistance, denial of loans or credits from the Export-Import Bank of the United States, direction of U.S. leadership of international financial institutions to oppose loans, restriction of exports, and a prohibition of major loans from U.S. financial intuitions to the offending government.[88] The IRFA also noted, to the disdain of many advocates, that large-scale and ongoing sanctions resulting from other human rights concerns could satisfy IRFA requirements. As opposed to the "one-size-fits-all" approach of the Wolf–Specter Act, these options were intended to provide the executive branch with ample opportunity to formulate a policy response tailored to the specifics of each case.

Finally, the IRFA amended Section 116 of the Foreign Assistance Act of 1961 to route funding to religious freedom advocacy and programming.[89] It included provisions to train U.S. officials adjudicating refugee cases to be informed and sensitive to religious freedom concerns.

IRFA's Critics

Much like the debates surrounding the passage of the IRFA, criticism of the legislation abounded on both sides, with some arguing the legislation was too expansive, and others that it was insufficient. The common criticisms fell into two categories: 1) criticisms of IRFA's purpose and its relation to U.S. foreign policy, and 2) criticisms of its effectiveness in achieving its stated aim. Subsequent chapters analyze the more granular, case-specific debates.

Criticisms of IRFA's Purpose

The first set of critiques, levied by many players with disparate views on foreign policy, involved the IRFA's stated purpose. They asked: Should the United States be doing this at all? Most times, they answered, emphatically, no. These criticisms typically involved allegations of cultural imperialism and hypocrisy, or idealism and naivete.

One of the most consistent criticisms against the legislation and international religious freedom advocacy was the claim that these efforts were a form of cultural imperialism. Even less generously, some claimed that the IRFA was but another attempt to exercise control over Muslim countries under the false pretense of humanitarianism and goodwill.[90] Critics maintained that religious freedom, at least as articulated in the legislation, was a Western concept without universal applicability. A common rebuttal to this line of inquiry was to point to international agreements that are not U.S.-specific, like the UDHR. However, as demonstrated by scholars like Anna Su, these lines are not immediately simplifying, as the United States played an outsized role in developing international human rights agreements in the first place, particularly in ensuring the inclusion of religious freedom as a protected right.[91]

Along these same lines was the enduring critique that the IRFA unfairly prioritized Christianity because it gave disproportionate attention to Christian groups suffering persecution, and that its design intentionally afforded Christian missionaries more latitude. This criticism and the surrounding conversation generated controversy. Most Americans in the late 1990s, when Congress passed the IRFA, identified as Christian. Pew Research Services reported that roughly 80 percent of Americans identified as Christian: 55 percent were Protestant, and 25 percent were Catholic.[92] Even if the operating assumption was that all people advocated on behalf of religious freedom equally, it would follow that, in the United States, most of the advocates would be Christian. Moreover, Christian philosophies—specifically Protestant theologies regarding individual conscience and free will—have contributed extensively to the conception of religious freedom in the United States and its role in U.S. foreign policy. As described earlier in the chapter, it is also true that evangelicals in the United States spearheaded the advocacy efforts leading to the IRFA's passage. These efforts began focusing specifically on ending Christian persecution. This is not to say that other groups were not crucial to the efforts; they were. As the previous section showed, the "unlikely alliance" of advocates, to borrow Professor Alan Hertzke's phrase, combined their efforts to push the legislation through the process. That said, Christians have dominated the conversation surrounding international religious freedom from the beginning. Speaking candidly, Laura Bryant, a fierce defender of religious rights and an instrumental figure in the IRFA's passage, noted: "The problem with the [original] bill was that it was focused on Christians. . . . It had this Christian focus. Now, I happen to be a Christian and I also work on this issue. You can't set up a foreign policy framework for the US government and isolate one group that you are going to write a bill for and not cover all these other groups."[93]

To be clear, the legislation developed, and its scope increased significantly from these original efforts. Nevertheless, the perception of the IRFA as being only from Christians and specifically for Christians remained throughout its passage and the early days of IRFA's implementation. Controversial appointments, especially of strident conservatives, to the IRF office and USCIRF exacerbated the tensions. Some have attempted to prove the bias quantitatively. For example, scholar Laurie Cozad, in her analysis of IRF policy in India, showed that the IRF reports in the early 2000s devoted considerably more attention to the plight of Christians in the country, who at the time made up just over 2 percent of the population than to the persecution of Muslims who made up approximately 12 percent. During this same period, violence killed thousands of Muslims. Christian deaths did not exceed ten.[94] This anecdotal evidence is not generalizable to IRFA's reporting of religious freedom conditions in India as a whole, let alone to IRFA's worldwide reporting. But, whether valid, the sentiment matters and has plagued IRFA from its inception. And the degree to which these initial efforts funneled into the policy itself, and thus to its implementation, remains contested.

Also controversial was the idea that the IRFA focused on protecting and expanding evangelical ministry efforts. In his book *For God's Sake:*

The Christian Right and U.S. Foreign Policy, Professor Lee Marsden argued that "an increased emphasis on religious freedom has provided Christian Right organizations with an opportunity to evangelize in areas previously inaccessible."[95] A bidirectional question emerged: Did Christianity spread because of religious freedom, or did the United States attempt to spread Christianity under the guise of international religious freedom? Since evangelical Christians focus on proselytizing as a core tenet of their faith, it followed that they would also take full advantage of opportunities afforded by greater levels of religious freedom. The subsequent concern of those against missionary activity abroad also followed.

A more widespread critique, in this same vein, argued that the IRFA encouraged the United States to intrude unnecessarily in moral debates across the world.[96] The rationale for wanting to avoid these types of moral entanglements was two-sided. Some made a distinctly moralist claim, pointing to perceived hypocrisy in U.S. policy. Acknowledging the United States' imperfect human rights record, they asked, How can the United States make self-righteous claims about religious freedom given its hypocritical record? This refrain quickly became a common tool used by foreign governments, too, in response to U.S. pressure.[97] Not specific to international religious freedom but applicable to all human rights challenges, this critique led to a preference to funnel all initiatives through existing international structures or to a more passive stance that precluded government involvement. Others who wished to avoid moral entanglements did so out of pragmatism. While grieved by the abysmal human rights abuses in much of the world, they argued for a limited scope in U.S. foreign policy.

Criticisms of IRFA's Effectiveness

The second set of critiques did not consider the purpose of the IRFA but its methods and tactics. Here, critics asked: Is this how the United States should promote religious freedom and curb persecution? Much like the arguments undergirding the first set of critiques, attacks on the efficacy of the IRFA came from many angles. As stated in the law itself, the goal was "to be vigorous and flexible, reflecting both the unwavering commitment of the United States to religious freedom and the desire of the United States for the most effective and principled response, considering the range of violations of religious freedom by a variety of persecuting regimes, and the status of the relations of the United States with different nations." On the question of how the United States should go about protecting religious freedom, some advocates found the legislation to be too flexible, rendering it "toothless" and ineffective. Others claimed that in attempting to be vigorous in its resolve, the legislation still excessively constrained the executive branch.

Madeleine Albright, while delivering a speech at Catholic University in 1997, argued that international religious freedom efforts, "although well-intentioned . . . would create an artificial hierarchy among human rights with the right to be free from torture and murder shoved along with others into second place."[98] This argument gained some traction, reappearing across news headlines. Why should there be a unique effort to promote religious rights while leaving the rights of the press and speech under the general jurisdiction of the human rights bureau? Advocates of international religious freedom responded in two different ways. First, some replied with a normative claim about the unique importance of religious freedom, the "first freedom."[99] They argued that religious freedom serves as a precursor and linchpin in securing other rights. However, others pointed to the State Department's relative inaction on religious freedom before congressional action in the 1990s. In this view, the IRFA was a response to religious freedom being left off the hierarchy altogether. Even so, what about other efforts that the United States had historically ignored? Some argued to expand IRFA's mandate to protect other marginalized and forgotten groups, like political prisoners.[100]

Of all the debates surrounding IRFA's effectiveness, those surrounding the proper role of the executive branch in matters of international religious freedom received the most attention. Some still thought the legislation unnecessarily tied the president's hands. This critique lessened from the Wolf–Specter Act since it gave the president more options and more broad waiver provisions, but some still thought the "mandatory action" required by the president was excessive. Alternatively, some saw the autonomy extended to the executive as sanctioning inconsistent policy. Reflecting on the early years of IRFA implementation, scholar Eugenia Relaño Pastor notes, "Where a violating nation can potentially be mined for some other benefit, the United States generally turns a blind eye to violations of religious liberty."[101] Again, as described earlier in this chapter, the Cold War–era debates shift back into focus.

Some claimed that the legislation, being about ending persecution and promoting religious freedom, was too broad and that the United States would be more successful if it handled these issues separately. Relatedly, many argued that, given the expansive aims of the act, it did not carry the resource allocation necessary to contend seriously with a problem as pervasive as religious repression. From an administrative standpoint, still others found the legislation to lack necessary strength.[102] Some advocates took issue with the "double-hatting" of sanctions, or the tagging of existing sanctions with the IRFA label to satisfy requirements. In short, they argued that nothing new would be done to stop egregious persecution. Instead, the IRFA became little more than a rhetorical tool rather than a serious mechanism supported by the force of American foreign policy. Even some fervent supporters of protecting religious freedom abroad questioned the efficacy of IRFA given broader constraints. Some argued that the foreign policy establishment in the United States was not adequately prepared to handle the evolution of public faith worldwide, despite the laudable rhetorical commitment of the IRFA.[103] In summary, while some thought the IRFA was foolishly grandiose, others believed its aim too limited.

IRF Purists and IRF Pragmatists

These initial debates and legislative battles surfaced significant tensions between members of the IRF community. One of the most consistent findings throughout the interviews for this book—across political parties and administrations—was the existence of two vastly different approaches to international religious freedom: the IRF Purists and the IRF Pragmatists.[104] Table 1 shows these distinctions. It should be noted that this frame is necessarily reductive, as all of the perspectives on international religious freedom cannot be neatly categorized nor perfectly captured by two groups. The IRF Purists, like Michael Horowitz and Nina Shea, still desired to make change for believers on the ground, and the IRF Pragmatists, like Bob Seiple and John Hanford, still often readily denounced religious repression. However, the approaches differed widely and caused significant tension.

TABLE 1.1. Different Approaches to International Religious Freedom

	IRF Purists	IRF Pragmatists
Ethical frame	Deontological	Teleological
Operating question	How can we stand against evil in the world?	How can we make significant, if incremental, change for believers on the ground?
Underlying premises	• We, as individuals and as a country, must vocally and publicly denounce evil. • Celebrating compromises on religious freedom is inadequate. We must, at all times and in all places, push for full respect for religious freedom.	• As individuals and as a nation, we must exercise caution and discretion when dealing with delicate diplomatic efforts like international religious freedom. • We must engage respectfully with other governments, providing encouragement for small steps forward.
Characteristics	• Often promotes black/ white thinking • Exclusively focused on international religious freedom • Demands immediate action	• Willing to recognize nuance • Contextualizes IRF with other foreign policy priorities • Uses long-term perspective

The following chapters rely on this frame to explain the often strained dynamics within the IRF community. The distinction, while blunt, also aids in understanding the relationship between USCIRF and the IRF office. USCIRF mostly adopted a Purist approach, partly because it was an independent organization focused only on international religious freedom. It was designed as a watchdog organization charged with analyzing and criticizing IRF's efforts and recommendations. Throughout the three administrations under study, it served an important public function, publicizing religious freedom violations and encouraging further progress. Conversely, the IRF office, by nature of its position within the State Department necessarily took a more diplomatic approach—it was more careful with its language, slower to recommend CPC designations, and more likely to celebrate even small wins. Chapter 3, which covers the bureaucratic elements involved in IRF policy, describes these tension points in greater detail. Part 2 of *Prioritizing Faith* shows how these bureaucratic tensions impacted policy implementation in China, Saudi Arabia, and Vietnam, respectively. The debates surrounding IRFA's passage did not evaporate in 1998. They affected bureaucratic arrangements, attention allocation, agenda-setting, and policy decisions at all levels.

2

Strategy and International Religious Freedom

In their book *The Politics of Attention*, political scientists Bryan Jones and Frank Baumgartner note that "decision makers, like all people, often ignore important changes until they become severe or until policy entrepreneurs with an interest in the matter highlight such changes."[1] As analyzed in chapter 1, the lead-up to the passage of the IRFA spanned several decades as policy entrepreneurs demanded the U.S. government pay more attention to the severe, and worsening, religious freedom conditions around the globe. But were these efforts, and the new congressional mandate, successful in bringing change? This chapter considers strategy and international religious freedom at the highest levels. Each presidential administration (Clinton, Bush, and Obama) articulated a commitment to international religious freedom, but they approached the subject differently. Some of this difference is personal. Each president had his religious convictions, way of incorporating religion into policymaking, and political party and constituencies to consider. External drivers also shaped the approaches as each president inherited a distinct foreign policy landscape and responded to world events outside his control.

The language of the IRFA purposely used internationally recognized definitions of religious freedom, as codified in the Universal Declaration of Human Rights (UDHR) and the International Covenant on Civil and Political Rights (ICCPR). Article 18 of the UDHR noted that "everyone has the right to freedom of thought, conscience and religion; this right includes freedom to change his religion or belief, and freedom, either alone or in community with others and in public or private, to manifest his religion or belief in teaching, practice, worship and observance."[2] Each of the presidents under study advocated for such an understanding of religious freedom despite the academic debates surrounding the universality of the concept. Instead, the contrasts in approach at the strategic level came from varied understandings of what constitutes adequate religious freedom promotion.

Distinct Contexts and Common Challenges

Each of the administrations occupied a unique moment in U.S. foreign relations. After the end of the Cold War, Clinton's era was marked by unchallenged American power, and Bush's presidency was defined by the aftermath of 9/11 and the wars in Afghanistan and Iraq. And for Obama, the focus shifted to the reemergence of great power competition in international relations.

With the dissolution of the Soviet Union and the end of the Cold War, Clinton intercepted a new iteration of American hegemony. But, without the fight against communism, which had dictated foreign policy and resource allocation for decades, the Clinton administration grappled with how to determine American foreign policy in the new unipolar era. Clinton attempted to focus on domestic issues, specifically strengthening the economy. But large-scale humanitarian disasters in places like Somalia, Rwanda, and the Balkans required policy attention.

During the 2000 campaign, Bush championed a foreign policy wary of nation-building—an approach that characterized the first few months of Bush's presidency.[3] However, the attacks of 9/11 disrupted this status quo and the administration's policy aims and military footprint expanded exponentially. Obama's foreign policy vision sought to decrease unilateral U.S. action and reduce military engagement. Obama also set his sights on Asia, hoping to establish a G-2 with China and pull attention away from the Middle East. But the Arab Spring forced him to change course.

Despite these divergences in approach and context, these presidents shared common strategic challenges. All three presidents sought a reset with Russia—efforts that proved largely unsuccessful. Each president undertook new military interventions, and each president, like all their predecessors, grappled with how to balance domestic and foreign affairs. Given these dynamic geopolitical considerations, the following section explains the unique approaches of each administration to international religious freedom efforts. But, in this arena, they shared similarities, too. Each president had to confront the deadly effects of religious extremism and the rise of militant Islam. And religious freedom, a counterbalance to pervasive repression and extremism, emerged as an attractive antidote—a "weapon of peace."[4] And, importantly, all three administrations designated China a CPC—a somewhat surprising development, given the competing strategic priorities involved (this case is discussed in detail in chapter 4).

The Clinton administration represented the final holdout of a previous paradigm that preferred avoiding religion in diplomacy. This trend was not in any way unique to Clinton himself. Instead, it represented the long-established dogma of the State Department, its roots in the realpolitik visions of foreign policy discussed in chapter 1. To be fair, the common discomfort of combining religion and foreign policy dissipated significantly throughout the Clinton years. With increasing congressional pressure and growing public awareness, international religious freedom became part of the foreign policy calculus. Between 1996 and the end of Clinton's time in office, the administration formed the Advisory Committee on Religious Freedom Abroad. Then, it appointed the first special representative of the secretary of state for international religious freedom. The IRFA, passed in 1998, elevated the position of special representative to ambassador-at-large for international religious freedom. It also created the Office of International Religious Freedom at the State Department and established the U.S. Commission for International Religious Freedom. Importantly, it was during this period that the U.S. National Security Strategy articulated international religious freedom as a foreign policy priority.

Because of his evangelical faith and the close relationship he shared with many in the international religious freedom community, George W. Bush was more vocal in his support for the cause. Bush was comfortable getting involved with religious freedom cases and spoke often of America's unique history and commitment to the "first freedom."[5] However, the War on Terror dominated his foreign policy agenda and highlighted the delicate tensions that can exist between religious freedom and religious extremism. In short, the geopolitical context of the Bush years made translating commitment to sustained policy outcomes difficult. International religious freedom under the Obama administration took on a decidedly more international approach, seeking to root America's commitment to international religious freedom in international law rather than American history. His strategy represented a new iteration of religion and foreign policy, best described as increased religious engagement. While many welcomed this broader approach, others lamented what they saw as a takeover of international religious freedom policy.

This chapter provides the context for the first two decades of IRFA policy—an important task, as it's easy to overstate the attention given a policy area when it is the only subject under study. But an honest account places international religious freedom relatively low on the priority list across the three administrations.[6] Lars Schoultz examines the tension of competing priorities in U.S. foreign policy. While he was considering the role of human rights, the sentiment likewise applies to international religious freedom efforts: "The importance of human rights is always a function of the other potential interests and values that impinge up on any given policy decision. . . . The question is not human rights versus no human rights; instead, it is human rights versus national security versus friendly relations with existing regimes versus economic benefits to the domestic economy versus humanitarian aid to impoverished people."[7]

Given this tension, this chapter considers how international religious freedom efforts fit within the broader foreign policy calculus. It considers the inclusion (or exclusion) of international religious freedom priorities within the National Security Strategies (NSS) of each administration. Mandated by Section 603 of the Goldwater–Nichols Department of Defense Reorganization Act of 1986, the NSS "is obligated to include a discussion of the United States' international interests, commitments, objectives, and policies, along with defense capabilities necessary to deter threats and implement U.S. security plans."[8] While not a perfect measure, inclusion or lack thereof in the National Security Strategy gives valuable insight into how the various presidents understood religious freedom efforts and its role in U.S. foreign policy.

This analysis of presidential strategy provides the groundwork for the case studies. Along with chapter 3, which considers bureaucratic changes, these chapters summarize the approaches to international religious freedom themselves. Part 2 details how these approaches were implemented on the ground. Part 2 will also provide the missing connective tissue between the large-scale strategic aims of the administration's respective foreign policy approaches and the bureaucratic agencies in charge of day-to-day decision-making and implementation.

Figure 2.1. President Clinton signs the Religious Freedom Restoration Act. Source: William J. Clinton Digital Library.

International Religious Freedom and Clinton's Vision

During his tenure, President Bill Clinton signed two sweeping pieces of legislation related to religious freedom into law: the Religious Freedom Restoration Act (RFRA) in 1993 and the IRFA in 1998. The RFRA enjoyed broad support from both political parties at the time, and the Clinton administration celebrated its passage. In his remarks at an interfaith prayer breakfast at the White House in 1993, Clinton lamented the secular policy environment of the time.[9] "The fact that we have freedom of religion," he said, "doesn't mean we need to try to have freedom from religion. It doesn't mean that those of us who have faith shouldn't frankly admit that we are animated by the faith, that we try to live by it, and that it does affect what we feel, what we think, and what we do."[10] He called upon the faith leaders present to exercise humility in this area to recognize their own human fallibility and work together for the common good. To use matters of faith to demonize the other side would be to "trivialize religion" and its role in policymaking. The results of the RFRA were extensive, preventing the government from impeding the free exercise of religion "even if the burden results from a rule of general applicability." That the RFRA drew such bipartisan support was evidence "that the power of God is such that even in the legislative process miracles can happen," Clinton quipped as he signed the legislation into law.[11]

Five years later, on October 27, 1998, President Clinton signed the IRFA and delivered a brief statement. As discussed in chapter 1, the Clinton administration challenged efforts to constrain or force executive branch action and initially opposed the Freedom from Persecution Act and the IRFA. Still, Clinton and his top leadership needed to signal that while they had problems with the legislation and disagreed with its prescribed methods, they supported the cause. As scholar Allen Hertzke notes, while the administration was more committed in its support for domestic religious liberty initiatives, Clinton "played a visible role in interpreting the significance and meaning of the "first freedom" in American domestic law and its application to international engagement."[12]

Despite the Clinton administration's initial misgivings about the legislation, international religious freedom advocates rightfully celebrate October 27, 1998, the day Clinton signed the IRFA into law, as a historic occasion. Still, it was but one of many priorities for the White House. Indeed, on the same day that Clinton signed the IRFA, he also signed legislation to strengthen Head Start programming; he delivered remarks at a roundtable on women and retirement security; and he attended a regional appointments event and gave a brief speech at a campaign reception held at Sharon and Jay Rockefeller's residence in advance of the midterm elections. In addition to the IRFA statement, the White House released statements on the Communities Opportunity Act, the Curt Flood Act, and the Crime Control and Safe Streets Amendment, and they released a letter to Congress concerning the ongoing emergency in Sudan.[13] International religious freedom remained a niche issue to be managed during a tense political moment in the United States.

What prevented Clinton from prioritizing international religious freedom during this time? The answer is multifaceted. First was the sheer number of issues vying for presidential attention, a consequence of a ballooning executive branch that affected each administration under study. With thousands of foreign and domestic policy issues fighting for a spot on the presidential agenda, something had to give. In 1998, Clinton faced an exceptionally crowded foreign policy landscape.

When Clinton came into office, he had little foreign policy experience. As former governor of Arkansas, he concentrated his efforts on domestic affairs, particularly economic growth. However, the post–Cold War geopolitical context required reevaluation. Priorities included extensive negotiations around trade policy. At the beginning of his presidency, Clinton supported an explicit linkage between China's human rights record and its status as a Most Favored Nation (MFN)—a position he eventually walked back. While the Reagan and H. W. Bush administrations laid the foundations for the North American Free Trade Agreement (NAFTA), Clinton formalized the agreement during his first term. Other large-scale foreign policy considerations vied for presidential prioritization, including a redoubling of counterterrorism agreements and ongoing negotiations for a Middle East peace agreement between Israelis and Palestinians.

From a human rights perspective, it is impossible to disconnect the activism that prompted the passage of the IRFA in 1998 from the atrocities that plagued the 1990s. While progress was being made in some regions of the former Soviet Union and South Africa, other places witnessed horror and genocide. In Rwanda, Hutu militias slaughtered over eight hundred thousand Tutsi civilians over only one hundred days beginning in April 1994. And, by the time Clinton became president, the conflict in Bosnia and Herzegovina was in full force, as Serb forces killed thousands of Bosnian Muslims in a brutal war. After years of unsuccessful mitigation efforts, the Clinton administration, under the leadership of Richard Holbrooke and Warren Christopher, helped negotiate the Dayton Peace Accords, an agreement successfully ending the conflict in the Balkans. In general, Clinton favored limited humanitarian interventions. He shifted away from broad democracy promotion efforts—especially after the terror of the Battle of Mogadishu in Somalia, the devastating loss of American lives, and the resulting outrage.

In the years after the Cold War, debates on how best to handle Russia and the former Soviet states continued. The Clinton administration wanted to ensure that the former Soviet countries could integrate into the global community without unduly aggravating tensions with Moscow, which resented the West's deepening relationships with Soviet satellite states. In the end, Clinton promoted the expansion of the North Atlantic Treaty Organization (NATO) and NATO's Partnership for Peace.

But not all the constraints on President Clinton's time and attention were policy-driven or political. They were personal. It is difficult to overstate the complexity of the year 1998 for Clinton. By the time he signed the IRFA, he was mired in scandal, with accounts of his inappropriate relationship with Monica Lewinsky surfacing in January. In August, Clinton testified about his actions, statements that would ultimately lead to his impeachment in December. And election season was well underway. Adding an unwanted layer of complication, many ardent supporters of international religious freedom in the Democratic Party were among the most vocally critical of Clinton's moral shortcomings.

At the end of 1998, *The Washington Post* recapped the year, noting that "the moral and religious implications of the Clinton affair overshadowed all other religion stories."[14] Here included was a description of the historic visit of Pope John Paul II to Cuba, the ongoing culture wars concerning gender and sexuality, confronting sexual abuse among clergy, and the passage of the International Religious Freedom Act.[15] Though there had been long-standing policy disagreements, Clinton's sex scandal significantly damaged his relationship with religious leaders around the country. Expectedly, he drew ire from conservative religious leaders, but, politically, Clinton's more significant problem came from within the Democratic Party. The sex scandal had alienated many in his party who defended the need for strong moral character and were unwilling to cede claims of moral superiority to the Republican Party. In a poignant speech on the Senate floor, Joe Lieberman issued a powerful rebuke: "But the president, by virtue of the office he sought and was elected to, has traditionally been held to a higher standard. This is as it should be because the American president, as I quoted earlier, is not just the one-man distillation of the American people, but today the most powerful person in the world. And as such, the consequences of his misbehavior, even private misbehavior, are much greater than that of an average citizen, a CEO or even a Senator."[16]

In an interview years later, Lieberman's chief of staff, William Andresen, noted that Lieberman "saw it as his obligation because of all the work he'd done on values issues. He felt he'd be a hypocrite if he let it go unremarked."[17] During the same period, he was championing international religious freedom efforts. International religious freedom appealed to 'values voters' and their congressional leaders on both sides of the aisle. Such a scandal, as publicized in painful detail by the Starr Report, damaged Clinton's reputation among this constituency. These voters lamented the threat to presidential legitimacy and feared that weaknesses in Clinton's character would limit America's ability to do good at home and abroad. This reality likely contributed to the Clinton administration's desire to reassert its commitment to the cause of international religious freedom, despite having vocally critiqued legislative efforts.

These political and personal challenges led to an overcrowded agenda, and a niche issue like international religious freedom rarely made the cut. Indeed, in Clinton's memoir, *My Life*, which is over one thousand pages, the IRFA gets one brief sentence, a note that he signed the act and appointed Robert Seiple, former CEO of World Vision, as the office's first ambassador-at-large.[18] After their second term, the Clinton–Gore team released a report entitled "The Clinton Presidency: Eight Years of Peace, Progress, and Prosperity," which chronicled the top accomplishments of the Clinton–Gore administration. The record of progress highlighted domestic initiatives to combat breast cancer, reduce class sizes, and expand Medicare, among many others.[19] On the foreign policy side, it included efforts to eliminate child labor, strengthen NATO, and combat sex trafficking. Of the 115 accomplishments listed, international religious freedom efforts was notably missing, as was the signing of the IRFA. Despite the omission, during Clinton's tenure, international religious freedom found a formal place within the U.S. foreign policy apparatus.

One of the most notable achievements for the IRF community within the Clinton administration was the introduction of international religious freedom in the National Security Strategy (NSS). The NSS distills a president's foreign policy priorities, and its inclusion of international religious freedom signaled an important shift. By the time Clinton included international religious freedom in the strategy, his second term was drawing to a close, but his successor drew upon those changes.

In the first NSS of the Clinton administration, "A National Security Strategy of Enlargement and Engagement," there were over twenty mentions of human rights and three mentions of religion. However, none of these centered on religious freedom or religious rights. Instead, it noted religious conflicts worldwide and, when describing the White House Conference on Africa, mentioned the inclusion of religious leaders. Over both presidential terms, the Clinton administration issued seven national security strategies.[20] Its final NSS, "A National Security Strategy for a Global Age," contains twenty-three mentions of religion and nine of religious freedom and rights, marking a significant shift from the earlier iterations. The first NSS to specifically include religious freedom was in 1997.[21] Though Congress had not yet passed the IRFA, by this point, pressure for the executive branch to act was mounting. This strategy, "A National Security Strategy for a New Century," stated that the U.S. "will work with international institutions to combat religious persecution" and specifically mentioned standing with the world's most vulnerable groups. However, the most significant shift occurred in 1999. Here the strategy read:

> Promotion of religious freedom is one of the highest concerns in our foreign policy. Freedom of thought, conscience and religion is a bedrock issue for the American people. To that end, the President signed the International Religious Freedom Act of 1998, which provides the flexibility needed to advance religious freedom and to counter religious persecution. In September 1999, we completed the first phase outlined in the Act with publication of the first annual report on the status of religious freedom worldwide, and in October, we designated the most severe violators of religious freedom. The United States is active throughout the world assisting those who are persecuted because of their religion and promoting freedom of religious belief and practice. We will continue to work with individual nations and with international institutions to combat religious persecution and promote religious freedom.[22]

To deem international religious freedom "one of the highest concerns" of U.S. diplomacy signaled a substantial transition point in U.S. policy. In addition, this strategy illuminated how international religious freedom might inform U.S. action across the foreign policy apparatus. It specifically mentioned the connection between religious freedom and displaced peoples, the necessity of acting against China's religious freedom violations, and the use of foreign aid to promote religious freedom across the globe. Largely rhetorical, and with little time to act on these new priorities, the inclusion of religious freedom on the NSS still set an important precedent. This strategic evolution compounded with the creation of new bureaucratic mechanisms, as outlined by the IRFA, and signaled a departure from the strict bifurcation of religion and diplomacy of years prior.

International Religious Freedom, George W. Bush, and the War on Terror

When George W. Bush prevailed over Vice President Al Gore in the contentious 2000 presidential election, conservatives were elated. Many saw Bush's win as an opportunity to restore dignity to the presidency. With Clinton's impeachment monopolizing the news in 1998 and 1999, Americans were eager to move on. Scholar Thomas Mann notes that while Clinton's job approval ratings were high, that did not necessarily capture the entire picture. He pointed out that Gore enjoyed a commanding lead (85 percent of the vote) among voters who approved of Clinton as a president and as a person. But among those who only admired Clinton's job performance and disapproved of him personally, Gore's vote percentage fell to 63 percent.[23] Gore attempted to distance himself from Clinton in the run-up to the election, and, though he won the popular vote, he could not secure the electoral college votes necessary to become the president-elect.

The election of 2000 featured religion prominently on both sides of the aisle. In an obvious dig at President Clinton, one of Gore's lead campaign officials announced on the trail that, with this election, "the Democratic Party is going to take God back."[24] Al Gore identified as a born-again Christian. He was wary of rigid orthodoxy and open to learning from a variety of denominations and spiritual approaches.[25] His running mate, Joe Lieberman, the first Jewish candidate on a national ticket, spoke frequently of his own devout faith.[26] Governor Bush articulated his faith often on the campaign trail, too. At a primary debate in Iowa during his presidential campaign, an audience member asked, "What political philosopher or thinker do you most identify with and why?" Bush replied resolutely, quickly responding, "Christ, because he changed my heart." When pushed to expand his answer, he noted, "Well, if they don't know, it's going to be hard to explain. When you turn your heart and your life over to Christ, when you accept Christ as the Savior, it changes your heart and changes your life. And that's what happened to me."[27]

Raised Episcopalian, the experience Bush mentioned happened later in his life. Heavily influenced by prominent evangelical Billy Graham, Bush recommitted his life to Christ when he was forty.[28] Deriving strength from his renewed faith, Bush quit drinking. Writing in his memoir, *Decision Points*, Bush noted that "God helped open my eyes which were closing because of booze."[29] Indeed, Bush attributed this life change to his ability to become governor of Texas and eventually president of the United States. While the most conservative wing of the Republican Party preferred Pat Buchanan, eventually President Bush secured support from some of the most prominent evangelicals, including Pat Robertson, Jerry Falwell, and Ralph Reed. On the campaign trail, he laid out his vision of "compassionate conservatism." Scholar Richard Holtzman noted that "this governing doctrine fused two principal strands of modern conservatism long at odds with one another—the neo-liberal championing of the free market and a faith-based concern with moral values, self-discipline, and community—into a coherent and complementary whole."[30] Bush's conservatism and vocal faith led to renewed hope among the international religious freedom community that religious rights might receive more attention than they did in previous decades.

In the early days of his administration, Bush expressed his unwavering support of international religious freedom. In a speech to the American Jewish Committee on May 3, 2001, he proclaimed: "It is not an accident that freedom of religion is one of the central freedoms in our Bill of Rights. It is the first freedom of the human soul—the right to speak the words that God places in our mouths. We must stand for that freedom in our country. We must speak for that freedom in the world."[31] While some critics dismissed these statements as mere rhetoric,[32] scholar and former NSC staffer William Inboden noted that "more than just elegant rhetoric, the President's declaration also empowered the officials and staff throughout the national security interagency working on religious freedom to elevate it as a strategic priority."[33]

Despite his vocal commitment, international religious freedom remained but one of many priorities for the administration as other human rights crises vied for presidential attention. These included the brutal conflict in Sudan and the subsequent negotiation of the Comprehensive Peace Agreement, fighting the AIDS epidemic through the

President's Emergency Plan for AIDS Relief (PEPFAR), and providing large-scale disaster relief after the 2004 tsunami in the Indian Ocean, which claimed over two hundred thousand lives. But nothing affected the president's foreign policy agenda more directly, or more extensively, than the terror attacks of 9/11 and the subsequent War on Terror.

When considering international religious freedom policy, it is difficult to overstate the breadth of the impact of the terror attacks of 9/11. While knowing exactly how President Bush's presidency would have unfolded is impossible, that tragic day reoriented everything about American foreign policy. It centered the connections between religion and politics and added unwanted complications to international religious freedom efforts. The deadly attacks forced Americans to face the brutality of extremist ideologies. As a result, many disavowed their commitment to religious freedom for all. In the weeks after 9/11, hate crimes against Muslims surged.[34] Some prominent religious leaders blamed Islam itself for the attacks. Franklin Graham, Billy Graham's son and successor in ministry, put it bluntly: "We're not attacking Islam, but Islam has attacked us." He continued, "The God of Islam is not the same God. . . . It's a different God, and I believe it is a very evil and wicked religion."[35] Other leaders of the Christian Right made similar accusations. Pat Robertson made sweeping claims against all Muslims,[36] calling Islam a "religion of violence" and noting that they wanted "control, dominate, and if need be, destroy."[37] Jerry Vines, leader of the Southern Baptist Convention (SBC), went further, calling the Prophet Muhammad a "demon-possessed pedophile" and inciting religious intolerance from the then-sixteen million members of the SBC.[38] These types of responses severely damaged the reputation of religious freedom advocacy, as they provided ample evidence that some of the very people advocating most ardently for religious freedom were quick to vilify entire religious populations.

For his part, President Bush vehemently rejected these attacks on the Muslim faith. As Bush's Deputy Assistant Secretary of Homeland Security James Norton noted, "President Bush went out of his way to wrap his arms around the Muslim community."[39] Indeed, within a week of the terror attacks, Bush chose to speak at the Islamic Center of Washington, DC—a decision that carried tremendous symbolic power. He said unequivocally: "The face of terror is not the true faith of Islam. That's not what Islam is all about. Islam is peace. These terrorists don't represent peace. They represent evil and war."[40] Bush acknowledged the anxiety and intimidation felt by American Muslims during this period and maintained that "those who feel like they can intimidate our fellow citizens to take out their anger don't represent the best of America. They represent the worst of humankind, and they should be ashamed of that kind of behavior."[41] In the month following the attacks, President Bush hosted an iftar dinner to celebrate the Muslim month of Ramadan, continuing the annual trend started in 1996 by First Lady Hillary Clinton. Bush continued the tradition each year of his two terms. Then, in a meeting with U.N. Secretary-General Kofi Annan in 2002, Bush lamented that "some of the comments that have been uttered about Islam do not reflect the sentiments of my government or the sentiments of most Americans. Islam, as practiced by the vast majority of people, is a peaceful religion, a religion that respects others. Ours is a country based upon tolerance and we welcome people of all faiths in America."[42] In 2005, President Bush added a Holy Qur'an to the White House library, the first in the nation's history. In speech after speech, Bush reiterated his admiration for the Muslim faith. And while many praised these efforts, some scholars have noted that Bush's efforts to make sure that he clarified that the War on Terror was not a war against Islam may have backfired, adding credence to the debate itself.[43]

In his address to the Joint Session of Congress on September 20, 2001, President Bush was unequivocal in his commitment: "Tonight we are a country awakened to danger and called to defend freedom. Our grief has turned to anger and anger to resolution. Whether we bring our enemies to justice or bring justice to our enemies, justice will be done."[44] The speech was confident and unambiguous. Scholars D. Jason Berggren and Nicol Rae note that this confidence was religious in its origin. They write that "evangelicals may be described as Christians of certainty. They are certain the Bible is the Word of God, Christ died for their sins, and that they have the 'blessed assurance' of a heavenly reward." Berggren and Rae connect this confidence to policymaking and argue that evangelicals are more likely to show confidence and express clarity when moral or spiritual matters are involved.[45] Indeed, as Bush finished his address to Congress, he asserted that America's efforts would have God's blessing: "Freedom and fear, justice and cruelty, have always been at war, and we know God is not neutral between them."[46]

The events of 9/11 changed the course of U.S. grand strategy in sweeping ways. In *Surprise Security*, John Lewis Gaddis argues that the events of 9/11 challenged the assumptions of existing U.S. grand strategy as global cooperation and ally-building proved insufficient to protect American interests.[47] Instead, the Bush administration resurrected a conception of American power and strategy marked by unilateralism and American hegemony. In a speech marking the twentieth anniversary of the National Endowment for Democracy in November 2003, less than seven months after the United States invaded Iraq, Bush made this renewed vision clear. Much of his speech centered on democracy in the Middle East and the role of the United States in its promotion. The speech showed an administration working to defend its actions in Iraq. Without weapons of mass destruction (WMDs), what was the justification for the war? The Bush administration's response: to end Saddam Hussein's reign of terror and to promote freedom and democracy. In the speech, Bush argued that the political dynamics within the Middle East were untenable: "Sixty years of Western nations excusing and accommodating the lack of freedom in the Middle East did nothing to make us safe—because in the long run, stability cannot be purchased at the expense of liberty. As long as the Middle East remains a place where freedom does not flourish, it will remain a place of stagnation, resentment, and violence ready for export."[48]

The events of 9/11 and the Bush administration's new muscular grand strategy profoundly impacted international religious freedom efforts and raised many new questions. What was the boundary between religious freedom and fomenting violence? How could the United States engage religious actors and form inroads, especially where the image of the United States was unfavorable? After decades of more restrained, incremental foreign policy of George H. W. Bush and Bill Clinton, the attacks of 9/11 renewed debates from the Reagan era. How should human rights and religious freedom, in particular, fit within a broader commitment to democracy promotion? Need U.S. policy in this arena be consistent across time and geographies? As President Bush sought to answer these tough questions, he redoubled efforts to promote democracy and articulated his Freedom Agenda.

George W. Bush is the only president who explicitly mentioned religious freedom as a foreign policy priority in all (or, in this case, both) of his administration's NSS documents. When comparing NSS documents across administrations, it is important to note that the documents differ in content, purpose, and form. Though Clinton's initial NSS was fewer than thirty pages long, his final NSS numbered eighty-four pages, almost tripling in size. This may be part of the reason that some found President Bush's first strategy, released in 2002, as incomplete, lacking "a coherent and concrete guide on how to achieve these objectives."[49] If eighty pages of detail were expected, the thirty-one pages offered likely seemed insufficient. Despite the brevity of the document, the 2002 NSS still mentioned international religious freedom specifically, noting that the U.S. would "take special efforts to promote freedom of religion and conscience and defend it from encroachment by repressive governments," and, again, "America must stand firmly for the nonnegotiable demands of human dignity: the rule of law; limits on the absolute power of the state; free speech; freedom of worship; equal justice; respect for women; religious and ethnic tolerance; and respect for private property."[50]

Also in 2002, President Bush signed Executive Order 13280, which called for the creation of a Center for Faith-Based and Community Initiatives within the U.S. Agency for International Development (USAID).[51] The purpose of the order was to make it easier for faith-based and community organizations to provide social services.[52] It removed obstacles that previously prevented religious organizations from obtaining federal funding. The most influential effect of the order was the ability for faith-based organizations to hire based on religious beliefs and standards. For religious freedom advocates, this signaled a renewed respect for the work of faith-based organizations around the world. It empowered organizations to live their faith more fully while making a meaningful difference. Critics argued that the move violated the rightful separation of church and state and feared that the order might cause more discrimination in hiring practices.[53]

As George W. Bush delivered his second inaugural address, he also solidified his Freedom Agenda. Here, he directly connected U.S. security to human freedom around the globe. He ended the speech with an ambitious aim: "So it is the policy of the United States to seek and support the growth of democratic movements and institutions in every nation and culture, with the ultimate goal of ending tyranny in our world."[54] Here, Bush articulated the Freedom Agenda, which committed the

United States to advance liberty to counter repression that, in this view, ultimately endangered the United States.

The second and final NSS of the Bush administration mentions religion 23 times, with five specifically considering religious freedom. It reinforced the Freedom Agenda and stressed the interconnectedness between political representation and religious and economic liberty.[55] The NSS went a step further, connecting the War on Terror to a lack of religious freedom. It noted: "Against a terrorist enemy that is defined by religious intolerance, we defend the First Freedom: the right of people to believe and worship according to the dictates of their own conscience, free from the coercion of the state, the coercion of the majority, or the coercion of a minority that wants to dictate what others must believe."[56]

Despite a solid rhetorical commitment to religious freedom amid the War on Terror, many lamented what they deemed to be a misalignment between rhetoric and policy. Some domestic advocates decried the Patriot Act, viewing it as an affront to civil liberties and a smokescreen for targeted racial and religious bigotry.[57] Others questioned the Bush administration's commitment to religious freedom around the world. Reflecting on the early years of IRFA implementation, scholar Eugenia Relaño Pastor writes, "Where a violating nation can potentially be mined for some other benefit, the United States generally turns a blind eye to violations of religious liberty."[58] This sensitive, often problematic, balancing act existed whether acknowledged explicitly. Some congressional leaders, like Republican Chris Smith, publicly vocalized their frustration. In an op-ed for the *Washington Times*, Smith condemned what he saw as the selective application of the IRFA and argued that the U.S. was ignoring egregious religious freedom violations out "of fear of offending our new partners in this war against terror."[59] The religious abuse in Pakistan, Saudi Arabia, Turkmenistan, and Uzbekistan, coupled with the perception that the United States was ignoring it, drew the most criticism.[60] Despite the religious hostility and intimidation of minority groups present in each of these states, they remained critical allies in the War on Terror.[61]

USCIRF also expressed concern that the War on Terror would force unwanted tradeoffs with long-term implications.[62] Perhaps the most controversial moment concerned U.S. involvement in setting up the new government in Afghanistan after overthrowing the Taliban. The new constitution, while heralded as an "important political development" by White House officials, explicitly stated that "no law can be contrary to the sacred religion of Islam."[63] USCIRF railed against the developments, adding that the constitution "envisions, provides for, and firmly guarantees the privileged place of Sharia law."[64] But, ultimately, it was Afghanistan's constitution—not a remake of the U.S. model. Moreover, religious freedom advocates within the Bush administration successfully advocated for the inclusion of Article 2 in the Constitution, which explicitly stated that individuals were "free to exercise their religious rites within the limits of the provisions of the law"—a significant, if modest, development.

Christian writer Richard John Neuhaus provides an incisive picture of the uncertain landscape:

> There is a justifiable anxiety that in the current war against terrorism, religious freedom is once again being put on a back burner as the U.S. cuts deals with some of the most notorious violators, China, Sudan, and Saudi Arabia, for example, in order to secure cooperation and gain momentary tactical advantages. Such maneuverings are understandable. Religious freedom is not and cannot be the only priority in foreign policy, especially in a time of war. But those who worked so hard to make it a priority are justifiably worried that this great achievement could be undermined by the foreign policy establishment's habits of facile expediency. The religious factor will be and should be vigorously debated in the months ahead. That debate does not pit "realists" against "idealists," but is, rather, a debate about the hard reality of religion in defining, more and more, the lines of conflict in politics among nations.[65]

As the next chapter will detail, practitioners who worked in the IRF office and at USCIRF during the Bush administration most quickly mentioned the unique difficulty of the foreign policy context after 9/11. Specifically, several interviewees noted the difficulty of translating the massive strategic goal of the Freedom Agenda into feasible policy options, particularly given severe resource limitations within the IRF office.

Despite criticisms from some congressional leaders and USCIRF, others have noted the support of the White House, especially President Bush himself, for religious freedom efforts. John Hanford, who served as Bush's ambassador-at-large for international religious freedom, argued that his efforts were never constrained by the White House, but were consistently affirmed and supported. He found President Bush's commitment to religious freedom to be sincere and enduring, emanating from his own deeply held religious convictions.[66]

Chapter 4, which considers international religious freedom efforts in China, discusses President Bush's bold affirmations of religious freedom at Tsinghua University in Beijing in February 2002 and again from the steps of Gangwashi Church in November 2005. In 2006, Bush welcomed Chinese Christians Yu Jie, Li Baiguang, and Wang Yi to the White House to discuss religious freedom conditions in China, sending another bold signal to the Chinese leadership. In May 2007, Bush hosted the Catholic archbishop of Hong Kong, Cardinal Joseph Zen, at the White House. The following month, President Bush met with prominent Uyghur activist Rebiya Kadeer at the Democracy and Security Conference in Prague. Bush's willingness to meet with dissidents and his consistent, vocal commitment to religious freedom gave the IRF office clout in its negotiations. Despite facing intense criticism, Bush met privately with the Dalai Lama in October 2007.

Breaking with precedent that required diplomatic caution after the Vietnam War, President Bush denounced religious freedom violations in Vietnam and, in 2005, signed a binding agreement with Prime Minister Phan Văn Khải, aimed at reforming the legal codes to open the religious landscape (this process, led by Ambassador-at-Large John Hanford, is discussed in detail in chapter 5). Despite the challenging foreign policy landscape, President Bush made a concerted effort to denounce persecution and promote greater religious freedom in some of the world's most hostile regimes. Often, these efforts came at significant political cost.

President Bush spotlighted the egregious human rights abuses in Sudan, and, in 2001, he appointed Senator John Danforth as its special envoy for peace.[67] The Bush administration exponentially increased foreign aid, vocally condemned the genocide with the signing of the Sudan Peace Act of 2002, and facilitated the Comprehensive Peace Agreement signed by the Sudanese government and the Sudan People's Liberation Movement (SPLM) in January 2005. And (as will be discussed in chapter 6), while often criticized for what was seen as capitulation to the Saudi regime, the Bush administration designated Saudi Arabia a Country of Particular Concern (CPC) in 2004.

IRF and the Obama Administration: Multilateralism and Religious Engagement

In his rousing speech at the Democratic National Convention in 2004, Senator Barack Obama confronted tropes about faith and partisanship. To a roaring crowd, he stated: "The pundits like to slice-and-dice our country into red and blue states. Red states for Republicans, blue states for Democrats. But I've got news for them, too: We worship an awesome God in the blue states."[68] His speech continued with a call for empathy and unity across geographic and partisan lines and concluded on a note about the importance of hope, a message that shaped his own political campaign four years later.

Obama came to faith later in his life. After years of exploration, he converted to Christianity and was baptized at Trinity United Church of Christ in Chicago in the early 1990s. He used scripture and metaphor throughout his speeches and made frequent reference to the social gospel—focusing on poverty reduction, addressing inequality, and fighting for justice as critical elements of the Christian life. Despite calls for unity, the Obama era ushered in new questions and controversies surrounding religious liberty. In analyzing Obama's legacy on international religious freedom, it's important to note the domestic political calculus involved. Religious freedom concerns, and even the language "religious freedom," resonates more strongly with the right. Indeed, a cursory search of news during Obama's tenure reveals headlines like "Has Obama Waged a War on Religion?"[69] Most of the domestic religious liberty issues that gained notoriety during the Obama administration, including the HHS Mandate as part of the Affordable Care Act or progressive reforms to sex education in public schools, involved issues with clear-cut partisan positions. Despite noteworthy exceptions like the Log Cabin Republicans, who have advocated for nondiscrimination protections for LGBTQ+ Americans at the federal level for years, for the most part, these debates fall on stark party lines.

A PEW survey released in 2009 noted that 48 percent of Americans viewed the Republican Party as friendly toward religion.[70] This number dropped to 29 percent for the Democratic Party. Obama attempted to create distance between domestic religious liberty issues and the pursuit of international religious freedom across the globe. As discussed in more detail in chapter 3, Obama's second ambassador-at-large, Rabbi David Saperstein, and his successor, Sam Brownback, made concerted efforts to reassert IRF's commitment to bipartisanship. Overall, Obama's international religious freedom strategy focused on engaging religious leaders worldwide and forming multilateral coalitions.

The international religious freedom community met Barack Obama's presidential candidacy with trepidation. The most overriding critique concerned his relationship with Reverend Jeremiah Wright. Among his many inflammatory sermons, Wright proclaimed that the attack of 9/11 represented "America's chickens . . . coming home to roost"—apparently speaking directly to American support for Israel and, earlier, American support for pro-apartheid movements in South Africa. In his most infamous sermon, Wright was quoted as saying, repeatedly, "God damn America," causing national outrage. Amid the controversy, Obama did his best to distance himself from Reverend Wright and assure the American people that he disagreed with Wright's incendiary comments.[71]

As he sought to contain Wright's damage, Obama did signal that his foreign policy agenda would depart sharply from the efforts of his predecessor. Obama favored multilateral partnerships and initiatives and was skeptical of U.S.-only action, especially regarding humanitarian and human rights issues. Like Clinton and Bush, there were many problems vying for presidential attention. Among other challenges, the Obama administration faced a worsening and egregious human rights crisis in Syria; a resurgent Russia, which annexed Crimea in 2014; negotiations of the Trans-Pacific Partnership (TPP); piracy off the coast of Somalia; intervention in Libya; and the widespread effects of the Arab Spring. Most significant, however, was the fact that the administration inherited the wars in Afghanistan and Iraq—and their geopolitical consequences.

Regarding religion and diplomacy, Obama attempted to ease existing tensions and elevate the image of the United States across the world. In his first major foreign policy speech at Cairo University in June 2009, he sought to redefine America's relationship with the Muslim world. In this speech, Obama explicitly stressed the importance of religious freedom: "People in every country should be free to choose and live their faith based upon the persuasion of the mind and the heart and the soul." The speech outlined seven sources of tension, ranging from bitter conflicts between Israelis and Palestinians to economic policy to debates on women's rights.

As Obama concluded, he clarified that his administration would approach things differently. "And finally," he stated, "just as America can never tolerate violence by extremists, we must never alter or forget our principles. . . . 9/11 was an enormous trauma to our country. The fear and anger that it provoked was understandable, but in some cases, it led us to act contrary to our traditions and our ideals."[72] Policymakers and scholars heralded the Cairo speech as a watershed moment for religion and U.S. diplomacy.

Given the overt cynicism of the Obama administration toward democracy promotion, it needed to rebrand and reimagine international religious freedom to align with its own agenda. To make this possible, Obama took intentional steps to restore America's image worldwide. Scholar Judd Birdsall, who also worked in the IRF office during both the Bush and Obama administrations, argued that these efforts successfully "enhanced America's ability to promote values like religious freedom."[73] A more detailed description of the bureaucratic mechanism employed by the Obama administration will follow in the next chapter, but the following section summarizes the shifts required by Obama's change in strategy.

In 2011, Secretary of State Hillary Clinton launched a Working Group on Religion and Foreign Policy as part of the Strategic Dialogue with Civil Society program, an initiative to form durable partnerships with leaders outside of official government roles. Maria Otero, then undersecretary for democracy and global affairs, noted the complexity of religion and the sobering fact that it is used by "human rights advocates and terrorists alike to defend their actions."[74] The working group rallied around the cause of leveraging religion to strengthen society. One recommendation of this group was to create a new office focusing on religious engagement worldwide. Elizabeth Prodromou, scholar and former USCIRF commissioner, noted that these efforts, which likely came at a political cost for the Obama administration, conveyed a deep commitment to better understanding of the role of religion in international affairs and to bipartisanship.[75]

In August 2013, Secretary of State John Kerry agreed that "we ignore the global impact of religion at our peril."[76] Taken on its own, one might expect this type of statement to elicit excitement and joy from the international religious freedom community. Here was a secretary of state finally highlighting the need to focus on religion. Before long, however, it would become clear that while the Obama administration would engage religion, it would not elevate the IRF office in particular. The administration focused its efforts on the creation of a separate office at the State Department, the Office of Religion and Global Affairs (RGA).

While the next chapter describes the relationships between these bureaucratic mechanisms in further detail, it is important to note that these substantial changes at the State Department reflected a major change in the approach of the Obama administration. To borrow Bob Seiple's metaphor, Obama funneled his efforts to lighting candles. He understood that this approach often felt unsatisfactory. As he accepted the Nobel Prize in Oslo in 2009, Obama stated, "I know that engagement with repressive regimes lacks the satisfying purity of indignation. But I also know that sanctions without outreach—and condemnation without discussion—can carry forward a crippling status quo. No repressive regime can move down a path unless it has the choice of an open door."[77]

In 2013, Congress passed H.R. 310, sponsored by Rep. Frank Wolf (R-VA), to create a special envoy to promote religious freedom of religious minorities in the Near East and South Central Asia. The legislation indicated that the new position would have ambassador-level rank.[78] Related Senate Bill 653, known as the Near East and South Central Asia Religious Freedom Act, became law on August 8, 2014, but the position outlined in the legislation remained vacant for over a year. Eventually, the Obama administration appointed Knox Thames on September 16, 2015, as special advisor for religious minorities in the Near East and South Central Asia.

In 2016, Congress amended the IRFA to be more inclusive, ensuring that the United States would advocate for nonbelievers, too. After all, freedom of religion includes the right not to believe. The move, which enjoyed bipartisan support, was a welcome relief to secular humanists concerned with violence against atheists and agnostics around the globe.

Despite its efforts, many in the IRF community wanted Obama to do more. They lamented that neither his 2010 nor 2015 NSS mentioned religious freedom. Some were angry by President Obama and Secretary Clinton's regular use of the term "freedom of worship" instead of "freedom of religion." Critics claimed that this choice of language communicated a weaker understanding of religious freedom—one that would narrowly protect believers' right to worship, but that would not extend to the right to evangelize or engage in the public square.[79] Regardless of support or criticism, Obama's approach represented a fundamental

Figure 2.2. President Obama receiving the Nobel Peace Prize in 2009. Source: Records of the White House Photo Office (Obama Administration).

departure from the Bush administration's efforts, and many were uncomfortable with the change.

Knox Thames maintained that though the Bush administration might have emphasized religious freedom more outwardly, the Obama administration deserved more credit for its efforts than it typically received. As president, Obama commended Turkey for reopening the Halki Seminary in 2009 and argued that "freedom of religion and expression lead to a strong and vibrant civil society that only strengthens the state."[80] Also that year, he proclaimed the necessity of respecting religious ministries at the U.S.-China Strategic and Economic Dialogue in July 2009. In January 2015, Obama called upon India's Hindu national government to confront its religious freedom violations. In a speech in May 2015, he spoke to the people of Vietnam, celebrating that religious freedom allowed "people to fully express the love and compassion."[81] In 2016, his administration, in conjunction with the IRF office, determined that the egregious treatment of Yazidis, Christians, and Shi'a Muslims under ISIS rule amounted to genocide.

Thames fondly recalled a quick exchange with President Obama over an Easter Prayer Breakfast. A smaller gathering than the annual National Prayer Breakfast, President Obama and Vice President Biden invited dozens of leaders in the faith community to gather in the East Room at the White House. Knowing he would have a brief moment to speak with the president, Thames debated on what to say. Ultimately, he thanked President Obama for raising religious freedom in India. During a major speech earlier that year, Obama, with the encouragement of USCIRF and the IRF office, insisted that India respect its founding documents. "Your Article 25 says that all people are equally entitled to freedom of conscience and the right freely to profess, practice and propagate religion. . . . In both our countries—in all countries—upholding this fundamental freedom is the responsibility of government, but it's also the responsibility of every person."[82] With rising reports of forced mass conversion, vandalism and arson against churches, and violence at the hands of Hindu nationalist groups like Vishva Hindu Parishad (VHP) and the Rashtriya Swayamsevak Sangh (RSS), Obama's remarks were pointed. While he did not mention Prime Minister Narendra Modi by name, the implications were clear. After an otherwise friendly visit, Obama stuck his neck out. Back at the prayer breakfast, he thought about Thames's expression of gratitude for a moment as he went to the next person in the line of breakfast attendees before he turned around, looked Thames in the eye, and said, "I meant it."[83]

Making sense of the strategic shifts over the first two decades of IRFA policy provides the necessary backdrop to understanding the environment in which the bureaucracy operated. While each president balanced his convictions and constituencies, they also grappled with how and when to highlight religious freedom concerns amid a chaotic and crowded foreign policy landscape. Still, as will be analyzed in the case studies to follow, when presidents prioritized religious freedom, the IRF office used the show of support and leveraged it to promote change. The following chapter considers the bureaucratic arrangements that facilitated, and more often constrained, effective policy.

3

Navigating the Bureaucracy

Within the U.S. State Department, the addition of the Office of International Religious Freedom was unwelcome. In addition to pushback from the White House, which was concerned that additional mechanisms would unnecessarily duplicate existing efforts and take away discretion from leadership, leaders at the State Department rejected the change.[1] Some viewed the creation of the office as a congressional attempt to force it to do better—force it to pay more attention to religious freedom concerns, despite preferring a more secular approach to diplomatic relations. They resented the overreach. Others, though, foresaw how the addition of the IRF office would complicate their own work.

More than most domestic policy areas, foreign policymaking involves complex bargaining among multiple organizations with different, sometimes conflicting, agendas. New bureaucratic agencies, like the Office of International Religious Freedom, must grapple with the preexisting actors that occupy the foreign policy space.[2] Political scientist Daniel Drezner describes the challenges facing newly formed "missionary institutions":

> Established agencies have an advantage over newly created institutions. Older agencies will possess more resources, information, skill, and expertise in the bureaucratic trenches. Newly established missionary institutions will certainly possess a strong sense of organizational mission, but may lack the other resources necessary to achieve their policies. When created, these institutions might have the backing of more powerful actors that can shepherd the bureaucratic unit through its infancy. However, as political fortunes change, these protectors can fall from power.[3]

As Drezner shows, missionary organizations must grapple with automatic disadvantages as they compete with preexisting and well-established institutions. However, the challenges facing the creation of the Office of International Religious Freedom were doubled. The IRF was a missionary institution lodged within another larger missionary institution: the Bureau of Human Rights, Democracy, and Labor (DRL).

DRL, originally called the Bureau of Human Rights and Humanitarian Affairs, was formed in 1977 to spread democracy and promote individual liberty worldwide. Its creation resulted from a sequenced set of actions beginning in 1975. With congressional pressure to act on human rights, the State Department created the position of coordinator for humanitarian affairs in the office of the deputy secretary. Eventually, this became the Office of Humanitarian Affairs but remained under the deputy secretary, Robert S. Ingersoll.[4] The International Security Assistance and Arms Export Control Act changed the position to coordinator for human rights and humanitarian affairs and made it a presidential appointee requiring Senate confirmation. In 1977, this coordinator position was elevated to an assistant secretary of state.[5] When officially established in October 1997, the Bureau of Human Rights and Humanitarian Affairs included the Human Rights Office and the Office of Refugee and Migrations Affairs, each with a corresponding deputy assistant secretary. A third deputy assistant secretary dealt with POW/MIA matters. Then, in 1994, the bureau was reorganized and became the Bureau of Human Rights, Democracy, and Labor. The reorganization "reflected both a broader sweep and a more focused approach to the interlocking issues of human rights, worker rights, and democracy."[6] Later, the Foreign Relations Authorization Act for Fiscal Year 1998 elevated the position to assistant secretary for human rights and humanitarian affairs.[7] In 1999, the secretary of state instituted a large-scale reorganization of the Department. Albright aligned independent offices with their functionally most related bureau to simplify the organizational structure and keep the number of direct reports to the secretary relatively few. Within this new structure, the IRF office found itself wedged within DRL.

As expansive as the revised mission of DRL, most diplomatic sway and institutional weight came from the regional bureaus. In keeping with Drezner's thesis, the "politics of bureaucratic structure can blunt the ability of an institution to propagate its founding idea."[8] A senior State Department official identified that the many functional bureaus vying for attention exacerbated tensions between functional and regional bureaus. For instance, within the jurisdiction of Civilian Security, Democracy, and Human Rights alone, there are eight functional bureaus: Conflict and Stabilization Operations (CSO); Counterterrorism and Countering Violent Extremism (CT); Democracy, Human Rights, and Labor (DRL); Office of Global Criminal Justice (GCJ); International Narcotics and Law Enforcement (INL); Office of International Religious Freedom (IRF); Office to Monitor and Combat Trafficking in Persons (TIP); and Population, Refugees, and Migration (PRM).[9] An ambassador-at-large, as is the case with the IRF office, or an assistant secretary leads each of these suborganizations.[10] Outside of Civilian Security, Democracy, and Human Rights, the landscape becomes even more crowded. The regional bureaus must also contend with bureaus for military affairs, nonproliferation, arms control, and economic and business affairs, among many others. A senior State Department official remarked: "If there were only one group knocking from the outside, maybe you'd get in."[11] As it stands, the knocking never stops.

The positionality of IRF within DRL constrained and limited its effective implementation of the IRFA. Despite the legislation specifying that the ambassador-at-large would enjoy direct access to the secretary of state, Assistant Secretary John Shattuck mediated his efforts instead. As will be discussed in the following pages, this tension negatively affected IRF policy in all three administrations under study, particularly during the Bush administration. Eventually, this arrangement shifted, and the IRF office enjoyed more autonomy, but questions of power and authority in this policy arena were constantly renegotiated. When Robert Seiple became the first ambassador-at-large for international religious freedom in 1999, he soon learned that navigating the bureaucratic maze at Foggy Bottom would be one of his most challenging tasks.

While chapter 2 discussed the high-level approaches to international religious freedom for each of the administrations, mid-level policymakers more often determined policy trajectories. Sure, sometimes a senior ambassador made religious freedom a cornerstone of their term, much to the delight of the IRF office. But, more often than not, the mid-level bureaucrats made the day-to-day decisions (and did the related daily work) to change policy.

This chapter considers the bureaucratic mechanisms used by each administration—sometimes at the direction of top leaders, but often because of competing priorities, without direct involvement from those at the top. Expectedly, most of the analysis centers on the IRF office at the State Department and the U.S. Commission for International Religious Freedom (USCIRF). It necessarily considers other adjacent bureaucratic mechanisms, such as the Office of Religion and Global Affairs, which was part of President Obama's Community and Faith-Based Initiatives Program. An analysis of the IRF office is an analysis of several organizations as it changed significantly and grew tremendously throughout the Clinton, Bush and Obama years.

This chapter also illuminates the people and personalities involved in IRF policy during the first two decades of the IRFA. The leadership of the IRF office shifted often, and several times, the position of ambassador-at-large for international religious freedom remained vacant for many months. These personnel shifts directly affected the organizational culture.

Bureaucratic Change During the Clinton Years

Robert (Bob) A. Seiple was the first ambassador-at-large for international religious freedom. When reflecting on the early days of the IRF office, Seiple recalls being "shown" his new office, since two people couldn't stand in it at the same time. In his typical good-humored way, Seiple recalled that his only companion in his office was a vacuum cleaner, which was a good thing because the office desperately needed it.[12] With his arrival and the creation of this new little office, Seiple attempted to clear away antiquated conceptions of the relationship between religion and diplomacy. For Seiple and other international religious freedom advocates, the only thing more diplomatically treacherous than engaging religion was ignoring it.

Seiple came to Washington amid an impressive and eclectic career. After serving in the Marines, which would profoundly shape his leadership of the IRF office, especially concerning Vietnam, he served as the president of Eastern College and Eastern Baptist Theological Seminary. Then, he became athletic director at Brown University before leading the prominent Christian NGO World Vision. World Vision, a privately funded organization dedicated to international development and humanitarian relief, gave Seiple experience and knowledge of the international system, making him an attractive candidate for the nomination.

Perhaps more than any specific qualification, Seiple had a command-ing presence and a magnetic personality. In many ways, Bob Seiple was precisely the type of man the Christian Right hoped might fill the posi-tion. In addition to his impressive resume, he was a man of unassail-able character and was well respected by political leaders on both sides of the aisle. He was a committed Baptist and a conservative. Indeed, Seiple himself cited his strong reputation with evangelical leadership[13] as a partial reason for his eventual selection for the ambassadorship.[14]

Seiple joined the Clinton administration before Congress passed the IRFA. In recognition that the United States needed to do more to tackle questions of religious freedom and attempting to head off the legisla-tive efforts that would constrain the administration, Secretary of State Warren Christopher announced the creation of the 1996 Committee on Religious Freedom Abroad.[15] One of the recommendations of the com-mittee was the appointment of a senior coordinator for international re-ligious freedom, a position that the Clinton administration asked Seiple to fill. These were the existing mechanisms that Assistant Secretary John Shattuck wanted to bolster instead of creating new institutions and new positions through the IRFA. Thus, when Seiple was appointed, it was unclear if the position would be temporary or long-lasting, or if it would have legislative backing.

Criticism from All Sides

Bob Seiple was not naive about the horrors of religious persecution nor the persistence required to make meaningful change in repressive regimes. However, he was frustrated by the State Department's bureau-cratic system. In reflecting upon his early days as ambassador, Seiple compared his position to his previous role at World Vision. In contrast to the fast pace of World Vision, where he enjoyed significant auton-omy and authority, the procedures and approval processes at the State Department drained Seiple's energy. After Congress passed the IRFA, Seiple wanted to release an op-ed to unify people in service of their common goals after the bitter legislative fight. He recalled, "I found that in the department, 55 different people had to clear such a document. Everyone wanted something edited. Unfortunately, I allowed that to happen and ultimately had an op-ed that I wasn't very pleased with. A good deal of the core was taken out."[16] Nevertheless, Seiple pushed it forward, and it was published—a move he would later regret.[17]

The politicization of international religious freedom caused Seiple much frustration. To signal his desire to work across the political spectrum, Seiple "went to the middle ground of undeclared" when he started his tenure in the administration.[18] But finding a middle ground would prove an arduous task. Blinded by ardent disapproval of Bill Clinton, many evangelical conservatives distrusted Seiple automatically given his new affiliation with the administration. Speaking of partisan tensions related to international religious freedom in 2020, Seiple noted "that some of the things you see today in spades were also present then, unfortunately. . . . They took energy and they wasted opportunity."[19]

The controversial op-ed published in *The Washington Times* on December 24, 1998, angered many on the Christian Right. Seiple himself likened it to "5-day-old piece of provolone."[20] Regardless of whether the op-ed articulated Seiple's true views or was a sanitized result of State Department procedures, the response to the piece clarified the continuing division within the international religious freedom community. Some lambasted Seiple for being soft on persecution, inflating the work of the Clinton administration, and discouraging sanctions for offending governments. Seiple recalled receiving pointed responses from leaders like Chuck Colson and John Richard Neuhaus, whom he regarded as dear friends. Despite his efforts for unity, the sharp debates that undergirded the ugly legislative fights of the late 1990s did not end with the passage of the IRFA. They concerned real differences of opinion, both in the scope of the goals and the methods of achieving those aims. But the disagreements often became personal. Jeremy Gunn, a political scientist and religious freedom advocate, summed it up this way: "While the motivations of many involved in this campaign are indeed sincere, and although the problems in the world are real and serious, the campaign unfortunately has relied too often on Washington-style attack politics."[21] Michael Horowitz was particularly merciless in his criticism. Given his close relationships with the leaders of the evangelical right, Horowitz wielded significant influence. Calling out Seiple particularly, Horowitz maintained that "persons favoring 'quiet diplomacy' strategies must bear the moral burden of, and responsibility for, the victimized believers who suffer and die on their watch."[22] Over the years to come, many IRF advocates and staffers would also find themselves in Horowitz's line of fire. The tense political environment added another tough element to Seiple's new role.

Resistance to Bureaucratic Norms

Seiple resisted many bureaucratic norms in his early days at the State Department, choosing a small office that provided more privacy over the statelier options offered. Disinterested in power plays, Seiple preferred to focus on the work itself. He recalled, "There were bad battles being fought, that I never wanted to participate in I thought they would be distractions. They were distractions."[23] Resisting institutional norms, even if they were distracting, ultimately left the IRF office vulnerable. Without the institutional protection it needed to thrive during presidential transitions, future leaders, like the second IRF ambassador, John Hanford, would have more difficulty.

The most challenging obstacle to overcome centered on the question of bureaucratic authority. Upon reflecting on his tenure as ambassador-at-large, Seiple recalled that religious freedom concerns often remained isolated from more extensive strategic discussions. Drawn together by Deputy Secretary of State Strobe Talbott, Seiple regularly joined the daily briefings with the assistant secretaries of state.[24] But in these "Talbott meetings" Seiple notes that he "was never once asked a question about religious freedom. Certainly, religious freedom indirectly came up in the context of disasters such as Afghanistan or Sudan, but the issue was never brought up in its own right—and this during an administration that cared deeply for human rights."[25] Seiple shared a warm relationship with then–Secretary of State Madeleine Albright. Still, his efforts were funneled through DRL, meaning he reported to Assistant Secretary John Shattuck and, later, Assistant Secretary Harold Koh. This chain of authority represented a sharp departure from the legislation itself, a bureaucratic decision that substantially limited the influence of the IRF office. It would be several years before the ambassador would report directly to the secretary, as the legislation intended. Tom Farr, who served as the first director of the IRF office, was the first full-time staff member.[26] He recalled the early days of his tenure as "exhilarating but a bit disorienting," with the lack of institutional support necessitating improvisation at every turn.[27]

Another Bureaucracy Mechanism Is Born: USCIRF

The IRF office at the State Department was not the only new organization forming. Nor was the IRF office the only bureaucratic arrangement needing managing. The IRFA also created an independent watchdog organization, the U.S. Commission for International Religious Freedom, or USCIRF, a group of experts meant to provide nonpartisan recommendations to the executive and legislative branches on matters of international religious freedom. The initial group of USCIRF commissioners included diverse religious leaders, including Rabbi David Saperstein, Baha'i activist Firuz Kazemzadeh, Cardinal Theodore McCarrick, and Mormon Michael K. Young. Nina Shea, a devout Catholic and decades-long proponent of religious freedom, and Leila Al-Marayati, a Palestinian American doctor and Islamic activist, also joined the inaugural commission.[28] Others included foreign policy professionals like John Bolton, who, before serving as a USCIRF Commissioner, was the assistant secretary of state for international organization affairs,[29] and Elliott Abrams, former assistant secretary of state for inter-American affairs and former assistant secretary of state for human rights and humanitarian affairs.[30] Interviews with several former commissioners indicated that while the group generally worked well together, there were several sources of conflict. It was a new organization forced to weather all the expected growing pains.

In describing the commission's early days, Elliott Abrams noted that while the establishment of the office was an important milestone, the work was only beginning. "You've got a congressional bill creating a commission, right? It's law. Now what?" he asked rhetorically. "You want space for an office. You want to hire a staff. The legislation permits this, but none of us knew how to do it. So, there we were, and one of us said, 'I've got an office. There's a conference table. Why doesn't everybody come over?' So, the first meetings of the Commission were held around that conference table with a speaker phone in the middle of the table."[31]

When asked about how USCIRF divided its attention across the many places where religious freedom violations occurred, former commissioners responded that they focused on egregious cases of persecution and countries moving in the wrong direction. Nina Shea recalled that most of the focus in the Commission's early days was on governments. In her view, the IRF reports could have done more to help identify where efforts should be focused. After the release of the first year's report, Shea testified in front of the House Subcommittee on International Operations and Human Rights that "the report itself contains an overwhelming and un-selective compilation of facts and information without reaching definitive conclusions, or conveying a sense of priority. In a report of this magnitude and type, prioritizing American concerns becomes essential. Not to do so is to lose sight of severe persecutors in a welter of detail."[32] With this in mind, Shea and her colleagues focused on three particularly egregious cases of persecution in the early years of the commission: China, Sudan, and Russia.[33] This decision did not come without criticism as the pressure from Congress to increase the breadth of focus mounted.

Some early challenges with USCIRF were internal to the new organization. For instance, Commissioner Laila Al-Marayati called herself a "counterbalance to neoconservative members like Elliott Abrams and John Bolton." In this capacity, she offered a vigorous dissenting view regarding the commission's findings on the religious freedom extended by the Israeli government. "I felt my role was to bring balance and to highlight the concerns and perspectives of Muslims living around the world who experience tremendous persecution," Al-Marayati explained. "I was able to have the Commission focus briefly on the religious freedom violations committed by Israel both within Israel and in the Occupied Territories. We were unable to come to a consensus due to the unwillingness of some of the Commissioners to criticize Israel under any circumstances."[34]

Nina Shea recalled the positive and negative effects of having individuals on the commission with specific ties to religious communities. When functioning properly, these individuals provided expert knowledge and understanding, leading to new relationships. Then, the commission leveraged these new connections to gather data and brainstorm potential policy recommendations. But sometimes, these ties could prove too close and obstruct USCIRF's work. Shea remembered one particularly egregious account involving Cardinal McCarrick, a commissioner deeply connected to the Catholic Church in China.[35] In advance of USCIRF's press release concerning the plight of bishops in China,[36] Cardinal McCarrick confused names and reported that Bishop Su Zhimin of the Baoding diocese was not imprisoned and had agreed to be ordained by the sanctioned Patriotic Association.[37] In reality, he remained loyal to Rome and was in prison without a trial date. When Shea contacted the commission's communication director, they deferred to McCarrick until Shea was able to provide documentation directly from the Vatican.[38] This type of confusion highlights the dangers of overreliance on commissioners' expertise.

Thorns in the Side

In some ways, the tension between IRF and USCIRF was intentional, providing a mechanism of accountability. However, the perspectives on the proper relationship between USCIRF and the IRF office varied dramatically. When describing the purpose of USCIRF and its mandate, Elliott Abrams responded wryly: "To keep jabbing the State Department and the administration to pay more attention to this issue."[39] Indeed, this may have been part of the design. This type of strategy sums up the IRF Purist approach. However, interview data from staffers in the IRF office across all three administrations note that when it (the IRF office) devotes the entirety of its time trying to elevate the issue, this "jabbing" can feel unproductive.

Former IRF staffer Lauren Woods described it this way: "USCIRF is the thorn in the side of IRF, IRF is the thorn in the side of DLR, DRL is the thorn in the side of the desk. The desk is king."[40] After she described this layered system, she acknowledged that some staffers recognized their location and knew when to push and when to back down. Others did not. Tom Farr noted that, at times, USCIRF's "jabbing" could be used to benefit IRF. "It's good when it's a good cop/bad cop thing. When the Commission is harshly criticizing the State Department about its failure to take to task one country or another, the State Department, if it is wise, can use that to its advantage with country X," leveraging that pressure for change.[41]

Ambassador Seiple recognized this strain immediately. He attributed the disagreements to differences in measuring success. The Countries of Particular Concern (CPC) list symbolized the differences in approach between the IRF office and USCIRF. Per the IRFA, the State Department designates CPCs after publishing annual reports on religious freedom conditions required for each country. To qualify as a CPC, the legislation indicates there must be "systematic, ongoing, egregious violations of religious freedom, including violations such as—(A) torture or cruel, inhumane, or degrading treatment or punishment; (B) prolonged detention without charges; (C) causing the disappearance of persons by the abduction or clandestine detention of those persons; or (D) another flagrant denial of the right to life, liberty, or the security of persons."[42]

But what constituted "systematic, ongoing and egregious violations"? And what was the goal of the CPC list? Here, opinions differed widely, often along organizational lines. The confrontations between USCIRF and the IRF office mimicked the debates surrounding the legislation itself. Many commissioners viewed themselves as courageously taking a "hard line" against persecution. They wanted to publicly and unapologetically rebuke offending governments. However, for Seiple and others who worked at the State Department and belonged to the IRF Pragmatist camp, the CPC list was a tool to leverage. The goal was to keep countries off of the list and to use its threat as an instrument to create positive change. Writing in 2001, Seiple blasted USCIRF, noting its efforts were redundant and claiming that USCIRF automatically distrusted State Department initiatives. Moreover, Seiple lamented USCIRF's apparent disinterest in discussing religious freedom promotion but argued, "They are ready to pick up the club when it comes time to punish."[43] Seiple was careful to note that most USCIRF commissioners were committed to the cause and wanted to work together. But, in his view, a couple of "grenade throwers" were "less than genteel" and hurt the efforts of the entire group.[44] Seiple believed USCIRF was only interested in "cursing the darkness" rather than "lighting candles."[45]

Seiple took a long view of religious freedom efforts and regularly lamented the short-sightedness of American foreign policy.[46] He viewed his role as playing a small but essential role in creating long-term change in some of the most hostile regimes. Under his tenure as ambassador-at-large, which lasted sixteen months, he and his small team laid the groundwork for the years to come.[47] Seiple worked with the Office of Country Reports and Asylum Affairs to create the International Religious Freedom Report. On May 1st of each year, the IRFA required a detailed report for each country in the world, including 1) the status of religious freedom, 2) violations of religious freedom, 3) U.S. policies and actions to promote religious freedom, 4) international agreements in effect, and 5) training of government personnel. The IRF office then delivered this report to Congress. This report identified Countries of Particular Concern, or CPCs, where persecution and limitations on religious freedom are severe. This was a remarkable achievement given the IRF office's limited resources and small staff.

In 1999, the Clinton administration identified Burma, China, Iran, Iraq and Sudan as CPCs.[48] Originally, Secretary Albright rejected the proposition of designating China as a CPC, fearing such an action would incur unwanted diplomatic costs. But, as Seiple recalled, she changed her mind. "She went off to a conference with Asian counterparts, and the Chinese insulted her. She came back and decided to go through with the CPC designation. . . . When that was announced, folks on the Hill were amazed and our office gained a great deal of credibility."[49] Still, others criticized the exclusion of other offending nations, especially North Korea, Saudi Arabia, and Vietnam.[50]

As will be discussed in further detail in chapters 5 and 6, Seiple also made significant inroads in Vietnam and Saudi Arabia. While many lamented his early resignation, he carried his work forward when he created the Institute for Global Engagement (IGE). He continued long-term projects like reconciliation work in Kosovo, Lebanon, and Indonesia in this new role. Today, IGE remains one of the leading NGOs promoting international religious freedom for all.

In reflecting on his tenure as ambassador-at-large in 2001, Seiple celebrated the inclusion of international religious freedom in U.S. foreign policy. But he also noted several troubling signs.[51] He believed that not including the United States in its yearly reports left room for hubris and arrogance. He stressed that humility was necessary to implement this sweeping legislation well. Lasting change would take time, especially in countries without a history of religious freedom. He expressed frustration at the annual reporting process, where Congress expects progress each year. He concluded, "The importance of patience and the applauding of small steps cannot be overstated." Ultimately, he called for greater cooperation between USCIRF and the IRF office and between the United States and other partner nations. He described the need for increased integration of religious freedom concerns across the policy landscape. Unfortunately, tensions at the State Department would worsen before they got any better.

Bureaucratic Tension During the Bush Years

When discussing the Clinton years, signs of tension within the State Department were clear but the strain increased in the early days of the Bush administration. As discussed previously, the first ambassador-at-large for IRF, Bob Seiple, had little patience for arduous State Department procedures or petty bureaucratic politics. But, by not engaging in the typical power plays, Seiple left the office vulnerable during periods of change. During the eight years of Bush's presidency, the IRF office changed dramatically, going from a handful of staffers to over twenty full-time employees.

George Bush nominated John Hanford in November 2001. By that point, the ambassadorship had been vacant for thirteen months. The Senate confirmation period took another several months, and Hanford finally became the second ambassador-at-large for international religious freedom in May 2002. With the longest tenure of any IRF ambassador, he held the position until January 2009. Before becoming the ambassador, Hanford served as a congressional fellow in international religious freedom in the Office of Senator Richard Lugar. An evangelical Christian, Hanford served in pastoral ministry before coming to Washington, DC, to work on Capitol Hill.[52] As described in chapter 1, John Hanford was one of the chief writers of the IRFA. He was intimately aware of its contents and was quick to point out when the law's implementation failed to align with its spirit.

Interview data regarding the early days of IRF showed the polarized atmosphere of the time. When asked about the culture of the IRF office in its early years, one State Department official described it as "collegial and warm" and another as "hostile and insular." Reflecting on John Hanford's leadership style, Knox Thames said, "He was great at thinking through every facet of an issue. . . . He could map out different scenarios about how policy battles might play out." In Thames's view, the natural downside to this precision and carefulness was that Hanford often took a long time to make decisions. The culture and bureaucratic challenges at the State Department impeded speedy progress. "It's a lot of trench warfare to get the simplest things done," he stated.[53] These bureaucratic challenges, and often outright hostility toward the IRF office, intensified during the Bush years. Former staffers cited several distinct but overlapping reasons for such hostility. First, they noted the intrinsic difficulties between the regional and functional bureaus. As Kyle Ballard, a former IRF staffer, recalled: "You almost inherently find that the people who set those offices up are kind of entrepreneurs come in with an attitude about government to say, I was sent here because you can't do the job that you're supposed to be doing and I'm here to make sure that you behave differently. These people were viewed as very zealous and dogmatic . . . which may be fair or unfair, but it is a reputation that has lived on in the bureaucracy."[54]

Tom Farr, who stayed on during the early years of the Bush administration as the Director of the IRF office under John Hanford, blamed the bureaucratic tensions on "an official, if sometimes implicit, reticence about addressing the religious factors in other culture and indeed in seeing culture as an expression of religion at all."[55] Relatedly, Judd Birdsall noted that the IRFA failed to integrate religion into the broader foreign policy process, and "the IRF office remained saddled with a congressional act that fossilized a 1990s vision of religious freedom."[56] In this view, the State Department still considered religious freedom a niche humanitarian issue, divorced from larger strategic and security goals. However, the Bush administration formed two new bureaucratic mechanisms to focus on religious affairs. The Global Anti-Semitism Review Act of 2004 established the special envoy to monitor and combat anti-Semitism. Then, in 2008, President Bush appointed Sada Cumber as the first special envoy to the Organization of Islamic Cooperation (OIC). The OIC brought together leaders from Muslim nations worldwide to "galvanize the Ummah."[57] Of the appointment, Secretary of State Condoleezza Rice stated, "It signals the deep respect for the values and the ideals of Islam that are held by the President and by myself, the U.S. Government and of course, the American people."[58]

Another factor contributing to the tension within the State Department concerned measuring success. To use Kyle Ballard's phrasing, "You're pitting something tangible against something that is very amorphous and nebulous." Having worked himself on the defense sales side of things, he recognized the tension between easily quantifiable exchanges with the much broader and more difficult-to-quantify questions of human rights. Questions surrounding measurement and success also involved disagreements about the rightful uses of the instruments outlined in the IRFA. Was the primary aim to keep countries off the CPC list and use it only when all other options failed? Or was the goal to ensure that the list included all offending governments? This may seem like a small and nuanced difference in approach, but it led to very different policy outcomes and contributed to tensions within the IRF community. Expectedly, IRF Pragmatists opted for the former approach, while the IRF Purists preferred the latter.

Finally, many critics claimed that the IRFA, and thus the IRF office, unfairly prioritized Christians. This practical problem intensified after 9/11 when religious extremism was at the center of the news cycle and the formidable challenge of separating the Muslim radicals who committed these egregious acts of terror from the religion of Islam more broadly. Domestically, controversial issues like the passage of the Patriot Act also contributed to heightened sensitivity surrounding international religious freedom. And some religious leaders who advocated for the IRFA most fiercely quickly gave way to islamophobia in the wake of 9/11.[59] While these leaders had significant influence, their discriminatory views were not representative of the perspectives of the IRF staff. Regardless of party affiliation or religious tradition, each interview with IRF staffers articulated a sincere commitment to religious freedom for all people and lamented the issue's politicization.

Even so, Birdsall noted that the lack of diversity among the IRF staff during the Bush administration confirmed this "Christian-only" bias and admitted that most of the high-profile cases pursued by the IRF at the time office involved Christians.[60] Other State Department officials noted that while evangelicals in the office, and Hanford himself, tried to support staff members who represented minority communities, representation remained an issue: "The issue was structural and not personality-driven."[61] Relatedly, self-selection bias likely continued to the IRF office's reputation. Instead of a general goal of working in foreign policy or diplomacy, many came to the State Department specifically to work on religious freedom issues.

Hanford himself was open about his faith. For some, this was a welcome expression of religious freedom in action. Still, others, even other staffers in the IRF office, were uncomfortable with the public nature of his religious expression. The internal dynamics of the IRF office mirrored the larger societal debates about the proper role of faith in diplomacy. Where should the line be drawn between protecting religious freedom and expression and separating church and state? When is religious expression appropriate in the public square?

Regardless of the merits of the criticism, these perceptions of U.S. efforts to promote international religious freedom continued to circulate around the world. Speaking in 2007, Former Assistant Secretary for DRL John Shattuck identified three major sources of this cynicism.[62] First, he acknowledged many nations viewed the IRFA, and subsequently the efforts of the IRF office, as an attempt to promote missionary activity and evangelism.[63] He also noted that many saw the specific promotion of international religious freedom as evidence that the U.S. cared more about religious rights than other rights. Finally, and perhaps most damaging, Shattuck stated that the United States insufficiently engaged with its partners and allies in this area. Thus, the IRF office was often seen as another attempt at U.S. unilateralism. Given the foreign policy landscape of the 2000s and the ongoing wars in Afghanistan and Iraq, perceptions of U.S. unilateralism were met with scrutiny and hesitation.

Structural Limitations

Despite these global perceptions, cultural considerations, and growing pains, the most difficult challenge the IRF faced was bureaucratic: its positionality within the State Department severely limited its ability to carry out its mission. The arrangement requiring the IRF ambassador-at-large to report to the assistant secretary was contentious because it did not follow the legislative intent of the IRFA, the State Department organizational chart, or the norms of existing precedent. The IRFA explicitly noted that the "Ambassador-at-Large shall be a principal adviser to the President and Secretary of State."[64] All the activities listed in the law spoke directly to the relationship between the secretary and the IRF ambassador. There were two brief mentions of consulting with DRL to produce accurate lists of religious prisoners and in making determinations on whether imports and exports were being used to carry out religious freedom violations in offending nations. Comparatively, there were twenty-six direct mentions of shared action between the secretary of state and the IRF ambassador-at-large. According to organizational structure, the State Department listed ambassadors-at-large as Level 1c, just below the secretary (1), undersecretary, (1a) and deputy secretaries (1b).[65] Assistant secretaries, who had authority at the bureau level, were considered level 2 and, thus, did not have organizational authority over ambassadors-at-large. In 2003, when the tensions between DRL and the IRF office reached a fever pitch, there were only two other positions with the rank of ambassadors-at-large within the diplomatic corps at the State Department: the coordinator for counterterrorism and the ambassador-at-large for war crimes issues.[66] Both positions reported directly to the secretary without mediation.

These inconsistencies have been present since the IRF office's inception, but because Seiple shared a warm working relationship with DRL Assistant Secretaries John Shattuck and Harold Koh, the negative implications of the fragile arrangement were less acute. However, relations between IRF and DRL quickly deteriorated when Lorne Craner became the assistant secretary. Craner and IRF office Director Tom Farr did not see eye to eye. Farr, dissatisfied with the current bureaucratic structure, wanted to establish IRF's autonomy whenever possible, especially while the ambassador-at-large position remained vacant. But Craner perceived his attempts to advocate on behalf of the IRF office as insubordination.[67] Without an ambassador-at-large, with its corresponding level 1c ranking, the IRF office lacked the bureaucratic leverage it needed to conduct its work successfully.

While Ambassador Hanford was aware of tensions within DRL, he hoped that he and Craner could work well together, but his hopes did not materialize:

> We need to be each other's biggest cheerleaders at the State Department. Because we understand that when we go home at night, each of us has problems on our conscience that we didn't get to that day that involved people's lives or whole nations. . . . Unfortunately, my hopes for goodwill were quashed almost immediately, and we found that Lorne and DRL treated IRF with what sometimes amounted to outright hostility. For one thing, I soon learned that the tensions between Lorne and Tom Farr ran much deeper than I had initially understood. When I told Lorne, in my second conversation with him, that I would be retaining Tom as the IRF office director, he got angry and said, "Then we won't be able to work together," and slammed down the phone.[68]

In some ways, these tension points were not unique to IRF. A report from the Office of the Inspector General (OIG) in 2003 showed that staff members across the bureau noted Craner's "own personal style and reserve, his penchant for holding information closely, and his habit of dealing directly and discreetly with individual staff members on particular issues" impeded internal communication and cooperation.[69] This type of "hub-and-spoke" configuration limited the success of the bureau. Indeed, while he may have "dealt directly" with many staff members, Ambassador John Hanford was not one of them. Senior leadership regularly excluded Hanford and the IRF office from bureau-wide meetings and communications. Some challenges were more personal: Hanford was initially denied a parking pass despite his rank, and DRL absorbed the secretarial position previously devoted to the ambassador-at-large.[70]

The disagreements between Assistant Secretary Craner and the IRF office went beyond questions of bureaucratic authority and into significant differences in defining religious freedom and articulating policy choices. Tom Farr notes that, early in his tenure, Craner clarified that he preferred a narrow definition of "religious persecution."[71] In his view, to qualify as religious persecution, religion must be easily identified as the causal variable involved. In practice, other forms of discrimination often accompanied religious freedom concerns. Religious freedom violations occurred alongside ethnic conflict. Discrimination against LBGTQ+ individuals often included a religious element. Likewise, religious tensions sometimes exacerbated violence against women. Offending governments paid attention to these linguistic distinctions, too. Just as "human rights groups may try to 'religionize' issues to use the CPC designation for leverage," Birdsall notes, "governments may try to 'dereligionize' issues because they want to avoid CPC designation."[72]

Again, this seemingly minor disagreement in language pointed to larger debates surrounding the role of international religious freedom in foreign affairs. Should the United States promote religious freedom as an essential but isolated goal? Or should the United States integrate it as a salient factor with far-reaching effects across the foreign policy apparatus? Even within the IRF office, there were contrasting perspectives. As mentioned previously, Farr favored a "capacious understanding" of international religious freedom.[73] Stephen Liston, who served after David Young as the office's third director, believed that the scope of religious freedom efforts should not have included development programming or religious awareness activities.[74] Liston was not the only one with this perspective. Indeed, years later, the Obama administration created an entirely different office, the Office of Religion and Global Affairs (RGA), to handle religious engagement issues that, in its view, did not directly relate to religious freedom. Ambassador Hanford answered these questions pragmatically. While he pushed back against Craner's attempts to redefine international religious freedom, he was also wary of adding extra activities that might steal attention: "I don't think it's in the best interest of the office to have the ambassador incessantly going to meetings all over the Department that have anything remotely to do with religion in general. . . . All that's going to do is dilute your ability to focus on religious persecution and suppression."[75]

When Hanford became the ambassador, the executive secretary at the State Department, Maura Harty, clarified that meetings and access would be streamlined under Powell's leadership. Harty noted that Powell wanted a more linear and direct organizational structure. She used the metaphor of a Christmas tree and indicated that Powell wanted to reduce extending branches and unneeded decor. For the IRF office, this meant exclusion from the morning briefing meetings.[76] Seiple, who had enjoyed access to these meetings, acknowledged that he rarely participated in them and was seldom asked his opinion.[77] Even still, access to these morning meetings provided a valuable opportunity for the IRF office to gather information about what was happening across the department. While Hanford would have welcomed the chance to take part, the change did not cause him outsized consternation.[78] He understood the secretary's dictate to streamline meeting attendance as an across-the-board change affecting various offices and not focused on IRF in particular. Others in the office, and particularly IRF Director Tom Farr, lamented this shift, viewing it as a signal about the seriousness, or lack thereof, with which the secretary considered international religious freedom.[79]

Hanford looked for other ways to elevate international religious freedom priorities. Without the help of DRL leadership, Hanford went directly to Deputy Secretary of State Richard Armitage. And, by 2003, Hanford secured IRF's ability to send memorandum directly to the secretary of state without DRL's mediation. The following year, Hanford worked to extract the responsibility of the annual IRF report from DRL. Dissatisfied with the fact that DRL leadership relegated the IRF report to summer interns, Hanford sought to obtain control over the report's content. He also negotiated several additional positions for the office.[80] Hanford spent considerable time looking for effective diplomats to join the IRF office.

IRF staffers also grappled with handling the tensions in the IRF office. Given the challenging institutional position, some met them with force, trying to get the bureaucracy to pay attention to IRF at every turn. Others took a softer approach and tried to form collegial relationships. Kyle Ballard noted his attempts at deepening relationships at the State Department. For instance, if a department official was facing congressional pressure and going to be meeting on the Hill, Ballard saw that as the perfect opportunity to help them prepare in advance. Sometimes, the result was simply to ease political tensions, but other times the preparation elevated religious freedom concerns on the agenda.

Expectedly, tensions between the State Department and USCIRF remained intense during the Bush years. Problematically, many in the U.S. media—and certainly overseas—misunderstood the organization of USCIRF and the IRF office. Some thought the groups were synonymous. For example, some misreported the CPC list from year to year, drawing instead on USCIRF's recommendations rather than the official State Department designations. Despite the independence of the commission, this misunderstanding afforded USCIRF more leverage, for better or worse.

Other points of contention were internal to USCIRF. While many of the inaugural commissioners, like Nina Shea and Michael Young, were reappointed, the commission welcomed several new commissioners during the Bush years. These included prominent evangelical Richard D. Land and Catholic Bishop William F. Murphy. The Honorable Shirin R. Tahir-Kheli joined in 2001. During this period, new allegations of anti-Muslim bias surfaced. Khaled Abou El Fadl, a legal scholar and former commissioner, said, "It was predetermined who the bad guys are and who the good guys are . . . there is a very pronounced view of the world, and it is that victims of religious discrimination are invariably Christian. It was rather suffocating."[81]

Within President Bush's first term, Burma, China, Iran, Iraq, and Sudan remained on the list before the administration removed Iraq in 2004 with the fall of Saddam Hussein's regime. In 2003, they added North Korea, and in 2004, Eritrea, Saudi Arabia, and Vietnam. As discussed in chapter 5, Vietnam entered a negotiated agreement and was removed from the list in 2006. The administration added Uzbekistan that same year.

A New Start: Bureaucratic Shifts During the Obama Years

The election of President Obama, and the return of Democratic control to the executive branch, equated to big changes for international religious freedom promotion at the State Department. However, new initiatives, including the new Office of Religion and Global Affairs, did not materialize overnight. It was not until 2011, when Secretary of State Hillary Clinton brought together the Religion and U.S. Foreign Policy Working Group, that bureaucratic changes were formalized. In addition, after John Hanford's term as ambassador-at-large ended, the position remained vacant for well over two years. This vacancy frustrated many in the IRF community, who viewed it as a signal that President Obama was unconcerned with international religious freedom efforts. Birdsall put this bluntly: "Everyone knows low priorities get slow appointments."[82] Because of this massive delay, the would-be ambassador-at-large faced added pressure. While the prolonged period between Hanford's term and the appointment of Suzan Johnson Cook impeded the IRFA's success, Knox Thames argued that the break between ambassadors also allowed for tensions between the IRF office and USCIRF to cool off and the relationship to heal.[83] Birdsall noted that, under the leadership of IRF office director Kurt Donnelly, the IRF office focused on rehabilitating its image and engagement with actors across the Department.[84]

During this interregnum, IRF staffers joined the State Department's Religion and Global Affairs Forum, a new initiative "to foster collaboration on religious engagement and socialize the Department to the growing salience of religion in international relations."[85] Out of these efforts, the White House created the Interagency Working Group on Religion and Global Affairs, and President Obama commissioned a worldwide survey to determine how embassies across the globe engaged with religious groups. Secretary Clinton also named Farah Pandith the first-ever special representative to Muslim communities in June 2009. These early efforts forged new relationships and worked to confront the reputation that the IRF office was only interested in protecting Christians. Years later, these efforts would culminate in large-scale changes in the organizational structure at the State Department.

An Ambassador Finally Arrives

Suzan Johnson Cook was the first and, at this writing, the only woman to hold the ambassador-at-large position. As some scholars have noted, this nomination held symbolic power, signaling that women could engage religious leaders on a global scale.[86] She joined the State Department in May 2011. Before she was appointed ambassador-at-large, Suzan Johnson Cook's efforts primarily concerned domestic religious engagement. A pastor and theologian, she served as senior pastor of the Bronx Christian Fellowship Baptist Church in New York City from 1996 to 2010. She also founded the Wisdom Women Worldwide Center, a faith-based network aimed at empowering female religious leaders in public life across the globe, and the Multi-Ethnic Center, which provided enrichment programming for youth. Previous experience also included serving as chaplain to the New York Police Department. In her words, Johnson Cook focused on "bringing women, faith leaders and multi-national NGOs to the table."[87]

Her political experience was also domestic-focused, as she served on President Clinton's Domestic Policy Council. Despite her strong track record with religious engagement in the United States, many lamented her lack of foreign policy experience or human rights advocacy.[88] Senator Jim DeMint (R-SC) questioned if international religious freedom was Johnson Cook's passion or her area of expertise. He went further, questioning if she had "the courage or the boldness to deal with this issue."[89] In his view, the ambassador needed boldness because he "didn't expect this administration or the next within the State Department culture to really take these issues as seriously as they should."[90]

After Johnson Cook became ambassador, many of these same criticisms followed her, and several of the staffers interviewed noted that her lack of foreign policy experience limited the efficacy of IRF's work. One staffer put it bluntly: "With completely failed leadership, the only reason the IRF office was saved was because of a good staff."[91] Another staffer noted that they focused on working with DRL Secretary Michael Posner. Others took a longer-term approach, fearing that excessive boldness or inflexibility, without the backing of an ambassador, would preclude them from future policy debates. One official recalled, "If I'm a pain in the ass, the desk will stop sending me paper. I just wanted to behave reasonably enough to have the opportunity to provide input."[92]

During Johnson Cook's tenure, the Obama administration ushered in new mechanisms to engage religion in global affairs. Secretary of State Hillary Clinton launched a Working Group on Religion and Foreign Policy, as part of the Strategic Dialogue with Civil Society program. While there was a subgroup focused on International Religious Freedom, Democracy, and Stability, the efforts of the working group were expansive and included efforts to "leverage [religion] in the pursuit of a stronger society."[93] The group was cochaired by Ambassador Johnson Cook and Joshua DuBois, the director of the White House's Office of Faith-Based and Neighborhood Partnerships. The working group put forth two recommendations in the first year. First, it recommended new literacy initiatives at the State Department, bolstering existing efforts to increase officers' understanding of religion, religious engagement and religious freedom efforts.[94] The group advised opening lines of communication to ensure that foreign and civil service officers understood when and how to apply the Establishment Clause to its diplomatic engagement efforts.[95] Second, the Working Group recommended a new structural solution via a new State Department mechanism that could increase existing State Department capacity. It identified five priorities when considering the new mechanism. It needed to focus on 1) integration across the department; 2) gaining access to high-level discussions and leaders; 3) addressing religious engagement across the department instead of limiting it only to questions of human rights; 4) collaborating with the IRF office;[96] and 5) ensuring the new mechanism be cost-effective.[97]

In August 2013, several months after becoming secretary of state, John Kerry agreed that "we ignore the global impact of religion at our peril."[98] Taken on its own, one might expect this type of statement to elicit excitement and joy from the international religious freedom community. Here was a secretary of state, finally highlighting the need to focus on religion. However, engaging religion at the State Department did not necessarily translate to elevating the IRF office. The Obama administration concentrated its efforts on creating a separate office at the State Department, the Office of Faith-Based and Community Initiatives.

In his brief interview after John Kerry gave remarks, Shaun Casey, the new special representative for religion and global affairs (RGA), noted that "the point is that our collaboration with my office is not to design and create a new silo that addresses religion in an isolated manner. Rather, we are seeking to multiply the engagement with religion that already exists across the bureaus and offices of this great organization."[99] Shaun Casey presented the role of the RGA as interrupting and adding complexity to reductive conceptions of religion in U.S. diplomacy. In an interview at Yale's Divinity School in 2016, he argued that "the US government historically has examined religion through two lenses: the evaluation of international religious freedom, or religion as a potential catalyst for violent extremism. While these are both important analytical lenses, they do not begin to exhaust the range of diplomatic and political implications of understanding religion. Our office was created to explore the vast territory between these two conceptualizations of religion in the realm of foreign policy."[100]

Some international religious freedom advocates rejected this dichotomy and argued that religious freedom, in its full expression, would allow for and encourage the full engagement of religious actors across the globe. The language of the IRFA extended beyond battling religious persecution; it also sought to promote religious freedom.[101] Religious freedom was necessary to make religious engagement possible. However, other IRF advocates welcomed the new addition.

It is important to note that the IRF office and IRF staffers were instrumental in forming the working group that led to the new office. Strictly separating the IRF office and the new RGA initiatives does not reflect history. Overall, the early Obama years brought significant change—whether it was welcome or unwelcome change depends on who you ask. Suzan Johnson Cook resigned her position in October 2013 and returned to the private sector.[102] This time, the position was vacant for just over a year. However, her successor, Rabbi David Saperstein, capitalized on the new bureaucratic changes at the State Department when he took the baton in December 2014.

A Familiar Face: Rabbi Saperstein's Tenure as Ambassador-at-Large

Rabbi David Saperstein, an ardent advocate for international religious freedom, helped ensure that the legislative efforts in the 1990s included all religious believers. Saperstein served as the director of the Religious Action Center of Reform Judaism for decades and *The Washington Post* designated him the "quintessential religious lobbyist on Capitol Hill."[103] Importantly, he also served as the first chair of the U.S. Commission for International Religious Freedom (USCIRF). These experiences uniquely positioned Saperstein to increase collaboration between the organizations.

During his confirmation hearing in September 2014, Rabbi Saperstein pledged that, if confirmed, he would integrate religious freedom into the nation's general strategy. He set the scene for broad engagement, noting religious freedom's connection to conflict stability efforts, human rights, and economic prosperity.[104] The newly formed RGA office took on some of these efforts. Even so, Saperstein focused on developing thematic competencies within the IRF office and developed the IRF office's structure to mimic the larger structure of the department, with regional and functional bureaus. Thus, in addition to staffers who focused on religious freedom issues in a particular region or country, the office had staff devoted to thematic issues, including blasphemy and apostasy laws, women's rights and religious freedom, and the countering of violent extremism. Overall, Saperstein was happy with the new structure. Unlike the notoriously tense relationship between the functional bureaus and the regional desks at the State Department, the staffers in the IRF office across regions and themes worked well together, and Saperstein's description of navigating the bureaucracy at the department differed dramatically from the experiences of previous ambassadors.

Protecting Religious Minorities in the Near East and South Central Asia

In 2013, Congress passed H.R. 310, sponsored by Rep. Frank Wolf (R-VA), to create a special envoy to promote religious freedom of religious minorities in the Near East and South Central Asia. The legislation indicated that the new position would have ambassador-level rank.[105]

Related Senate Bill 653, known as the "Near East and South Central Asia Religious Freedom Act," became law on August 8, 2014, but the position outlined in the legislation remained vacant for over a year until the administration appointed Knox Thames on September 16, 2015, with the title of special advisor for religious minorities in the Near East and South Central Asia.

President Obama appointed Thames at the recommendation of Ambassador Saperstein. Impressed with his qualifications and long-standing commitment to international religious freedom, most praised the selection of Thames to lead the new efforts. However, others expressed dismay that the administration downgraded the position to special advisor instead of special envoy, as the original legislation directed. In a letter to Secretary Kerry, Senator James Lankford (R-OK) expressed his frustration and asked, "How does creating a lower-level position reflect that promoting and protecting religious freedom is a key objective of U.S. foreign policy?"[106] Lankford also noted his concern about the length of time it took to fill the vacancy for this position. The method of announcing Thames's appointment, a Twitter post from Ambassador Saperstein, also drew particular ire from the senator.

But an interview with Thames told a less controversial version of the story. He expressed some confusion at the appointment process but described the conversations with senior administration officials during this time as productive. Thames suggested that the Obama administration convert the position to a nonpartisan (Schedule B) instead of a political appointment (Schedule C). Careful to note that he would have accepted an ask to serve at Obama's request, Thames preferred to continue his work in a nonpartisan way.[107] After many years of working together with a shared purpose, the relationship between Saperstein and Thames was strong. Despite being "downgraded" from special envoy to special advisor, it was unlikely that Saperstein would impede Thames's efforts. This also meant that the Obama administration could fill the position immediately instead of waiting for a lengthy Senate confirmation process. Thames started just two weeks after his appointment.

The work of Knox Thames during this period represents what scholars Sharon Alvarez and Jay Barney term a "discovery" approach to entrepreneurial action.[108] Here, Thames recognized a new opportunity and took action once the policy window aligned. He thought creatively about how better to integrate religious freedom concerns throughout the State Department. Human rights atrocities in Iraq and Syria led him to connect with cultural preservation efforts. At the same time, ISIS was committing physical genocide; it was also erasing, or attempting to erase, the cultural landscape of Iraq and Syria. Holding tightly to a radically exclusive version of Islam, ISIS deliberately destroyed Christian, Yazidi, and non-Sunni Muslim sites.

Beyond this expected iconoclasm, ISIS also destroyed significant artifacts from ancient periods, the cultures of which no longer existed. Scholars debated the motivations of these rampages. Arguing that religion was but one dimension of ISIS's motivation for destroying heritage sites, anthropologist Chiara de Cesari contends that the violence was "a symbol of the failure of the post-colonial state," and that ISIS sought to build anew, without the sins of ancient pasts of the past haunting the newly established caliphate.[109] Alternatively, historian Christopher Jones argues that ISIS's expansive attacks originated with a rejection of the idea of the nation-state itself. In this view, since the nation-state required to citizens obey its laws and commanded its own authority, it inherently violated Islamic code, which reserved all loyalty and authority for God.[110] Regardless of the complexities of ISIS's motivations or the details of its strategy, beginning in 2012, the destruction of cultural and religious sites was monumental. ISIS leveled cultural sites in places like Aleppo in Syria, and Hatra and Ashur in Iraq entirely.

Recognizing the magnitude of this problem and its acute effect on religious minorities, Knox Thames described asking several organizations involved with cultural preservation, including the Cultural Heritage Center (CHC) at the State Department, the U.N. Education, Scientific, and Cultural Organization (UNESCO) and the Smithsonian Institution, how they engaged religious communities at historical sites. The answer was largely the same: They didn't. Thames identified this as an opportunity to make tangible progress.[111]

President Obama bolstered efforts to connect religious freedom concerns with cultural preservation on May 9, 2016, when he signed the Protect and Preserve International Cultural Property Act. This bill, sponsored by Representative Eliot Engel (D-NY), instructed the president to "impose import restrictions with respect to any archaeological or ethnological materials of Syria."[112] The legislation also called for interagency efforts to strengthen executive branch activity to preserve cultural property. The impetus for this new legislation was partly because of the growing understanding of the connections between preservation and countering violent extremism. "In many ways, it helps to frame it as a national-security issue to make it more important," writes law professor Mark Vlasic, who specializes in "blood antiquities." "When you observe that stolen cultural heritage is funding ISIS," Vlasic continues, "and that these terrorists could kill more Americans based on the money they have, then all of a sudden, it becomes something we need to pay more attention to."[113] The connection between terrorist financing and the smuggling of blood antiquities received increased publicity as Hobby Lobby, a major arts and crafts company in the United States, illegally purchased almost four thousand Iraqi artifacts from the UAE and Israel, in violation of federal law.[114]

Months later, in September 2016, the State Department convened a panel discussion, "Today's Struggle to Protect and Preserve the Cultural Heritage of Religious Minorities," at the Metropolitan Museum of Art. Here, Thames lamented the uptick in violence at the hands of ISIS and the "destruction of churches and monasteries, Sunni and Shi'a shrines and mosques, Yazidi temples, Jewish cemeteries and other historic sites."[115] After the panel, the Bureau of Educational and Cultural Affairs announced a series of coordinated efforts in response.[116] This announcement included increased funding for the Cultural Antiquities Task Force to combat the looting and trafficking of culturally significant objects. In addition, it included expanded support for the Iraqi Institute for the Conservation of Antiquities and Heritage (IICAH) and particularly for training IICAH leaders to equip them in restoration and education efforts.

The State Department also undertook several initiatives with the Smithsonian Institute. In 2016, they collaborated to put together a handbook, *The Guide to Mosul Heritage*, which was then distributed to coalition forces. The handbook provided rich detail of the cultural sites at risk during their operations. In addition, it summarized expectations and guidelines for protecting cultural property, as identified in the 1954 Hague Convention for the Protection of Cultural Property in the Event of Armed Conflict. The collaboration continued the following year as the organizations published another guide, this time describing heritage sites around Raqqa and Deir ez-Zor. The Smithsonian Institution partnered with the State Department to convene a special workshop, "Protecting the Cultural Heritage of Religious Minorities," for representatives of persecuted groups in northern Iraq.

Reforms at USCIRF

During the Obama years, USCIRF expressed concern that their efforts were becoming too intertwined with the work of the State Department's IRF office. Nina Shea, who served on the commission from 1999 to 2012, expressed frustration that USCIRF reports were overrelying on the State Department reports, recycling the "boilerplate" language year after year. "Since the whole concept of the Commission was to be a watchdog organization that can independently propose new issues and identify new trouble spots," Shea argued, "this trend is very disturbing."[117] Suzan Johnson Cook was not immune to ongoing criticism of USCIRF, though, since she was not as directly involved as Ambassadors Seiple and Hanford, the tensions surrounded what she did not do rather than what she did. Shea scrutinized Johnson Cook, arguing that the ambassador "is supposed to be an early warning signal before massacres break out, and I think she missed some of the biggest crises of our day," Shea maintained.[118] She expressed particular frustration with Johnson Cook's inaction on behalf of Coptic Christians in the Near East. Johnson Cook responded to the criticism, noting that the secretary of state and president constrained her actions and decisions. She also noted that security clearance issues prevented her from sharing the complete picture of diplomatic negotiations.[119]

There was a common understanding among the USCIRF commissioners that they would keep as much agency regarding the priorities of the commission and the subsequent recommendations and publications. Rather than have a staff-led organization with commissioners serving as a de facto board of directors, they wanted to retain autonomy. In this view, as appointed commissioners, it was their responsibility to make the judgment calls, not the staff.[120] From the perspective of some IRF officials, the disconnect between staff members and the commissioners constrained USCIRF's success. During the Obama administration, IRF staffers held USCIRF staffers in high esteem. Occasionally, USCIRF staffers even transitioned to positions at the State Department.

But, in February 2010, tensions within USCIRF reignited. While allegations had swirled for years, a new report from *The Washington Post* drew significant attention, especially from congressional leaders.[121] It included allegations from former commissioners and charged that US-CIRF's tribalism, in-group thinking, and anti-Muslim bias impeded its efficacy.[122] One high-level department official accused USCIRF of being short-sighted. The IRF office had to pragmatically consider the entire diplomatic picture, while USCIRF's laser focus on religious freedom violations ignored the broader geopolitical context. While the official recognized that, in some ways, this was the legislation's design, he lamented the challenges that resulted: "Commissioners were deeply entrenched in their own agendas without proper understanding of the political dynamics involved." The official continued, "Perhaps there is a reason that Congress did not set up another watchdog organization when it created it's Anti-Trafficking Office."[123]

After a long battle, where it was unclear if Congress would reauthorize USCIRF, Congress mandated several new reforms in 2011.[124] These reforms included a significant budget cut lowering the commission's annual budget from $3 million to $2 million. More notably, however, was the introduction of two-year term limits for commissioners. By this point, most of them had been on the commission for many years. As a result, it forced seven of the nine to resign within ninety days of the reauthorization. One former USCIRF commissioner argued that these reforms were short-sighted: "You need to develop both institutional memory when you arrive at the Commission and institutional capacity."[125] This capacity-building process, which entailed learning USCIRF's position among all of the moving parts within the U.S. government, took time. In this commissioner's view, these reforms created a "revolving door" of commissioners and severely weakened USCIRF's capacity.[126]

After the series of reforms, USCIRF entered a new period with a fresh start. This coincided with Ambassador Saperstein's appointment as ambassador-at-large. Given his vast experience with the commission, Saperstein focused on building strong, collaborative relationships. During this period, USCIRF asked what role they might play in coordinating efforts with parliamentarians in other countries. About this same time, the All Party Parliamentary Group for International Freedom of Religion or Belief (APPG FoRB), under the leadership of Lady Elizabeth

Berridge, released a report, "Article 18: An Orphaned Right."[127] Intrigued by it and hopeful for opportunities to collaborate, Thames reached out and coordinated a meeting in Oxford in June 2014 with a small group of parliamentarians from around the world to discuss ways to work together to confront religious freedom abuses abroad.

These initial meetings resulted in the establishment of the International Panel of Parliamentarians for Freedom of Religion or Belief (IPPFoRB) in 2014. The following year, IPPFoRB, along with Konrad Adenauer Stiftung, the Church of England, the Norwegian Foreign Ministry, and USCIRF, convened a group of almost one hundred parliamentarians from over forty-five countries, with the goal of creating and solidifying a plan to take an international approach to promote religious freedom.[128] The resulting document, "The New York Resolution on Freedom of Religion or Belief," serves as the foundation for IPPFoRB's work that continues today. This success was possible "because we had staff expertise, with the expertise of Commissioners working hand in hand and complementing each other," Thames maintained. "Those Commissioners could reach up high and get headlines, we [the staffers] provided the expertise."[129]

By the time Obama left office, many of the bureaucratic challenges analyzed in this chapter approached resolution. The IRF office transformed its reputation within the State Department with a more diverse staff and efforts to increase bipartisanship. Increased support from top leadership aided in these efforts.

These bureaucratic details deserve consideration because they impacted the IRF office's capabilities. The acute tensions originating from the early legislative debates of the 1990s carried forward. While one might assume that advocates would rally in unison behind the cause of protecting the world's most vulnerable, history reveals a more fractured and bitter story. Indeed, many of the former staff and commissioners expressed enduring frustration and sometimes pain when recalling their experiences in the international religious freedom space. Perhaps most important, albeit difficult to quantify, is what the IRF office was unable to accomplish because of the time, mental space, and emotional energy automatically, if reluctantly, devoted to handling bureaucratic challenges. Across the three case studies that follow, the tenuous bureaucratic situation constrained the IRF office's ability to carry out its mission.

PART TWO

4

International Religious Freedom in China

In the 1992 presidential campaign, then-Governor Clinton lambasted President George H. W. Bush concerning his foreign policy toward China. Upon accepting the presidential nomination, Clinton envisaged "an America that will not coddle tyrants, from Baghdad to Beijing," a blatant affront to the Bush administration's restraint.[1] James Mann put it this way: "On China, Clinton took office believing that he could have everything and please everyone. He saw no conflict between American ideals and American commerce, or between his desire to please the Chinese students, whom he had so carefully courted during the campaign, and the business community whose support he had also assiduously cultivated. . . . At the beginning of 1993, everything seemed possible."[2] But, Clinton would soon understand, everything was not possible. He could not please everyone at the same time, and tensions between American ideals and American commerce were real and unavoidable. Much to the chagrin of most international religious freedom advocates, Clinton's tough stance on China's human rights record proved too difficult to maintain.

There is a long history of religious and political oppression under the communist regime in China. While scholars debate the specific reasons for the ongoing assault on religion, at its core are questions of power and control. Still-dominant ideology within the CCP views religion as a mechanism of "foreign domination"—a symptom of Western imperialism. As scholar Zhou Qi notes, Chinese leadership term U.S. human rights efforts as "human rights diplomacy," tying human rights promotion to larger U.S. foreign policy goals—namely, to increasing American power.[3] While much of the CCP's trepidation concerns geopolitics and power dynamics, some fears transcend international relations. Religious convictions, especially those deeply held, can challenge loyalty to the state. Thus, despite the rhetorical commitment to freedom of religion affirmed in Article 36 of the Chinese Constitution, religion remains highly restricted. State interference, surveillance, and government-sanctioned persecution affect hundreds of millions of religious adherents in the country.

Stories of appalling persecution filled the pages of human rights reports throughout the 1980s and 1990s.[4] Religious freedom violations in China outraged congressional leaders, church members, and the activist community. With recent memories of the atrocities of Tiananmen Square in 1989 in mind, groups mobilized. A powerful movement emerged as a result of strong condemnation of the H. W. Bush administration's unemotional response to human rights abuses coupled with an escalating wave of persecution across different faiths. When advocates pressed for legislative action, they often used the China case, because of the severity of the atrocities committed. Indeed, the horrors of abuse contributed to IRFA's passage.

This chapter considers U.S. foreign policy toward China during the Clinton, Bush, and Obama years, focusing specifically on efforts, or lack thereof, to combat persecution and promote religious freedom. In many ways, it is a story of how international religious freedom policy gets lost in the middle of larger strategic shifts and conflicting interests. Throughout the three administrations, competing visions of U.S. foreign policy in China, ranging from constructive engagement to more hardline containment strategies, caused dissension.

Despite his hardline campaign rhetoric, Clinton reversed course and articulated a "comprehensive engagement" strategy. Clinton elevated trade policy, granted China Most Favored Nation Trade status (MFN) and helped facilitate China's entry into the World Trade Organization (WTO), despite China's ongoing human rights abuses. Still, under the Clinton administration, Ambassador Seiple and his small team created new inroads that his successor, Ambassador John Hanford, built upon. President Bush, who vocally supported increased religious freedoms in China, bolstered Hanford's efforts, as the administration focused on combating terrorism and called upon the CCP to be a "responsible stakeholder" in the region. Faced with a rising great power rivalry, President Obama pivoted to Asia. The administration engaged significantly with the CCP, as it combatted Chinese aggression in the South China Sea and worked toward global climate change policy. However, the pivot did not automatically translate to an increased focus on religious freedom issues. This next section outlines the sources of religious intolerance in contemporary Chinese history and considers the strategic dynamics that shaped U.S. policy toward China and constrained international religious freedom efforts.

Historical Context

With the communist takeover of China in 1949, Mao Zedong began a decades-long process to try to decrease religion's control in China. He was steeped in Marxist aversion to religion and desired complete political control. Chairman Mao, and the CCP writ large, saw religion as threatening for three reasons: 1) it viewed religion as a tool of capitalism that would hinder economic progress and prevent communism's flourishing; 2) it viewed religion—and particularly eschatological beliefs—as weakening the state's control; and 3) it feared that foreign governments were exploiting religious belief to foment separatism. As the pages that follow detail, during the period under study the CCP's response to religion was cyclical. As religious groups gained momentum, the CCP cracked down. Then, slowly, religious groups were afforded more latitude, before, again, the government intervened.[5]

Religious intolerance in China did not begin with the toppling of the KMT. Apprehension about the spread of Christianity, combined with fear of increasing Japanese and Western influences, led to bloody confrontations in the late 1800s. By 1899, the confrontations had reached Beijing, culminating in the Boxer Rebellion.[6] Three decades later, the anti-Christian movement of the 1920s erupted across the country. Here, members of the Anti-Christian Federation destroyed property, occupied Christian schools and churches, and, in some places, murdered missionaries.[7]

Then, in 1949, as the People's Republic of China was founded, so too was the State Administration for Religious Affairs Bureau (SARA). Through a complex bureaucratic system, the CCP employs various mechanisms in order to control religion, including burdensome registration processes, intense surveillance and monitoring of religious activity, preapproval of all religious materials and sermons before distribution, and the forced infusion of Chinese propaganda in religious services. The Chinese Constitution suggests that its involvement in religious affairs is to protect the public order, health of citizens, and the education system.

However, the inexactitude of these goals allows the Chinese government to have constitutional backing to become involved at will. The Public Security Bureau handles implementation of these regulations.[8]

Beginning in the late 1950s, with Mao Zedong's Great Leap Forward and the Cultural Revolution, religious groups of all types, and particularly Christian congregations, were decimated. The CCP destroyed religious schools, executed clergy and missionaries, and methodically murdered citizens unwilling to denounce their faith. After two brutal decades of persecution, religious communities in China felt relief when Deng Xiaoping ushered in new reforms. During this time, China experienced explosive religious revival, especially of Protestant churches. Fearing religion's growing influence, the CCP responded by increasing its controls of religious practice. Since the late 1970s, China has witnessed widespread growth of religion and widespread persecution.

Registration of religious groups is mandatory. However, China will only recognize state-sanctioned versions of Buddhism, Catholicism, Daoism, Islam, and Protestantism.[9] As such, religious groups that fall outside of these state-sanctioned faiths cannot register. Thus, simply by existing, these unregistered groups violate the law.

While all religious adherents face repression from the state, some fare better than others. Religions considered indigenous to China, like Confucianism or Daoism, enjoy slightly higher levels of freedom. But because of the CCP's fierce desire for control, it targets religious sects that are also seeking some level of political autonomy with particular vigor. Hostility against the Uyghur population in the Xinjiang Province stems, in part, from perceived connections to the East Turkestan Islamic Movement (ETIM).[10] Their commitment to national identity also makes the Tibetan Buddhists another target of special, though unwanted, attention from the CCP. Given a history of struggle and war combined with an enduring reverence of the Dalai Lama, Tibetan Buddhists are routinely subject to imprisonment and "reeducation" for minor violations of religious codes.

Throughout the time period under review, the CCP persecuted Christian communities with varying levels of intensity. These restrictions included, but were not limited to, the forbiddance of teaching Christian eschatology and the mandatory final assent to the Communist Party in matters of faith and conduct.[11]

In short, restrictions on belief and practice have threatened the rights of all religious believers in China, regardless of faith or creed. This abysmal human rights record, particularly regarding religious expression, has complicated U.S.-China relations for decades. To varying degrees, each president has expressed outrage, imploring the CCP to abide by international norms as codified in the Universal Declaration of Human Rights. If acknowledged at all, the CCP meets these appeals with denial and anger. When directly confronted on questions about labor camps and religious prisoners, government officials will issue the now predictable response: they detain citizens for political reasons—trying to disrupt the public order—rather than due to sincerely held religious convictions. The CCP leaves religious regulations intentionally vague, claiming to "protect normal religious activities" without ever defining normality. This deliberate vagueness in the law gives the government "legal" permission to discriminate while still making a rhetorical nod to freedom to appease the international community.

When Clinton won the 1992 presidential election, the images of Tiananmen Square remained fresh in America's collective memory. Only three years prior, in May 1989, the Chinese Communist Party declared martial law as pro-democracy protesters coalesced in Beijing. Inspired by the death of a prominent reformer, Hu Yaobang, the demonstrators, many of them students, pushed for democratization, a free press, and the freedom of conscience. They also demanded political autonomy. The CCP sensed the power undergirding the movement and met the peaceful protest with fury. On June 4, 1989, the tension reached a breaking point as troops moved into Tiananmen Square, firing indiscriminately into the crowd. Death tolls from the massacre vary widely, ranging from several hundred to several thousands of lives lost.

A rare internal CCP document encapsulated the party's perspective on religion after the massacre. The document, issued February 5, 1991, stated plainly: "We must realize that hostile forces beyond our borders have all along been using religion as an important means to carry out their strategy of bringing about 'peaceful evolution' in our country. They have continuously engaged in infiltration and disruptive activities against us."[12] The document alleged that splittist movements have "used religion to stir up trouble," and that some religious actors were resorting to oppressive feudal structures, aimed at siphoning power away from the

CCP. Finally, it lamented that some illegal religious actors are "trying to compete with us for the hearts and minds of young people."[13]

In the wake of the violence at Tiananmen Square, President Bush attempted to condemn the massacre without sacrificing American interests in China. But, many Americans sought an impassioned, and immediate, castigation of the CCP and criticized Bush's restraint. In his presidential campaign, then-Governor Clinton capitalized on these critiques of the Bush administration and vowed to change course if elected.

IRF Policy During the Clinton Years: 1993–2001

When Bill Clinton became president, religious believers in China were facing a crackdown on religious activity and expression. In 1992, the State Administration for Religious Affairs (SARA) bulldozed churches, imprisoned clergy, and sent congregants to "reeducation facilities."[14] Catholic Bishop Liu Difen was killed in a labor camp in November 1992, and the following year, Human Rights Watch (HRW) released a report detailing the gruesome beatings of worshippers in Shaanxi Province.[15] Also that year, police arrested Fathers Guo Xijing and Miao Lehua along with a group of devout Catholics as they observed mass in an unregistered house church.[16] HRW also provided evidence of organ transplant operations performed on executed prisoners—many of whom were in prison for unsanctioned religious activity.[17] Report after report detailed stories like these: of men and women whose lives were upended or brutally cut short. Unsurprisingly, throughout the early 1990s, asylum claims due to religious persecution rose, especially among unsanctioned Christian congregations.[18]

As the United States and the international community expressed outrage, Chinese officials continued to deny the allegations. Zhang Shengzuo, the director of Religious Affairs at the State Council, maintained that religious activities existed, in part, to maintain social unity and promote China's economic prosperity. He vigorously denied that the CCP had detained anyone for practicing their faith. Instead, he claimed that those arrested threatened China's stability.[19] When questioned about the thousands of political dissidents imprisoned, he repeated a familiar refrain: they detained individuals for breaking the law, not because of their religious or political beliefs.[20]

Another mechanism for total control was new regulation, which loosened the legal criteria used to charge citizens for unsanctioned religious activity. A 1994 update to the 1987 Regulations on Government Public Order Offenses made it illegal to hold social gatherings without registration.[21] Regulation No. 145 created a new commission to monitor religious activity, making the registration process for new churches even more cumbersome.[22]

Debating MFN Status

From a strategic perspective, the primary point of contention in the U.S.-China relationship in the mid-1990s revolved around trade and, specifically, the granting of Most Favored Nation (MFN) status. Decades earlier, the passage of the Jackson–Vanik Amendment linked human rights and trade regulation. Unless the United States issued a waiver, Jackson–Vanik prevented nonmarket economies that abused human rights from achieving MFN status.[23] With China, the U.S. granted provisional MFN status in 1980. But the status required annual renewal. In subsequent years, vigorous debate would center on China's human rights record, and many would call for the privileged status to expire.

As China tightened its regulations stipulating religious activity, Clinton vowed to take a tough stance on human rights. In the early days of his term, his assembled team seemed unified in its approach. He appointed Winston Lord, a vocal supporter of leveraging economic ties to promote human rights change, as assistant secretary of state for Asia and the Pacific. During his confirmation hearing, Warren Christopher, Clinton's first secretary of state, stated with striking candor, "Our policy will be to seek to facilitate a broad, peaceful revolution in China, from communism to democracy, by encouraging the forces of economic and political liberalization in that great and highly important country."[24] Throughout his campaign, Clinton signaled his support for legislative actions to connect MFN status to human rights progress—a strategy promoted by Congress since the H. W. Bush presidency.

Economic interests in China multiplied during the first years of Clinton's presidency, making his hard-line approach more challenging to sustain. On the one hand, Clinton was under significant pressure from Congress, who threatened to take action if they were dissatisfied with the administration's approach to human rights.[25] But, with the changing economic calculus, the business community pushed for unconditional MFN status. In an attempt to appease both groups, Clinton announced an executive order.[26] In a jubilant ceremony in May 1993, Clinton signed a detailed plan that involved new human rights criteria that the administration would use to determine China's trade status. The demands were specific: China needed to release peaceful dissidents, protect Tibetan religious and cultural traditions, and grant access to radio and media outlets.[27]

In September 1993, National Security Advisor Anthony Lake introduced the Clinton administration's new foreign policy strategy. He explained that the U.S. would move from containment to enlargement. Here, he identified four components of the new strategy. Enlargement meant 1) strengthening market democracies; 2) fostering new market democracies where possible; 3) countering belligerence against market democracies; and 4) promoting a bold humanitarian agenda that included aid and democracy promotion.[28] Lake argued that "our strategy must be pragmatic. Our interests in democracy and markets do not stand alone. Other American interests at times will require us to befriend and even defend non-democratic states for mutually beneficial reasons."[29] This pragmatic approach did not align with the hard-line criteria outlined in the May 1993 executive order. Former National Security Council (NSC) staffer Michael Green put it this way: "Clinton turned campaign pledges and untested academic theories into inflexible policies that contradicted his core foreign policy theme of enlargement and engagement."[30]

Predictably, Clinton's economic advisers disapproved of linking human rights conditions to MFN status. For Clinton, who campaigned on economic revitalization, the tensions were acute. Within the administration, views on the MFN question diverged significantly. For instance, Deputy National Security Advisor Sandy Berger favored prioritizing the business interests involved. His boss, Anthony Lake, took a harder line in favor of the linkage.[31]

With Washington scrambling for a coherent strategy, conditions worsened in China. Secretary Christopher traveled to Beijing in March 1994, hoping to make enough progress on human rights to satisfy congressional leaders.[32] But, before Christopher's visit, and without his knowledge, Assistant Secretary for DRL John Shattuck met with prominent dissident Wei Jingsheng.[33] Outrage ensued.[34] Seemingly in response, Chinese officials detained several dissidents involved in the Democracy Wall demonstration of the late 1970s and the Tiananmen Square protests of 1989. They interrogated several American journalists. Years later, Christopher would call the "visit . . . as frustrating as any [he] made as Secretary."[35]

As conditions worsened and tensions grew, policymakers and activists encouraged President Clinton to maintain his position, as articulated in the 1993 executive order. IRF Purist Frank Wolf, who spearheaded early legislative efforts at curbing religious persecution, argued emphatically:

> There is no way that the Clinton administration can send up MFN for China. I am here to announce that if the Clinton administration sends up MFN for China, President Clinton's credibility will be zero. I am predicting that we in this body will never vote on the issue, because he has spoken out strongly in favor of human rights, and if he means what he says and he says what he believes, there is no way this body can ever deal with this issue of human rights, because frankly, we should never ever, ever, ever grant this barbaric nation MFN because of what it is doing to those of the Christian faith, those of the Dalai Lama and Buddhist, and also to the human rights activists in China.

In the following months, much to the dismay of Representative Wolf and much of the human rights community, the Clinton administration walked back its hard-line position. Shortly after signing the executive order, Clinton himself came to believe that China was "too big to punish and too important to isolate."[36] With China's military and economic power rising, and the relative position of the United States weakening, the explicit linkage between trade and human rights proved too difficult to maintain.

Thus, the Clinton administration adopted a new strategic approach, which it coined as "comprehensive engagement."[37] This approach opened dialogue across all levels of government, including a summit between President Clinton and President Jiang. These new dialogues did not lead to any immediate progress. Still, economic leaders in the administration pushed for MFN's renewal. Secretary of the Treasury Lloyd Benson, Secretary of Commerce Ron Brown, and Robert Rubin, the director of the newly created National Economic Council, each petitioned Clinton to prioritize U.S. economic interests. In the end, they persuaded Clinton, and, despite China's failure to fulfill the criteria outlined by the executive order to renew its trade status, China remained an MFN.[38]

In a press conference in May 1994, Clinton called for a delinking of human rights and the MFN trade status and maintained that "the best path for advancing freedom in China is for the United States to intensify and broaden its engagement."[39] Of the debacle, Christopher noted that "linking human rights to MFN has taken us as far as it can. It is not likely to yield more progress on human rights."[40] Expectedly, the Clinton administration faced intense criticism of this shift in policy direction. AFL-CIO President Lane Kirkland put it plainly: "No matter what America says about democracy and human rights, in the final analysis profits, not people, matter most."[41] This, of course, was not a novel line of criticism. However, Clinton's strong campaign promises and vocal condemnation of his predecessors' approach cast a heavy shadow. The policy reversal and subsequent outrage damaged Clinton's credibility, particularly with the international religious freedom community.

Tensions Loom: Taiwan and Tibet

While China considered the renewal of its MFN status a notable victory, the mid-1990s brought other challenges. The most pressing challenge concerned Taiwan. Beginning in 1979, the United States prevented any Taiwanese president from visiting the country, signaling its view that the PRC was the only government in China. But, in May 1995, Clinton reversed course. Facing unyielding pressure from Congress, the administration allowed Taiwanese President Lee Teng-hui of the Nationalist Party to attend an alumni event at Cornell University, enraging Beijing. By June, China had announced it would conduct a series of missile tests, beginning the Third Taiwan Strait Crisis.

After years of fighting for democracy, Taiwan was preparing for its first direct presidential election in 1996. Before then, the presidents were elected indirectly by the National Assembly. The missile tests were an attempt to dissuade Taiwanese citizens from voting for Lee, who promoted "Taiwanization," which aimed to strengthen Taiwan's identity and reduce the influence of the PRC. Despite Chinese intimidation efforts,

Lee won by a large margin. During the crisis, the Clinton administration contributed naval support and warned of grave consequences should China attack Taiwan.[42] In the end, a major crisis was avoided. Still, the U.S. commitment to the One China Policy would frame debates for years to come. Years later, President Clinton's second secretary of state, Madeleine Albright, would note for Chinese officials to be happy, all diplomatic meetings could be reduced to one line: "The U.S. supports the One China Policy."[43]

Also, during the mid-1990s, tensions between the CCP and Tibetan Buddhists intensified. Beijing was intent on curbing the religious commitment of Tibetan Buddhists as it viewed allegiance to the Dalai Lama as antithetical to the control it desired. Years before IRFA's passage, the CCP and the Dalai Lama engaged in separate, parallel processes to choose the next Panchen Lama, one of the most important spiritual authorities in the Gelug tradition, a prominent branch of Tibetan Buddhism. The Panchen Lama and the Dalai Lama are essential in determining who rightfully, through reincarnation lineage rituals, will become the next Dalai Lama or Panchen, respectively. The Dalai Lama declared Gedhun Choekyi Nyima, an eight-year-old child, the eleventh Panchen Lama of Tibetan Buddhism on May 14, 1995, causing great controversy.[44] In an attempt to reassert control in Tibet and weaken the influence of the Dalai Lama, the State Council rejected the choice of Gedhun Choekyi Nyima. The CCP immediately took him and his family into custody, and his whereabouts remain unknown. Instead, the CCP installed Gyaincain Norbu as the eleventh Panchen Lama. He now serves as the vice president of the Buddhist Association of China, though many Tibetan Buddhists do not recognize him as legitimate.

Formalizing International Religious Freedom Efforts

By the late 1990s, signs of modest human rights progress emerged. China signed the International Covenant on Economic, Social, and Cultural Rights in 1997 and the International Covenant on Civil and Political Rights (ICCPR) in October 1998. In addition, China released prominent dissidents like Wei Jingsheng and Wang Dan. While the release of prisoners was a cause for celebration, some scholars argued that these types of releases constituted a form of "hostage diplomacy," whereby the CCP used prisoners as bargaining chips.[45] And, without changing the underlying policies involved, China apprehended dissidents at a much faster rate than it released them. Scholar Ann Kent chronicled China's selective compliance with international norms as it deemed beneficial. While she noted that there were some modest successes, international efforts "have not succeeded in breaching the divide between China's international human rights policy and its domestic human rights practice."[46]

At home, Washington responded to Clinton's policy reversal and the renewal of China's MFN status, and pressure from Congress to stand up against China's human rights violations intensified. As international religious freedom legislative efforts gathered steam, senators like Don Nickles and Joe Lieberman repeatedly cited abuses in China to awaken lawmakers to the urgency of their efforts. In hearings preceding the passage of the IRFA, they lamented the plight of Christians in the mainland forced to worship in secret, the startling number of Chinese citizens imprisoned for their beliefs, and the barbaric treatment of Uyghur Muslims in Xinjiang. Before the IRFA's passage, President Jiang Zemin explicitly called into question the universality of religious freedom, maintaining that different social systems and values would necessarily affect how freedom was defined or implemented. Then he took this logic further, arguing that these differences represented "the manifestation of democracy."[47] To Chinese leaders, the IRFA reeked of foreign domination—an attempt by the United States to co-opt China's internal affairs. These realities led legal scholar Darin Carlson to assume that legislative efforts to promote international religious freedom would be unsuccessful: "China would rather suffer the economic impact of U.S. sanctions than suffer the ideological impact of ceding some of its policy power to the United States."[48]

As discussed in chapter 1, President Clinton signed the IRFA into law in 1998 after an arduous process. The first IRF report, issued in September 1999, designated China a CPC, showing "systemic, ongoing, egregious violations of religious freedom." The first report covered 1998 and the early months of 1999. Primary grievances laid out in the report include the baseless denial of religious registration, destruction of religious sites, imprisonment of religious officials, and rigid control of religious materials.[49] In 1999, the Clinton administration designated four other countries as CPCs: Burma, Iran, Iraq and Sudan.[50] As expected, the CPC designation frustrated Beijing. As Ambassador Seiple recalled, the designation was particularly unwelcome, since the U.S. failed to designate North Korea.[51]

Contesting Religious Prisoners

During the Clinton administration, information on a few particularly heinous cases of persecution made headlines around the world and prompted U.S. action. One such case was Protestant minister Xu Yongze, who led a revival in Chinese house churches as part of the Born-Again Movement (BAM). In March 1997, police arrested Xu, his wife, and six other parishioners for disrupting the public order. They accused Xu of engaging in "illegal and even criminal activities under the signboard of religion."[52] Years following Xu's arrest, Freedom House released a report analyzing seven internal documents of the CCP regarding religious freedom. Here, the CCP accused Xu and the All Sphere Church of maligning the name of China and causing widespread disruption to the public order through their expressive worship services.[53] They claimed that productivity was being hampered because worshippers were neglecting their work and instead focusing only on spiritual matters.[54] Often referred to as the "Billy Graham of China," Xu was not unfamiliar with the risks involved in his continued religious activism. Indeed, Xu served time for attempting to meet with Reverend Graham in the late 1980s.[55]

Bishop Su Zhimin's case also received considerable notoriety during the first years after Congress passed the IRFA. Deemed a counterrevolutionary as early as the 1950s, Bishop Su refused to join the Patriotic Association, China's national Catholic Church.[56] As such, his Catholicism was unregistered and, thus, unlawful.[57] Arrested on October 8, 1997, in Hebei Province, local officials turned him over to the Public Security Bureau.[58] Before his arrest, he had spent over twenty years in prison or labor camps for his illicit religious activities. Like Xu, he was all too familiar with the potential consequences of his religiosity. Another Catholic priest, Li Qinghua, was arrested in a night raid in November 1998. Soon afterward, reports of brainwashing and torture surfaced. The Vatican reported that Chinese officials employed sexual blackmail tactics to cause Li to break his vocational vows.[59]

Secretary of State Madeleine Albright brought these cases forward as she met with President Jiang and other senior Chinese officials in February 1997 and April–May 1998. In addition, she accompanied President Clinton on his state visit to China in the summer of 1998. Here, Clinton raised the case of Bishop Su directly but could not secure a sufficient answer as to his whereabouts or condition. Similarly, then–special representative Bob Seiple failed to secure an adequate answer during his January 1999 trip, nor did Assistant Secretary of State Harold Koh during the official human rights dialogue with China.

During this tenure, Ambassador Seiple focused on alleviating the plight of Tibetan Buddhists. In January 1999, Koh raised concerns about China's attempts to "reeducate" Tibetan Buddhists, and frequently senior U.S. officials raised the cases of Abbot Chandrel Rinpoche, Jigme Sanpo, and Ngawang Sangdrol. One bright spot of these international religious freedom efforts occurred before Clinton's 1998 visit. Senior officials successfully negotiated the early release of Catholic Bishop Zeng Jingmu, who was arrested in 1995 for leading unauthorized religious activities. James R. Sasser, the U.S. ambassador to China, touted this release as a sign that President Clinton's engagement strategy was "bearing fruit."[60] Unfortunately, the CCP rearrested Bishop Zeng Jingmu the following year.

Persecuting the Falun Gong

Many of the conditions listed in the 2000 IRF report, which analyzed conditions beginning in July 1999, were similar to the inaugural report. One key difference, however, was the crackdown against the Falun Gong.[61] While Chinese leadership tolerated many indigenous and folk religions, they banned others.[62] Falun Gong originated as a group of *qigong*, an ancient Chinese practice that relies on physical activity, breathing exercises, and meditation to improve its adherents' overall health. The popularity of Falun Gong increased in the latter half of the twentieth century, prompting concern about power consolidation from the CCP. In the summer of 1999, they banned Falun Gong, deeming it a dangerous cult. With the passage of the anti-cult laws in October 1999, the Chinese government laid the legal foundation upon which they would defend the detention and execution of the Falun Gong practitioners for years to come.[63] The well-organized Falun Gong continued to operate and staged massive protests against the government, particularly between 1997 and 1999. Predictably, this perceived lapse in control of religious life in China resulted in more stringent laws and further restrictions. As outlined in the first annual IRFA report, embassy officials and the State Department fiercely criticized this persecution, as the CCP temporarily detained Falun Gong parishioners in July 1999 and sentenced many of the group's leaders later that year.

Belgrade Bombing

Within the China case study, perhaps no event more immediately constrained IRF policy than the bombing of the Chinese embassy in May 1999 in Belgrade by NATO forces during the Serbian occupation of Kosovo. The bombing killed three Chinese journalists and wounded twenty others. In the wake of the bombing, President Clinton issued an apology, noting that the attack was an accident, but it had little effect. Outraged Chinese officials called the attack a "barbarian act."[64] Anti-American protests erupted throughout the country. In light of the bombing in Belgrade, China suspended human rights dialogues in May 1999, complicating the work of the State Department and the IRF office. The suspension of human rights dialogues effectively tabled any large-scale discussions about religious liberty and societal change. Instead, the U.S. focused on protesting specific cases. This suspension constrained activities for the years to come, including after President Clinton's term concluded. The official human rights dialogues recommenced in the summer of 2000.

China Joins the WTO

In the final months of his presidency, Bill Clinton focused on bringing China into the World Trade Organization (WTO). Clinton sought multilateral involvement, hoping to depressurize the zero-sum game that characterized Sino-U.S. relations. In the fall of 1999, the United States agreed to China's participation if China opened its markets to the United States. But, for China to officially join, the United States first needed to give China Permanent Normal Trade Relations (PNTR) status. The annual review process, and annual waiver, which had been in place since 1980, did not satisfy WTO protocol. Thus, Clinton needed Congress to act. In a speech at Johns Hopkins School of Advanced International Studies (SAIS) on March 9, 2000, Clinton praised the economic opportunity: "This agreement is the equivalent of a one-way street. It requires China to open its markets . . . to both our products and services in unprecedented new ways. All we do is agree to maintain the present access which China enjoys."[65]

Human rights activists, and many within the international religious freedom community, countered, arguing that without a yearly review, the U.S. would cede its influence on the dire human rights abuses in China. After all, even though congressional efforts to overrule the president's waiver were unsuccessful, China's human rights record was thrust into the national spotlight each year. IRF Purists at USCIRF were most vocal in their opposition, arguing that "the unconditional grant of PNTR at this moment may be taken as a signal of American indifference to religious freedom."[66] Ambassador Seiple did not comment publicly, but the State Department released a statement in response to the USCIRF's 1999 report. It argued that failing to grant PNTR would "severely restrict our ability to positively influence the course of China—including our ability to promote religious freedom."[67] Predictably, actors within the international religious freedom community were not perfectly aligned. Prominent evangelical Billy Graham, for example, argued that increased trade connections with the West increased religious freedom. Graham's son, Ned, also publicly supported deeper trade ties with China, noting that economic reforms beginning in the 1990s made his mission work possible.[68]

Workers' rights groups pushed against the legislative efforts, fearing that the opening would allow China to usurp important manufacturing jobs from the United States. But, after months of bitter debate, Congress passed the U.S.-China Relations Act of 2000. George W. Bush, the then-presumptive Republican presidential nominee, celebrated the vote, noting that it meant "more opportunity for liberty and freedom in China."[69] But, in the years to come, it would become clear that political liberalization did not accompany economic liberalization.

IRF Policy During the Bush Years: 2001–2009

In the run-up to the 2000 presidential election, then-Governor Bush took a harder line on China, separating himself from the Clinton party line. On the trail, Bush diverged from using the familiar term "strategic partnership" to describe U.S.-China relations and instead called China a "strategic competitor." As such, he added, "we need to be tough and firm."[70] Similarly, in a speech in January 2000, Condoleezza Rice argued that what was needed vis-à-vis China was "a kind of realism—optimism about what's possible, but realism about where we are." Then she levied her critique, "It means that you don't call them the 'butchers of Beijing' one day and the next day a 'strategic partner.' That confuses the Chinese and it confuses us."[71]

Ultimately, the Bush administration faced the same set of questions as its predecessors—questions made more urgent and more complicated by China's ascendence and by the War on Terror. How should the United States handle its deepening economic interdependence without sacrificing its leverage in other policy arenas? When Bush became president, many strategic challenges existed between the United States and China. Still, President Bush remained hopeful that shared interests and global engagement could improve the status quo. Underpinning Bush's trade policy in China was a belief that economic freedom would expand into other arenas too. Bush spoke of this belief with candor:

> Trade with China will promote freedom. Freedom is not easily contained. Once a measure of economic freedom is permitted, a measure of political freedom will follow. China today is not a free society. At home, toward its own people, it can be ruthless. Abroad, toward its neighbors, it can be reckless. When I am president, China will know that America's values are always part of America's agenda. Our advocacy of human freedom is not a formality of diplomacy. It is a fundamental commitment of our country. It is the source of our confidence that communism, in every form, has seen its day.[72]

The Bush administration adopted a strategic approach toward China that it characterized as "cooperative, constructive, and candid."[73] And, in the aftermath of the terrorist attacks of 9/11, President Bush faced the arduous task of denouncing violent extremism while reasserting a firm commitment to religious freedom, both at home and throughout the world. Some religious minorities claimed that China used 9/11 to defend the crackdown of unregistered religious groups. Indeed, "defending against terrorism" became a familiar, though largely unfounded, reason to defend religious persecution in many places across the world as the War on Terror raged. In the years that followed, the United States would call on China to be a "responsible stakeholder" and to use its growing influence to encourage Sudan, North Korea, and Iran to engage with the international system.

An analysis of IRFA policy between 2001 and 2008 includes confronting an unwelcome truth: that economic liberalization in China did not lead to political liberalization the way that many hoped, or at least at the speed that many hoped. Moreover, the CCP continued to arrest, detain, and persecute its people arbitrarily for living out their faith convictions. Still, under Ambassador John Hanford's leadership, there were important steps forward—prisoners released, a policy change that extended greater religious rights to minors, and, perhaps most importantly, a deepened understanding of the Chinese system.

The IRF office leveraged President Bush's vocal support of international religious freedom. Laura Bryant Hanford, who helped craft the IRFA itself, analyzed this dynamic and observed how Bush's support influenced the cost-benefit analysis: "When President Bush spoke of the importance of religious freedom, especially in China, it signaled that the U.S. cared about religious freedom, at the highest levels, which translated into a greater willingness on China's part to engage with the IRF office."[74]

Another point of leverage during this time was the closeness of the relationship between Clark "Sandy" Randt, the U.S. ambassador to China, and President Bush. Randt, who served for almost the entirety of the Bush administration, knew Bush well, their relationship dating back to Yale and their membership in Delta Kappa Epsilon. Hanford, who also served during both of Bush's terms, deepened the stability of the relationship.

A Difficult Start

Tensions between the United States and China were high during the early days of Bush's term. Within the first few months of his presidency, Bush signaled that the United States would sponsor a U.N. resolution condemning China's human rights record. Human rights dialogues between the United States and China to discuss religious rights were still semiregularly turned down. For instance, the CCP prevented two diplomats from the IRF office from meeting with religious leaders on their visit to China.

Tom Farr, one of these diplomats, recalls the tension at the time—March 2001—and the message he received from Ye Xiaowen, the director of the State Administration for Religious Affairs: "Stale fried rice. For Mr. Farr to think Chinese officials are going to meet with him after all this reminds me of stale fried rice."[75] Despite discouragement from Chinese officials, Farr and his colleague Paul Martin traveled to China. It had been almost two years since the IRF office had made official contact with senior Chinese officials, an unfortunate side effect of a vacant ambassadorship. During this transition, conditions facing the Falun Gong and other unregistered spiritual movements worsened.[76] The effects of this tightening rippled outward. In Wenzhou, authorities destroyed churches and temples in 2000. Chinese authorities defended these actions claiming that the churches were operating illegally in the first place, and that the clearing was part of a larger community renewal project.[77]

In response to the U.N. resolution, Chinese officials responded with a white paper on human rights in April 2000. Human rights groups claimed that this report "white-washed" the realities on the ground.[78] This paper continually referred to citizens' rights instead of human rights, showing a fundamental misalignment between the CCP and the broader human rights community; it also conflated economic progress with human rights promotion, treating economic accomplishments as paramount.[79]

But the U.N. resolution was not the only point of contention. In his first few months on the job, Bush actively supported Taiwan, approving a major arms sales package in April 2001 and pledging that the United States "would do whatever it took" to defend Taipei should Beijing attack it.[80] The next month, Bush met personally with the Dalai Lama. Each of these actions enraged Beijing.

But the largest crisis of Bush's early days occurred in April 2001. During a high-level reconnaissance mission, a U.S. Navy aircraft collided with a Chinese plane, killing its pilot. The American plane made an emergency landing on China's Hainan Island and a twelve-day stand-off ensued, where the CCP held the plane's crew of twenty-four Americans. President Bush expressed regret at the situation, but Chinese officials were incensed. Other American officials, including a leader of U.S. Pacific forces, Admiral Dennis Blair, argued that responsibility to avoid collision was on the Chinese plane, because it was more maneuverable.[81] Colin Powell advocated for a diplomatic approach to secure the crew's release. In response to his proposal, Vice President Cheney quipped that it would be better if Powell said, "Pretty please."[82] While the crew was eventually returned to the United States, the Chinese obtained sensitive intelligence information and technology. The aircraft was an advanced EP-3, one of the most sophisticated in the U.S. military. President Bush himself admitted that "this was not the way he wanted to start his relationship with China."[83]

Glimmers of Progress

After a tough start, tensions cooled in early 2001. By July, the Chinese government agreed to resume the official human rights dialogues, beginning with a dialogue in October 2001, where religious freedom was on the agenda.[84] But, in February 2002, Freedom House published a report analyzing seven classified Chinese documents that described the internal CCP policies to crackdown on religious activity, especially among unregistered groups.[85] Considering these documents, Freedom House, among other institutions, pleaded for a vocal protest during President Bush's visit to China later that month. The visit which included First Lady Laura Bush, Colin Powell, and Condoleezza Rice, commemorated the thirtieth anniversary of Richard Nixon's visit to China, which had opened dialogues between the nations after years of disconnection. Overall, both leaders saw the trip as a great success. They declared a willingness to work together despite differences. Dialogue during this visit centered on a commitment to combating terrorism and to revisiting the stalemate over the Clinton-Jiang November 2000 nonproliferation pledge. Here, the CCP claimed that all now-illegal exchanges occurred prior to the signing of the agreement. While they achieved no formal resolution, the visit signaled a positive change in atmosphere between the two nations.[86]

In a speech at Tsinghua University in Beijing on February 22nd, which was broadcast across China, President Bush made note of the importance of faith in the United States, remarking that "someone once called us 'a nation with the soul of a church'" and testified to his own personal faith. He continued: "When I met President Jiang Zemin in Shanghai a few months ago, I had the honor of sharing with him how faith changed my life and how faith contributes to the life of my country. Faith points to a moral law beyond man's law, and calls us to duties higher than material gain. Freedom of religion is not something to be feared, it's to be welcomed, because faith gives us a moral core and teaches us to hold ourselves to high standards, to love and to serve others, and to live responsible lives."[87]

President Bush's speech came only a day after President Jiang defended his country's commitment to the rule of law. In response to a pointed question about Catholics detained for religious activity, Jiang asserted that "whatever religion people believe in, they have to abide by the law. So, some of the law-breakers have been detained because of their violation of law, not because of their religious belief."[88]

The uptick in persecution in the months preceding President Bush's state visit highlights the differences between the two presidents' approaches. USCIRF drew direct connections between the granting of PNTR with China, which was granted in 2000, with the sentencing to death of Pastor Gong Shengliang.[89] Without a review of China's human rights record before Congress, USCIRF asserted, the conditions for religious adherents were worsening in China. Still, there were glimmers of progress. John Hanford, who had become ambassador in May 2002, chose China as his first official visit, signaling the IRF office's prioritization of religious freedom issues in China. This visit, in the late summer of 2002, laid important groundwork for the continuation of official dialogues on human rights, which were slated for December 2002.

Hanford and his team had the difficult task of simultaneously calling out the CCP's behavior while also celebrating small steps forward. "I negotiated hard on problems, but that never undermined my ability to continue working with officials and make progress," Hanford stated. "What could destroy trust was if I was perceived as stabbing them in the back by going outside of our negotiations and blindsiding them with public statements to make myself look tough at their expense."[90] And, often, in a place like China, the expense is personal. Chinese officials working on these issues with IRF must answer to their superiors. To build trust, Hanford attempted to get to know his interlocutors personally—asking about their families, knowing the culture. In this vein, Hanford was quintessentially pragmatic; even when dealing with some of the world's most hostile regimes, he believed that respect and cultural sensitivity could lead to meaningful change on the ground.

This approach angered some IRF Purists, and especially USCIRF commissioners. But what they saw as capitulation Hanford considered effective diplomacy. Hanford described his negotiations as thorough and, when necessary, intense. However, in his experience, tough talk for its own sake could be "very counterproductive to making progress," particularly in a country like China, which has a strong sense of national pride and defensiveness toward perceived humiliation.[91]

One success story during this time concerned Ngawang Sangdrol, a Tibetan nun who had been convicted at only thirteen for her calls for Tibetan independence. With the help of the IRF office's negotiations, the CCP released her from prison in October 2002. A year later, she traveled to the United States for medical treatment. Her ardent activism continues today.

In December 2002, Ambassador Hanford accompanied Lorne W. Craner, assistant secretary for human rights, democracy, and labor (DRL), and a small U.S. delegation to China to discuss human rights. The dialogues, which lasted four days, were "marked by incremental yet unprecedented progress."[92] The Chinese government showed willingness to collaborate and assented to unconditional visits by the U.N. special rapporteur on religious intolerance in addition to the U.N. Working Group on Arbitrary Detention.[93] Chinese officials also agreed to welcome, for the first time, a delegation from the USCIRF. During the 2002 visit, U.S. officials focused on the Xinjiang Uyghur Autonomous Region. Here, under the guise of fighting terror, Uyghur Muslims were being persecuted, often held indefinitely in reeducation camps. In particular, the delegation advocated for the release of Rebiya Kadeer, a Uyghur prisoner arrested in August 1999 on charges of sharing confidential information with U.S. congressional representatives as well as funneling separatist propaganda to her husband, Sidiq Rouzi, who worked for Radio Free Asia and Voice of America.[94] While they made no initial progress to secure her release in 2002, the Chinese government would reconsider in the years to come.

Despite the success of these dialogues, its internal handling revealed the extent of tensions within the State Department. Hanford reflected on the process years later:

> IRF was heavily involved in the dialogues, and the Chinese announced that they were agreeing to some of my specific requests from my visit to Beijing four months prior. These were some of the only meaningful areas of progress in the dialogue that year. And yet I found out—after the fact— that Lorne had excluded IRF from the press conference in Beijing where he personally announced our successes. In fact, Lorne had originally informed me he planned to exclude religious freedom from the Human Rights Dialogue altogether.[95]

Two Steps Forward, One Back

In February 2003, USCIRF began initial talks to coordinate a visit to China. From the beginning of these negotiations, the CCP assured USCIRF that a trip to Hong Kong would be part of the plan. However, in late July, the Chinese government recommended Hong Kong's exclusion from the trip. Despite USCIRF's protests, this recommendation became a directive, striking Hong Kong from the itinerary. USCIRF postponed the visit.[96] After rescheduling the trip later in the year, with a Hong Kong visit included, USCIRF postponed again, this time because Chinese officials directed them not to take any meetings during their "stopover" in Hong Kong.[97]

An ongoing concern, which resurfaced in 2003, regarded the religious repression of minors. As seen in the stringent rules surrounding Chinese schools, the CCP sought to control all aspects of the education and development of minors.[98] The Chinese curriculum, which only taught atheism in its state-sponsored schools, undergirded this reluctance to allow minors to participate in religious activity.[99] John Hanford and his staff focused on extending religious freedom to individuals under the age of eighteen, and to allow parents to educate their children as they saw best. In 2005, the tides turned as a foreign ministry spokesperson showed that the limitations concerning religious instruction only applied when such instruction interfered with the public education system—an important step and an important win for the IRF office. Still, implementation of this policy was not automatic. And, at times, the SARA excluded minors from religious activity and prevented them from attending services across the country and especially within the Xinjiang Province.

Persecution worsened for several groups as the CCP continued its decade-long crackdown on illegal cults. For example, they targeted the Three Grades of Servants Church in 2003. Officials imprisoned dozens of parishioners, beating one prisoner, Gu Xianggao, to death in a security facility in Heilongjiang Province.[100] After being detained, the CCP sentenced three church members to death, including the group's leader, Xu Shengguang. Many others received sentences from three to fifteen years.[101]

Conflicting Visions and Presidential Leadership

While the IRF office continued to push where possible, debate within the administration as to how best to approach its relationship with China continued to rage. In September 2006, Deputy Secretary of State Bob Zoellick gave a clarifying speech. In the wake of the War on Terror and decades of work to integrate China into the international system, Zoellick maintained that "the dragon emerged and joined the world."[102] But an important question was left still outstanding: How would China use its growing influence? Here, Zoellick called on China to become a "responsible stakeholder," which meant that "China would be more than just a member—it would work with us to sustain the international system that has enabled its success."[103] Though initially confused by the terminology, China was pleased with the development.[104] Some found Zoellick's frame to be too accommodating and positive. The 2006 National Security Strategy took a decidedly more pessimistic view, noting that "China's leaders must realize . . . that they cannot stay on this peaceful path while holding on to old ways of thinking and acting that exacerbate concerns throughout the region and the world."[105]

Figure 4.1. President Bush welcomes Chinese dissidents Li Baiguang, Wang Yi, and Yu Jie to the White House on May 11, 2006. Source: George W. Bush White House Photo Library.

Amid the internal debates on how to approach China, President Bush personally signaled that religious freedom would remain a priority regardless of other goals and objectives. In November 2005, he returned to China and attended worship services at the Protestant Gangwashi Church. After the visit, he gave a short, yet bold, statement from the church steps: "It wasn't all that long ago that people were not allowed to worship openly in this society. My hope is that the government of China will not fear Christians who gather to worship openly. A healthy society is a society that welcomes all faiths and gives people a chance to express themselves through worship with the Almighty."[106]

Then, in 2006, Bush welcomed Chinese Christians Yu Jie, Li Bainguang, and Wang Yi to the White House to discuss religious freedom conditions in China. Expectedly, China resented the move, calling the activists "enemies of the state" rather than religious believers. The label carried with it the threat of retribution—a threat made explicit by an urgent message sent from a high-ranking Chinese official on the morning of the meeting. Advisers at the State Department and the NSC grappled with what to do, with most in the regional bureau pushing to forgo the meeting. But, after giving the dissidents full knowledge of the gravity of the situation, it went ahead as planned. Of the situation, NSC staffer Michael Gerson noted, "It is still sobering to facilitate a decision that may cost a life, or result in terrible punishment."[107] President Bush greeted the dissidents, discussed the conditions on the ground, and ended the meeting with a prayer. "Now I've seen your faces and know your names," Bush continued, "from now on, whenever I talk about human rights in China, I'll be thinking about you."[108] In yet another bold signal, in 2007, President Bush attended a ceremony in celebration of the Dalai Lama receiving the Congressional Gold Medal, diverging with precedent by meeting publicly with the Tibetan leader, much to the CCP's disdain.

The choice for Beijing as the site for the 2008 Olympic Games sparked criticism from human rights activists, with many calling for a boycott of the opening ceremonies. Even officials of the games themselves, like the president of the Olympic committee, Jacques Rogge, urged Chinese officials to expand press freedoms and protect the rights of protesters in the days before the Olympics began.[109] Pressure to boycott the games directly involved the question of religious freedom, as many demanded that China open a dialogue with the Dalai Lama. In March 2008, five months ahead of the games, violence erupted as Tibetan protesters clashed with police. Chinese officials blamed the Dalai Lama for inciting the protests, once again framing the exiled leader as a separatist terrorist. Bush faced criticism for not boycotting the games from some human rights activists but he assured the public that he would "carry the message of freedom as he travels to Beijing."[110] In the days before he left for Beijing, Bush welcomed Harry Wu, Wei Jingsheng, Rebiya Kadeer, Sasha Gong, and Bob Fu, prominent dissidents from several faith traditions, to the White House. Writing in his memoir years later, Bush stated optimistically, "The Olympics gave the world a chance to see the beauty and creativity of China. My hope is that the Games also gave the Chinese people a glimpse of the wider world, including the possibility of an independent press, open internet, and free speech. Time will tell what the long-term impact of the Beijing Olympics will be. But history shows that once people get a taste of freedom, they eventually want more."[111] His hope mimicked Clinton's words eight years prior—a refrain Obama would pick up in the years to come.

Figure 4.2. President Bush visits the Kuanjie Protestant Christian Church on August 10, 2008. Source: George W. Bush White House Library.

IRF Policy During the Obama Years: 2009–2017

Soon after Barack Obama became president, he explained that his foreign policy would increase attention and resources toward Asia. Recognizing China's growing influence in the world and its status as a great power, the Obama administration focused on forming an informal Group of Two (G-2) with China. Some foreign policy heavyweights like Zbigniew Brzezinski promoted the effort, noting that the two countries possessed "the most extraordinary potential for sharing our collective future."[112] Rhetorically, Chinese officials welcomed a deepened relationship, but were quick to note its limits. After meeting with President Obama in November 2009, Chinese Premier Wen Jiabao stressed the importance of "keep[ing] sober minded over it."[113] An official press release from the visit also noted the need for diplomatic ties across the globe and reiterated that "China pursues the independent foreign policy of peace and will not align with any country or country blocks."[114]

Obama faced challenging dynamics in his foreign policy toward China that reflected larger questions surrounding America's role in the world. As Michael Green notes, the Obama administration grappled with two competing drivers.[115] On one side was a commitment to democracy and the universality of human rights, while on the other was a commitment to improving the image of the United States around the world. Writing for *Foreign Policy* in 2011, Secretary of State Hillary Clinton noted six action items. Besides increased military presence, Clinton's priorities included bolstering security alliances, increasing diplomatic efforts toward multilateral institutions and emerging powers, focusing on trade, and, finally, promoting democracy and human rights.[116] Despite this commitment, Obama also focused on improving the global perception of the United States after the Iraq War. And, without the presence of WMDs, democracy promotion became the primary reasoning behind Operation Iraqi Freedom. This reality, combined with hesitation about unilateralism and imperialism, made Obama wary. Still, in Obama's first term, the administration put forth a new vision for the U.S.-China relationship. Whether Barack Obama was actually "America's first Pacific President," as he boldly claimed in November 2009, his policy toward China featured prominently, especially in his first term.[117]

After initial talks of a G-2 with China, Obama formally announced a broader vision for his foreign policy: a "pivot to Asia." Tom Donilon, Obama's national security advisor, argued that the pivot was a result of a strategic assessment, whereby Obama's security team determined, "Where are we over-weighted? Where are we underweighted?"[118] They concluded that the pivot was necessary to rebalance American foreign policy after years of wars in the Middle East.

Janine Davidson, who served as President Obama's deputy assistant secretary of defense for plans from 2009 to 2012, summed up the military shift this way: "The rebalance is meant to promote the general long term stability of this critically important economic zone by committing to patrol the sea lanes, promote responsible norms of maritime behavior, and engage with allies and partners to promote their own self-defense and resilience."[119] The strategy aimed at leveraging U.S. investments, hoping that "the American military posture could have a cascading effect on stability."[120] With the withdrawal of troops from the Middle East, the U.S. had a new opportunity to capitalize on military opportunities in Asia, especially in the face of China's increasing territorial expansion and aggression in the South China Sea and North Korea's provocative development of its nuclear program. But the military rebalancing was only one element of the changing relationship between the U.S. and China.

Solidification of Great Power Politics

A return of great power politics characterized the Obama era. The foreign policy landscape moved in this direction since the short-lived unipolarity of the latter days of the George H. W. Bush presidency and the early days of Bill Clinton's term, but solidified in the Obama administration. During the Obama years, China's influence in the world expanded significantly. China flexed its military strength in the South China Sea as the U.S. cut back military spending. China extended its economic reach, especially in the developing world. Moreover, action to combat climate change, a top priority of President Obama, required Chinese participation.

As Obama grappled with how best to manage the global financial crisis of 2008–9, China's leverage over the U.S. economy increased. In particular, China's ownership of U.S. debt climbed, reaching $1.3 trillion in 2011. The effects of this increased interdependence reverberated beyond questions of trade and economics. After a tense naval confrontation in 2009, one commentator noted that were the United States to respond to perceived Chinese belligerence, it would first "have to face that its defense is crucially supported by the very country it wanted to confront."[121] While some scholars noted that this new level of interdependence amounted to greater risk for the China rather than the United States, fears about China's growing influence, and its potentially constraining effect on American foreign policy, loomed large.[122]

Inasmuch as presence signals priorities, the Obama administration made clear from the beginning that it would prioritize Asia. Obama himself decided to forgo the celebration for the twentieth anniversary of the fall of the Berlin Wall, angering Germans and prompting questions about whether America "had turned its back on a crisis-stricken Europe."[123] Instead, he traveled to Asia, meeting with leaders in Japan, Singapore, China, and South Korea. Secretary Clinton attended every

ASEAN Regional Forum meeting, and President Obama chose to attend the East Asia Summit in November 2011 after administration officials convinced Indonesia to schedule the summit directly after the annual APEC meeting.[124] The Obama administration's commitment to the region translated to significant policy wins. At the APEC in 2011 meeting, President Obama celebrated the negotiations and eventual agreements of the Trans-Pacific Partnership (TPP) between nine member countries, including Australia, Brunei, Chile, Malaysia, New Zealand, Peru, Singapore, Vietnam, and the United States. Later, President Obama and President Xi announced a joint commitment to reducing carbon emissions, an important step that laid the groundwork for the U.N. Meeting on Climate Change for 2015.

But, in his first term, while Obama focused on the Asia-Pacific region and before the Arab Spring diverted focus back to the Middle East, the IRF office lacked sufficient leadership to be effective. Without an effective ambassador, or an ambassador at all for the first sixteen months of his presidency, the IRF office struggled. By the time Rabbi David Saperstein, a widely respected leader and creative policy entrepreneur, became the ambassador, the crisis in the Middle East had recaptured the administration's attention.

The first IRF Report of the Obama era, issued in 2009, praised Secretary Clinton's visit to Haidian Protestant Church in Beijing, where she addressed Chinese dissidents and women's right activists. However, during this trip, human rights groups and international media lambasted Clinton for what they saw as a "callous" capitulation to economic growth. To calm tensions and make progress in other areas, Clinton maintained that contentious issues like human rights "can't interfere with the global economic crisis, the global climate change crises and the security crisis."[125] It seemed the return of great power politics would constrain U.S. action to promote human rights. She added later that it "might be better to agree to disagree." Of the statement, one former IRF office staffer said, "That put quite a damper on our efforts, not just because of the morale issue but because it showed the Chinese government that we don't really take this issue seriously."[126]

Mixed Progress and Deteriorating Conditions

The 2009 IRF report noted modest, yet significant, progress regarding the registration of churches in China. It observed that "government officials allowed increased space for some unregistered religious groups it viewed as non-threatening."[127] Importantly, the report also states that the State Council held a meeting with Protestant house church leaders to discuss opportunities for registration outside of the officially sanctioned churches. These meetings did not produce a formal agreement, but the dialogue itself represented an important step forward. It should be noted that during this period, there was no ambassador-at-large for international religious freedom. Secretary Clinton declined John Hanford's offer to stay on until a new appointment was made, and the process of appointing and confirming the next ambassador, Suzan Johnson Cook, took years.[128] She was not confirmed until May 2011. Even then, she lacked the foreign policy experience necessary to pick up the tenuous situation.

It is difficult to talk about religious rights across China in broad terms because some religious groups enjoyed increased protections and rights while others faced worsening conditions. For instance, the Chinese government helped to promote sanctioned Buddhist activities and even to organize a Second World Buddhist Forum in Wuxi, Jiangsu, in March 2009. In a modest improvement in 2011, the IRF report noted that, while CCP officials were technically required to be atheists, more government officials were attending church services without punishment.[129] In February 2012, the SARA published a joint opinion with other governmental entities permitting religious organizations to offer social programming and disaster relief. But other groups experienced deteriorating conditions. As Xi Jinping visited Shenzhen in December 2011, Chinese officials arrested Christian missionary Cao Nan, along with ten others.[130] Another group charged with disrupting social order was the millenarian sect called the Church the Almighty God, or Easter Lightning, which taught of an impending apocalypse. In 2012, religious police arrested or detained approximately one thousand sect members across the country. Believers in the Tibetan Autonomous Region (TAR) and Xinjiang Uyghur Autonomous Region (XUAR), faced intense repression during Obama's first term.[131]

The summer of 2009 proved particularly bloody and set the stage for systematic persecution of the Uyghurs in the years to come. The uptick in violence stemmed from an online post that surfaced in late June. In it, a worker at a toy factory in Shaoguan claimed that a Uyghur Muslim migrant worker raped a Han Chinese woman. Outraged by the charges, a fight broke out at the factory in July 2009, leaving two Uyghurs dead and over one hundred people injured. Later that month, Uyghurs protested, demanding a full investigation of the events. Police confronted the protesters in Urumqi, the capital of Xinjiang Province, and a massive riot broke out. The violence left almost two hundred people dead and over a thousand injured. The bloody riots of summer 2009 marked the beginning of new stringent controls on China's Uyghur population, as authorities pledged to crackdown on "illegal religious activities."[132] Over the next decade, these controls intensified and compounded, creating a full-fledged surveillance state.

The IRFA reports from 2009 to 2011 noted the often thin line that separated religious repression and political repression. The 2011 report, for instance, stated that "it remained difficult to determine whether particular raids, detentions, arrests, or judicial punishments targeted those seeking political goals, the right to worship, or criminal acts."[133] This distinction became especially tenuous for Uyghur Muslims in XUAR and Buddhists in TAR. Repression against Uyghurs was brutal. In June 2011, the Korla police killed eleven-year-old Mirzahid Amanullah Shahyari.[134] While the details concerning his death remain unknown, his body showed signs of torture. Authorities forced the boy's mother to bury him without allowing for customary Islamic burial rites.[135] The CCP prevented teachers and civil servants from observing Ramadan, barring them from fasting or attending religious services. Societal trends matched the government-sanctioned repression. In one case, a Han Chinese man lifted the veil of a Uyghur girl, sparking intense protests. Over the next decade, brutal repression of Uyghurs would only worsen, with the United States acknowledging it as a genocide.[136]

The Implications of Chen Guangcheng's Escape

During President Obama's tenure, no single case in China garnered more public attention than that of Chen Guangcheng. While not charged or detained for religious reasons, his case surfaced the fragility of America's response to Chinese dissidents. Though his activism covered many subjects, Chinese officials detained him for protesting China's repressive family planning regime. Eventually, he was put on house arrest. Despite changes in the law that leveraged fines and fees to bring about compliance to its family planning vision, Chen Guangcheng alleged that forced sterilization and forced abortions were still occurring in Shandong Province.

In April 2012, Chen escaped house arrest and, relying on a dedicated network of activists throughout the country, fled to the American embassy in Beijing. The events sparked a diplomatic crisis, as U.S. officials negotiated for Chen's release. Citing injuries occurring during the escape, and Chen's blindness, Senior State Department officials noted they accepted Chen on "humanitarian grounds."[137] In a series of rapid negotiations, U.S. diplomats negotiated Chen's release to the United States, where he studied law at New York University. Originally, Chen was intent on staying in China, but, after threats to hurt his family, he agreed to come to the United States. The event represented a flash point in U.S.-China relations as the U.S. attempted to balance its priorities. Notably, the U.S.-China Strategic & Economic Dialogue, held in Beijing on May 3–4, occurred even as U.S. and Chinese officials completed negotiations. Chen and his family arrived in New York on May 19, 2012. Chen did not meet with President Obama after he fled to the United States. Indeed, in a sharp contrast to the Bush administration, Obama chose not to meet with any dissident leaders from Asia in the Oval Office throughout his presidency.[138]

Presidential Politics and Changing Leadership

A major feature of the presidential campaigns of Obama and Mitt Romney in 2012 concerned trade policy with China. In particular, Romney criticized Obama for what he considered insufficient action to constrain China. As the Obama administration submitted a formal complaint against Chinese auto subsidies to the WTO, Romney dismissed it as "too little, too late."[139] Still, Obama pushed forward with his plans to define U.S.-China relations as the new great power rivalry solidified.

Chinese leader Xi Jinping became president in March 2013, several months after becoming the general secretary of the CCP. Much to the disdain of Tibetan and Uyghur activists who protested the summit, President Obama and President Xi met at Sunnylands, a two-hundred-acre estate in Rancho Mirage, a beautiful setting nestled in the Coachella Valley in California. The purpose was to deepen personal ties between the leaders in hopes of greater cooperation in the years to come. But the relationship was tenuous, and Xi made clear that he would prioritize stability, especially in Xinjiang. Addressing the Congress of the XUAR in 2016, Xi stated that "we must always treat counter-terrorism efforts and stability maintenance as the overriding political task."[140]

Scholars Sheena Chestnut Greitens, Myunghee Lee, and Emir Yazici argue that between 2014 and 2016, fears of radicalization of Uyghur Muslims by transnational terrorist groups increased significantly, leading the CCP to a more collectivist strategy whereby it would detain and "reeducate" millions of Uyghurs. In analyzing the perceived terrorist threat of Uyghurs seriously, Greitens and colleagues were careful to note that "invoking counterterrorism . . . does not provide the CCP with a moral 'blank check' for human rights abuses," and that they aimed to separate "empirical explanation from moral justification."[141] But the explanation includes sincere fears of security breaches and terrorism. Pragmatic voices in the IRF community during Obama's tenure, especially IRF Ambassador Rabbi Saperstein, understood this distinction and tried, with varying levels of success, to leverage it. Saperstein became the ambassador-at-large in December 2014. The following year, Saperstein traveled to China, calling for an end to persecution against Christians in Zhejiang Province and advocating for Tibetan Buddhists and Uyghur Muslims. He worked with the CCP's national security team to try to convince them that religious freedom could increase their security, rather than threaten it. Despite these efforts, the CCP continued to view the Uyghur population as a threat, and, by the end of Obama's tenure, conditions in the XUAR would be worse than ever before.

The China case highlights the difficulty of prioritizing international religious freedom when the policy agenda is crowded. With China's rise and the return to great power politics, trade policy and security concerns often overshadowed human rights promotion. Zooming out, this case shows that economic liberalization does not automatically translate to greater human rights protections. The first section of this chapter, which detailed Clinton's MFN debacle, showed the tensions that can arise when connecting international religious freedom progress to other policy goals. In the dynamic foreign policy environment between the U.S. and China, where the trade relationship was constantly in flux, hardline positions proved too difficult for Clinton to maintain. In turn, the debacle damaged American credibility.

The case of China also highlights the importance of symbolic power in the executive branch. Rhetoric, especially at the highest levels, carried meaningful weight. As President Bush vocally supported religious freedom expansion, senior officials took notice. They had to. And the IRF office could then leverage Bush's support. Instead of promoting a niche foreign policy issue, they carried the message and mission of the president himself. Conversely, rhetoric without leverage, from lower-level officials or USCIRF, often inflamed tensions, ending dialogues and stopping forward progress. Through IRF's concerted efforts, especially as persecution of the Uyghurs intensified, to monitor and publicize the crisis in the XUAR translated into large-scale attention of the international community, the American public, and congressional leaders.

5

International Religious Freedom in Vietnam

Over the last three decades, the story of religious freedom in Vietnam has been one of progress and deterioration, of empty rhetoric and meaningful change. The same could be said of the bilateral relationship between the United States and Vietnam during this time. In the late 1990s and early 2000s, as Vietnam sought closer relations with the United States and further integration into the world economy, it was forced to reckon with its deplorable religious freedom conditions, highlighting how changing geopolitical landscapes can enable or constrain international religious freedom policy.

The Vietnam case stands out as a time when the United States successfully employed the International Religious Freedom Act as intended: to compel an offending regime to make widespread policy changes in favor of religious freedom. During the Clinton years, the United States normalized its diplomatic relationship with Vietnam. Motivated by his own strained history from the Vietnam War, the first IRF ambassador, Bob Seiple, devoted outsized attention to the country, forming deep relationships with Vietnamese diplomats. His successor, John Hanford, leveraged Seiple's network but religious freedom conditions remained abysmal. Eventually, Hanford argued for Vietnam's designation as a Country of Particular Concern (CPC). Anxious to be removed from the list, Vietnam negotiated with the United States on a binding agreement, which yielded remarkable results almost overnight.

The next section gives a brief historical overview, covering the nature of religion and religious persecution in Vietnam and the U.S.-Vietnam relationship. Then it analyzes how the United States leveraged the geopolitical context of the time, specifically a rising China and Vietnam's desire to integrate into the world's economy, to make meaningful progress for religious freedom. But it also reveals how elusive lasting policy change can be, especially when the conditions that made the initial reforms possible fade away. In this sense, the

Vietnam case is sobering, as conditions worsened significantly during the Obama administration.

Historical Background and Religious Context

The history of religion in Vietnam is vast and syncretic. Historical Vietnamese religion combines elements of Confucianism, Taoism, and Buddhism. Other traditions, like animism, folk religions, and ancestral worship, contribute to Vietnam's complex and vibrant religious landscape. Jesuit missionaries brought Catholicism to Vietnam in the sixteenth and seventeenth centuries. While successful in gaining converts, many Vietnamese resented Catholicism, believing it to be a tool for colonialism and a threat to Vietnamese unity.[1] Protestantism did not arrive until the early 1900s as the Christian and Missionary Alliance (C&MA) evangelized, planted churches, and trained indigenous people to lead the church, leading to the significant growth of Christianity. While this growth was widespread geographically across the north and south, it was most significant among the Hmong people in the North Highlands and the Montagnards in the South Central Highlands. Another important Vietnamese religious tradition is Hòa Hảo Buddhism, a denomination founded in 1939 by Huỳnh Phú Số. Originating in the Mekong Delta region of southern Vietnam, it is an accessible form of Buddhism aimed at encouraging religious practice among the working class. It venerates its founder as a living Buddha, charged with protecting Vietnam. Other minority religions include Hinduism, Islam, and Baha'i, each contributing to the fabric of religious life in Vietnam. Taken together, these traditions form an intricate and sometimes strained religious landscape.

Before his death in 1969, Ho Chi Minh tightened his control on political rights and civil liberties throughout the country. He tolerated religion so long as it "did not confront the aims and political order of the communist system."[2] With the communist takeover in 1975, under the leadership of Lê Duẩn, religious freedom in the south evaporated overnight. Vietnam's religious repression is similar to the Chinese model: built upon militant atheism in keeping with a Marxist-Leninist ethic. Political scientist Ani Sarkissian argues that the "regime bases itself on ideals that advocate the eventual demise of religion altogether. Yet because the regime recognizes that eliminating religion completely is a long-term goal, it copes with its continuing presence by imposing state control over all religious institutions."[3] Much like the Chinese system, Vietnam identifies six "patriotic" religions. These include government-sanctioned versions of Buddhism, Catholicism, Protestantism, Islam, Cao Đài, and Hòa Hảo Buddhism.

Legal scholar John Gillespie contends that the religious landscape in Vietnam is best understood within the narrative framework of Đại Đoàn Kết (DDK), which means Great Unity. The Vietnamese government uses DDK to "inculcate the belief that Vietnamese people are bound together by a common culture and spiritual destiny—by a national identity."[4] One outgrowth of this narrative is a strictly controlled religious system, so that the sole source of authority and identity rests in the state rather than faith. Vietnam challenges what it views as Western understandings of human rights, arguing that the West uses the idea that "human rights rank above State sovereignty" to "justify their policies of invasion and military intervention in other countries."[5]

The Communist Party of Vietnam (CPV) views religion as a mechanism for foreign domination—a smokescreen for imperialism. Of course, the bloody history of the Vietnam War looms large in collective memory. As scholar Reginald Reimer writes, "Christians are still suspected of being related to the ongoing nefarious goals of the unnamed 'enemy', which everyone knows to be the United States."[6] The CPV singles out other groups, like the Hòa Hảo Buddhists, for supporting anti-communist forces during the Vietnam War. Moreover, the government banned the Unified Buddhist Church of Vietnam (UBCV) after its leaders called for democratic reform. Vietnamese officials assert the inextricable linkage between cultural expression and human rights, thus arguing that there are many valid interpretations of the true nature of human rights. Throughout the period under study, Vietnamese officials repeatedly used this line of argument to defend the country's poor human rights record, particularly regarding religious freedom conditions.

Since the reunification of Vietnam in 1975 under communist rule, the government has maintained strict control over its citizens' public and personal lives. Political and religious oppression and poverty characterized the decade following the reunification, often called the "dark decade" or the "dark years." The CPV razed churches, forced adherents to renounce their faith, and imprisoned religious leaders. Those imprisoned faced abysmal conditions, harsh forced labor, and torture. Many religious believers stopped attending church or worshipping together for fear of punishment.

While the CPV tightened control over all religious practice during this period, it explicitly singled out the Montagnards in the Central Highlands. The CPV targeted the Montagnards for several reasons. First, as an ethnic minority, they remained somewhat removed from Vietnamese society. Moreover, because of their Protestant beliefs, the CPV suspected the Montagnards of being negatively influenced by Western forces. Finally, they actively supported the United States during the Vietnam War, a fact not soon forgotten by the CPV. During this time, they experienced brutal persecution, with almost all their churches closed and religious leaders arrested.[7]

The economic conditions of Vietnam during this time were dire. Years of expensive military engagement, the addition of a U.S.-led trade embargo, and the almost automatic collectivization of rice production devastated Vietnam's already struggling economy. In addition, Vietnam faced significant foreign policy challenges. After Vietnam invaded Cambodia to depose the Chinese-backed Khmer Rouge in 1978, the Sino-Vietnamese War erupted at the border.

Desperate to improve economic conditions in Vietnam, the CPV passed a series of reforms in 1986 called Đổi Mới, or "renovation." These reforms modernized the Vietnamese economy and opened up global trade opportunities. But these reforms rippled outward, profoundly affecting all sectors of society. Oppressed religious groups seized on the newfound freedom, and, between 1986 and 1999, Vietnam experienced dramatic religious growth, particularly among Protestant groups in the North and Central Highlands. The religious resurgence brought new temples, churches, and religious schools. But the CPV feared this growing momentum and again cracked down on religious activity. Even as Vietnam debated how best to handle religious activity in the 1990s, it had other foreign policy aims—namely, how to integrate into the world economy.

The following section details IRF policy toward Vietnam during the Clinton administration, as Vietnam sought to normalize its bilateral relationship with the United States. As the United States considered new trade agreements with Vietnam, advocates and the growing international religious freedom community pushed for human rights to be on the agenda.

International Religious Freedom Efforts During the Clinton Years

As Clinton took office, the U.S. relationship with Vietnam was deepening. After the complete dissolution of diplomatic relations at the end of the Vietnam War, Clinton's predecessor took incremental steps to reestablish a bilateral relationship. President George H. W. Bush set up a field office for Missing in Action Affairs in Hanoi, hoping to find missing prisoners of war and bring them home. In 1990, Secretary of State James Baker welcomed Nguyễn Cơ Thạch, Vietnam's foreign minister, in the highest-level talks since 1975. In 1991, the United States constructed a road map for improving U.S. relations with Vietnam. The U.S. promised political and economic benefits and the possibility of normalized relations with Vietnam in exchange for supporting the U.N.-led peace talks in Cambodia. In October 1991, Vietnam signed the Agreement on a Comprehensive Political Settlement of the Cambodia Conflict. The road map also demanded full cooperation with American efforts to repatriate fallen soldiers. Clinton picked up these efforts with zeal, noting that the status of the U.S.-Vietnam bilateral relationships "should be guided by one factor and one factor only: gaining the fullest possible accounting for our prisoners of war and our missing in action."[8] This commitment led Clinton to lift the trade embargo against Vietnam in February 1994, believing that increased diplomatic relationships might bolster forward progress. Clinton also announced the establishment of a new liaison office in Vietnam to begin a new human rights dialogue. Despite the positive steps, Clinton clarified that these steps did not translate directly to normalization. "Before that happens," he stated, "we must have more progress, more cooperation, and more answers."[9]

On July 11, 1995, President Clinton formally announced the normalization of diplomatic relations with Vietnam. Clinton celebrated the progress, noting that more American families could receive critical answers about their loved ones with increased cooperation from Hanoi.

Sometimes, they could locate the remains and send them home for a proper burial. While, again, Clinton focused on POW and MIA cases, he also recognized that normalization might bring progress in other areas too. Normalization ushered in new opportunities for trade with Vietnam and many agreements and programs associated with established human rights standards. In another historic development in the summer of 1995, Vietnam joined the Association of Southeast Asian Nations (ASEAN). In a statement announcing the normalized relations, Clinton expressed his hope that increased contact between the nations would improve human rights conditions in Vietnam, using Eastern Europe and the Soviet Union as historical examples.[10]

One of the early pushes for freedom during this time concerned Vietnamese emigration. In April 1996, the CPV agreed to a new initiative called the Resettlement Opportunity for Vietnamese Returnees (ROVR), in which the United States offered resettlement interviews to Vietnamese refugees seeking asylum in Hong Kong or Southeast Asia. The provision also extended to refugees who recently returned to Vietnam. From the beginning, the ROVR initiative faced significant challenges to successful implementation. Allegations of corruption mounted, with local officials offering resettlement interviews to refugees who could pay. Attorneys with UNHRC, who monitored the situation at the refugee camps, noted instances of sexual bribery and rape.[11] The CPV also instituted an arduous clearance process, one for which it did not have the adequate logistical support to carry out.

But U.S. officials, including the newly appointed U.S. ambassador to Vietnam, Pete Peterson, and Secretary Albright, stressed the importance of the ROVR initiative's success and its implications for the future of Vietnam's economy. Existing law, including the Jackson–Vanik Amendment, restricted U.S. trade relations with nonmarket economies that restrict emigration unless the president waived the requirement. The ROVR was the key to securing this waiver.[12]

Feeling the pressure, by October 1997, the CPV had streamlined its clearance process and cracked down on government corruption. In the months that followed, the CPV cleared over thirteen thousand applications for interviews with the U.S. Immigration and Naturalization Service (INS). Because of these improvements, President Clinton granted the waiver in March 1998, paving the way for a new bilateral trade agreement (BTA).[13] The United States and Vietnam negotiated the deal between 1998 and 1999 and eventually formalized the agreement in 2000. Comprised of five sections, the agreement outlined 1) increased market access for industrial and agricultural goods; 2) increased protection for intellectual property; 3) market access to service industries; 4) provisions to protect U.S. investments; and 5) provisions to increase transparency within the trade relationship. The BTA, which became official in December 2001, granted Vietnam conditional Most Favored Nation (MFN) trade status—a critical benchmark necessary for further integration into the global economy and, specifically, for entry into the World Trade Organization (WTO).

As the negotiations for the BTA took place, activists in the United States and Vietnam, IRF Purists, opposed the agreement. They saw an opportunity for the United States to use its leverage to encourage human rights improvements. During this time, reports of persecution proliferated. The CPV demolished churches, broke up religious services, and imprisoned believers for sharing their faith. In 1997, Vietnam passed Directive 31, authorizing the Ministry of Interior to detain individuals, without trial, for up to two years. One dissident who received significant notoriety was Catholic priest and democracy advocate Father Nguyễn Văn Lý. After meeting with human rights groups in 1999–2000, Father Lý submitted detailed testimony to USCIRF in February 2001. In it, he discouraged the United States from signing the BTA and pressed for political and religious freedom. Eventually, he was sentenced to fifteen years in prison. His case highlighted the difficulties involved with classifying human rights issues. Was Father Lý's case primarily a religious freedom issue or a political freedom issue? Throughout all three administrations under study, Ambassadors Bob Seiple, John Hanford, Suzan Johnson Cook, and David Saperstein each advocated for his release.

The normalization process of U.S.-Vietnam relations occurred alongside the international religious freedom movement in the United States. When Bob Seiple became the first ambassador-at-large for international religious freedom, he had a long and storied history with Vietnam. Given the small office and limited resources in the IRF office at the time, Seiple quickly began defining key priorities. In some places, like Saudi Arabia and Vietnam, the persecution was so overt and extreme that they automatically demanded attention. But another reason elevated Vietnam and Laos on Seiple's priority list: his desire for reconciliation and closure.

Bob Seiple served as a captain in the U.S. Marine Corps and served in the Vietnam War from 1966 to 1968. Seiple reflected on his experience some years later: "Vietnam was an event that most completely impacted my generation, including those who said they weren't or were going to go. The results have been with us for most of our lives. There were no winners or losers, only victims."[14] The Vietnam War left almost 60,000 Americans dead and over 150,000 wounded. Two million Vietnamese civilians perished in addition to one million Vietnamese military deaths. And the long-term effects of herbicides like Agent Orange devastated the country. Over the course of the bloody war, Seiple completed over three hundred flights. He earned twenty-eight Air Medals, a Vietnam Campaign Medal, the Navy Commendation Award, and the Distinguished Flying Cross.

After the war, Seiple continued an impressive, if eclectic, career, leading Eastern College, Eastern Baptist Theological Seminary, and prominent Christian NGO World Vision before he joined the State Department. During his tenure at World Vision, he grappled with the past. Given the horrors of the Vietnam War and the death that occurred on all sides, Seiple questioned, "How do you bring war to closure? How do you reconcile what happened here?" Seiple maintained that "unreconciled conflict undermines the victim and, in Vietnam, everyone was a victim."[15]

Despite his deeply held convictions, Seiple was humble in his approach and eschewed any sense of triumphalism. But this humility sometimes meant he focused on the quality of his efforts over measurable outcomes.[16] Combining his experience on the ground with World Vision, Seiple deepened his relationships with Vietnamese leaders across the country. But these relationships did not form overnight. Seiple recalled one of his initial meetings with State Department officials and Vietnamese foreign officials. As Ambassador Pete Peterson introduced him, he said sarcastically: "I want to introduce you to the guy who is here to punish you."[17] Seiple rebuffed the assertion but would fight that reputation throughout his tenure.

This initial meeting shows one of the results of long-standing infighting between the IRF Purists and the IRF Pragmatists. Seiple, a quintessential Pragmatist, wanted to be seen as a team player, not as an antagonist. But, since the Purists, like many commissioners at USCIRF, regularly controlled the bully pulpit, it was difficult to shake the presumption that all IRF advocates were hardliners.

After the IRF office released its first annual International Religious Freedom report in 1999, Representative Chris Smith (R- NJ) blasted Seiple and the IRF office for its failure to recommend Vietnam as a CPC: "Where is Vietnam, which brutally suppresses Buddhists, Protestants and others who will not join official churches run by the government itself and which attempts to control the Catholic Church through a Catholic Patriotic Association modeled closely after the Chinese institution of the same name?"[18] Representative Benjamin Gilman (R- NY) added a layer of skepticism, suggesting a connection between CPC designations and the Clinton administration's hopes for normalizing trade relations in Vietnam and Laos. He concluded: "Our Nation's foreign policy must never be to ensure that business comes before the right to freely practice one's religion and the freedom of assembly."[19]

The criticisms from these congressional leaders continued the following year. Smith claimed that while the IRF report is generally "clear and honest about denials of religious freedom by governments with which our government enjoys friendly relations, such as Saudi Arabia, France, Austria, and Belgium," for countries with more fragile relationships with the United States like North Korea, Laos, and Vietnam, "somehow the statements become less clear." Smith railed against the report's description of official religions in Vietnam, arguing that they were mere smokescreens to prevent authentic expressions of faith. He continued, "A careful reading of these reports suggests there was a struggle in the State Department between people who wanted to tell it like it is and those who did not want to say anything that would set back the relationship between the United States and whatever odious regime happens to be in power in the country to which they were posted."[20]

As compelling as the dichotomy Smith paints may be, it is also reductive, failing to account for the effects of a CPC designation on IRF's work. Seiple used Laos as an example to prove his point when asked about this tension. He told the story of being part of a delegation to Laos where American diplomats met with Laotian officials over the course of two weeks. They forged deep relationships. The delegation went from

Figure 5.1. President Clinton Greets a Large Crowd in Hanoi, Vietnam in November 2000. Source: William J. Clinton Library.

province to province and negotiated the successful release of dozens of prisoners. Shortly thereafter, USCIRF issued a report recommending the addition of Laos to the CPC list,[21] which, Seiple concluded, "would have just destroyed everything that we had created."[22] The challenge of maintaining relationships with foreign governments and maintaining credibility at home continued throughout Seiple's tenure.

Seiple became the first IRF ambassador in 1999 and stayed on for about eighteen months. Still, Seiple and his small team were able to make meaningful inroads in Vietnam in the name of increasing religious freedom. Seiple focused on convincing the Vietnamese regime that it was in their security interests to advance religious freedom. Seiple broke down the argument this way:

And our job was to try to get folks to initially grab onto their own vested interest and realize why this was important for them to embrace. And it basically came down to security issues. If a minority or person in a society feels their government has their best interest at heart, a lot of times that is portrayed as allowing them to worship as they want to worship, believe what they want to believe. If they have their best interest at heart, they will be loyal to the government and when there is loyalty, there is stability. When there is stability there is security.[23]

But, in Vietnam, this was a challenging feat. After decades of persecution, religious believers distrusted the CPV. Repairing these relationships required long-term attention, a reality Seiple understood well. During his short tenure, Seiple visited Vietnam, meeting with foreign ministers and religious groups. The IRF office advocated tirelessly for religious prisoners, most of whom were Catholics, Protestants in the North and Central Highlands, and members of the banned UBCV. Seiple and his team secured the release of eight prisoners in 1998.[24] Perhaps Seiple's most enduring accomplishment was how he set the stage for his successor, John Hanford. In an interview years after leaving the State Department, Seiple noted, "I think legacy is determined by the success of your successor—what you leave him/her to move forward."[25]

Vietnam's Binding Agreement: International Religious Freedom Efforts During the Bush Administration

President George W. Bush intercepted an exciting time for U.S.-Vietnam relations. In his first year, the United States and Vietnam officially entered the BTA after many years of negotiations. Still, as economic ties between the countries deepened, extensive human rights concerns remained. Economic liberalization did not translate to increased human rights protections. And the Bush administration clarified that it would avoid compartmentalizing policy issues in Vietnam. Assistant Secretary of State for East Asia and Pacific Affairs James Kelly acknowledged that disagreements on religious rights had "the potential to impede the forward momentum in our ties more than any other issue."[26] In short, Vietnam could not ignore its abysmal religious freedom conditions and continue with business as usual.

When John Hanford became the ambassador-at-large for international religious freedom, he prioritized the Vietnam case. He believed that the situation offered more potential for real and systemic change because of the IRF office's preexisting work and the unique geopolitical moment that gave the U.S. leverage. But external pressure from IRF

Purists at USCIRF, who repeatedly denounced the IRF office's perceived inaction, likely contributed too.[27]

Cycles of uprising and government crackdown characterized the early 2000s. Adding to religious grievances, new large-scale economic projects led to the forced displacements of hundreds of thousands of Vietnamese. Lacking resettlement support, these displaced persons experienced financial distress and acute food insecurity without resources to adapt agrarian practices to new lands.[28] During Easter 2001, thousands of Montagnards gathered in the capitals of Đắk Lắk, Gia Lai, and Kon Tum provinces to advocate for religious freedom and the return of their ancestral lands. The CPV met these demands with fury and quickly extinguished the demonstrations using military force. These events prompted increased controls by the CPV, which immediately banned protests and church gatherings outside of sanctioned regular worship.

Between 2002 and 2004, Ambassador Hanford and other officials from the IRF office traveled to Vietnam repeatedly to witness religious freedom conditions and raise concerns in person. In his first year as ambassador, Hanford focused on observation and data collection. The hard-liners in the Vietnamese government denied charges of religious persecution. But, over time, the IRF office provided overwhelming evidence that made confronting their denial possible.[29] In February 2004, Ambassador Hanford testified about these efforts and his "hands-on approach" to the Senate Foreign Relations Committee. While he expressed gratitude to the CPV for their willingness to discuss religious freedom with the American delegations, he acknowledged significant problems in the country, starting with the circularity of the legal system: "We knew that many other churches had requested registration and asked about their prospects. The authorities gave us the rather circular response that these churches could not be registered until they had approved pastors and approved buildings, but the pastors and buildings could not be approved until they were registered with churches."[30] While this registration problem was widespread across the country, it was acute in Đắk Lắk and Gia Lai provinces, where, combined, fewer than ten churches served approximately two hundred thousand Protestant parishioners.

In June 2004, the CPV released the Ordinance on Religion and Belief, which restated that "citizens have the right to freedom of belief and religion, to follow or not to follow a religion,"[31] and noted that "the State guarantees the right to freedom of belief and religion of its citizens. Nobody is allowed to infringe upon that right." In theory, the ordinance aimed to improve registration processes. But, in practice, the process remained challenging to navigate and impossibly slow. Article 8 explicitly prohibited the use of religion "to undermine the peace, independence, and unity of the country. . . . or to sow division . . . disturb public order . . . carry out superstitious activities, or to commit other breaches of the law."[32] Left intentionally vague, this article afforded local governments space to crack down on religious activity.

Competing Priorities and the Choice to Designate

The decision on whether or not to designate Vietnam as a CPC proved to be a controversial one. The many differing opinions swirling around the State Department and the White House during Bush's first term were emblematic of fundamental disagreements on the purposes and rightful usage of the IRFA. Raymond Burghardt, the U.S. ambassador to Vietnam, represented a familiar State Department perspective that viewed the designation with hesitation. Burghardt was a foreign service officer in Vietnam in the early 1970s and returned in the early 2000s. Burghardt denied the pragmatism of congressional human rights rebukes or the CPC designation. Unsurprised by Vietnam's approach to religion, Burghardt viewed the problem as intractable:

> I could see that we might be able to make some progress on the issues of the Montagnards, but there were some issues we are not going to make much progress on, such as the freedom to organize, the need to register with the state to begin with. We were never going to change that. That's basic Leninism 101. They do not believe in civil society. They may compromise on the role of it, but they are never going to truly accept it. They saw what happened in Poland, first the Churches advocated for change, then the unions, and they felt they were not going to allow that to happen in Vietnam. It's delusional to believe that the fundamental situation is going to change as long as the overall communist structure is in place. As a political scientist, I expect Leninists to behave like Leninists.[33]

This thinking led Burghardt to disagree with the CPC designation, believing it would do little besides interfere with other strategic priorities. He concluded: "You don't get any leverage; all you do is piss them off." It should be noted, however, that, with this line of logic, his disagreements likely surrounded the IRFA in its entirety, not simply its application to Vietnam in the early 2000s. Ambassador Seiple, who by this point had founded the Institute for Global Engagement, a nongovernmental organization that promotes religious freedom worldwide, also opposed the designation. Emblematic of the IRF Pragmatist approach, Seiple urged caution, fearing that undue pressure "could play straight into the hands of the hardliners." Instead, he described a way forward: the creation of a space, without the threat of sanctioning. Seiple resisted the IRF Purist instinct to punish offending governments and instead saw the primary role of the IRF office as to "demonstrate why it was in their naked self-interest to embrace the concept of religious freedom."[34]

But many disagreed. Within the IRF office, staffers like William Inboden and Tom Farr argued that diplomacy could continue even after they made the CPC designation. Senators like Sam Brownback, who would eventually become the IRF ambassador under the Trump administration, demanded action within Congress. The Congressional Human Rights Caucus, the Taskforce on International Religious Freedom, and the Congressional Caucus on Vietnam all supported the designation.

In the end, John Hanford, also an IRF Pragmatist, took a more incremental approach and did not seek the designation in 2003. Instead, he tried to develop support for the designation at the State Department while persuading the Vietnamese government that improvement was necessary if they were to avoid being named a CPC in the future. "We spent an enormous amount of time forming trusting relationships, so Vietnamese officials would believe we were dealing in good faith, that we were not discussing religious freedom issues to rub their nose in it, but that we were pursuing the interests of the United States."[35] Hanford noted another reality he faced: convincing others at the State Department. He carefully crafted a case and gathered evidence, hoping to drum up support within the building. Hanford also argued that this prudence translated into increased policy options once this designation was in place. "I'd rather take a little heat from USCIRF for one extra year over a country that they feel should be designated but then make a lot more progress after that." In short, Hanford sought to avoid surprising anyone. "Within the State Department, people respected that they were not blindsided," Hanford reflected some years later. "When we all work together, it bears greater fruit."[36] But improvement was still out of reach.

Ambassador Burghardt actively tried to undermine IRF's efforts and sent a preemptive memo to the secretary arguing that Vietnam should not be designated a CPC. Thus, it came back to the secretary of state. Powell listened to the ambassador, but he also listened to the assistant secretary of state for East Asian and Pacific affairs, James Kelly, who supported the designation. Powell raised religious freedom issues in Hanoi himself, but the situation did not improve and worsened in many places. This reality led staffers like Michael Green, the director of Asian affairs at the National Security Council, to support Vietnam's designation. After weighing the case and the evidence Hanford and his office had assembled over the years prior, Powell agreed to designate Vietnam.[37] Unsurprisingly, news of the designation enraged the CPV, who deemed it "a wrongful decision, based on erroneous information."[38] Angry as they were, they were not dismissive. They understood that the designation carried unwanted implications and were determined to have Vietnam's name removed from the CPC list.

A Creative Agreement

The IRFA required the U.S. government to take action within 180 days of the CPC designation. Unlike previous CPC designations, it could not rely on preexisting sanctions to prevent further action, since no such sanctions existed with Vietnam.[39] Given the fierce debate over the designation in the first place and the direct opposition to the designation by many in the State Department, levying new sanctions proved undesirable, if not bureaucratically untenable. Instead, Hanford and members of the IRF staff focused on formulating a binding agreement with the government of Vietnam that would outline a series of tangible goals to curtail religious freedom violations.[40] These negotiations took place in February 2005 over ten days. As part of the team that traveled to Vietnam, staffer William Inboden recalled the response of a senior Vietnamese foreign policymaker as negotiations began:

We are changing. Look, you Americans have been badgering us on these religious freedom issues for a while, and we're tired of it. We still don't quite get why you care about it a lot, but we sit in a difficult neighborhood. We are concerned about the rise of Chinese power and growing pressure from China for us to be a sort of satellite state of theirs, and we would prefer to have better relations with the U.S. as a counterbalance. And so we have decided we are going to improve religious freedom conditions. We are going to take steps the U.S. recommends to get off the CPC list.[41]

These security concerns and hopes of further integration into the global economy gave the United States significant leverage, illustrating how geopolitics can aid or constrain the success of international religious freedom policy.

With this newly established unity of mission, they worked out the agreement's details. Matthew Schmolesky, another IRF staffer who worked closely with Ambassador Hanford in drafting the binding agreement, reflected on the challenges of determining the benchmarks to ensure they would promote the desired changes in Vietnam. "If you are too specific," Schmolesky said, "you might get the specific things you asked for but miss out on some larger opportunities because they weren't specifically asked for. If you go too general, there may be latitude for the other party to live up to the letter but not the spirit."[42] The legal office at the State Department vetted the terms of the agreement, which was written in conjunction with the government of Vietnam, per the IRFA.

Hanford focused on negotiating with the Ministry of Public Security. Even though he met with the Religious Affairs Bureau, Hanford understood that "the decision on where to loosen up the stranglehold on religious practice wasn't coming from that office, it was coming from people that were in the state security apparatus." The IRF office was persistent in its efforts to reach a negotiation. Hanford wanted to convince the Vietnamese that he was serious, and he recalled one time "where we just camped out in Hanoi" after discussions seemed to stall. His interlocutors soon realized he was not going away and that he would stay as long as he needed to make progress. "Vietnamese food is pretty good," Hanford quipped.[43]

While the entire agreement has never been fully released, the White House summarized its contents in a press statement, marking it as a "key component of the President's freedom agenda."[44] In the end, the agreement banned forced renunciations, released many prominent prisoners, significantly changed the registration process for churches, and reopened houses of worship. It also included notable legislative changes. Among those was the "Ordinance on Religion." The National Assembly initially passed this legislation in November 2004, but the binding agreement included provisions to ensure its proper implementation.[45] The agreement also included large-scale commitments from the government of Vietnam: to declare existing legislation contradicting newly established religious freedom protections invalid and to focus on ensuring the proper implementation of these new legal changes at the local level.[46] They completed the agreement in May 2005. Two months later, on the tenth anniversary of normalized relations between the United States and Vietnam, President Bush welcomed Prime Minister Phan Văn Khải to the White House, where they signed the landmark agreement. National Security Council staffer Michael Greene used this visit as leverage to secure CPV buy-in.

Removal of the Designation

Throughout 2005, Vietnam made significant progress toward religious freedom. While the reports still showed problems, Vietnam had "turned a corner." Vietnam modernized its legal codes through the prime minister's "Instruction on Protestantism" and an implementation decree pertaining to the 2004 Ordinance. These developments restated Vietnam's prohibition of forced renunciation of faith and instructed provincial governments on how to help religious groups through the registration process so they could worship publicly.[47] By 2006, previously outlawed congregations, including Buddhist groups, the Baha'i, and some Christian sects, who once gathered underground, could meet openly. During this year, the Vatican appointed fifty-seven new Catholic priests, and the Southern Evangelical Church of Vietnam established a new training facility to develop its clergy. Between 2005 and 2006, Vietnam released dozens of religious prisoners, many of whom had been in jail for many years. In 2005, a large-scale presidential amnesty program allowed for the release of prominent Buddhist activist Thích Thiện

Mihn. These developments led the Bush administration to lift the CPC designation in November 2006.

IRF Purists at USCIRF lamented the decision to remove Vietnam as a CPC after such a short period. And while commissioners praised Hanford and his team for their efforts on the binding agreement, they wanted to see more concrete improvements before lifting the designation: "The key words here are 'might' and 'future,'" said Commissioner Nina Shea in a hearing before the House International Relations Committee.[48] "The actions taken only signal promises of improvement and not actual measurable progress. And, these actions do not address the human rights violations that landed Vietnam on the CPC list in the first place."[49] USCIRF Chair Felice Gaer argued that the United States was giving away its leverage for further change: "The designation of Vietnam has been a positive incentive for engagement on religious freedom concerns. Lifting the designation removes that incentive."[50]

Hanford disagreed, asserting that "major progress has been achieved on all points of concern that led to Vietnam's initial designation." The willingness to lift the CPC designation after such a short time exemplified the pragmatism of Hanford's approach. In a press conference marking the 2006 CPC list, Hanford spoke unequivocally:

> Designation as a CPC is not and must not simply be an exercise in naming and shaming. We find no satisfaction in heaping criticism on a country. The purpose of the designation is to signal to a country that it has severe problems related to religious freedom that need to be addressed. And it's also a signal that the United States wants to work with that country to help overcome those problems. The decision not to designate Vietnam is an important indicator that this is our goal and it should serve as a signal to other countries as well that our purpose in this process is to improve conditions for religious believers and that we will recognize progress when it occurs. We hope that the successes achieved in Vietnam can be a model for improvement and bilateral relations as we continue to press for religious freedom reform in other nations around the world.[51]

Again, this debate surfaced fundamental disagreements between the IRF Purists and the IRF Pragmatists on how the CPC process should function, and how the United States might best maintain political leverage. Laura Bryant Hanford, who was instrumental in writing the IRFA, noted that the IRF office clarified the exact reasons for the CPC designation. While she recognized that problems still existed, the impressive improvements meant that the violations no longer warranted CPC designation. In this view, to uphold the designation in the face of vast improvements would create a credibility problem. "First, you're going to lose credibility with the people in the government that are on your side," Hanford stated. "And then they're going to lose credibility and the ability to push for the right things within their own government. If there's no reward for progress, there's no leverage."[52] From her perspective, while challenges within Vietnam still existed, the threshold to remove the designation was not perfection. Ambassador Hanford reiterated: "You're going to get lifted from CPC once you've dealt with CPC-level problems sufficiently." Others, including many IRF Purists at the Commission, viewed the CPC process differently. They hoped to "squeeze" the designation and get as much progress as possible on every front. The problem, though, from Hanford's view, was that this undermined credibility with the offending governments. If other governments felt like the United States was constantly moving the goalposts, they might be unwilling to cooperate at all.[53]

In the end, the negotiations and signing of the binding agreement exemplified how the writers of the IRFA, including Laura and John Hanford, envisioned the legislation working. The process showed how the IRF office, with the president's full support, could successfully facilitate positive change even in one of the world's most challenging regimes.

After the CPC designation was lifted, President Bush traveled to Vietnam and worshipped with Laura Bush at the Cửa Bắc Cathedral in Hanoi. Here, he reiterated the importance of religious freedom in society: "It's our way of expressing our personal faith and, at the same time, urging societies to feel comfortable with, and confident in saying to their people, if you feel like praising God, you're allowed to do so in any way you see fit."[54]

Without the designation holding it back, Vietnam obtained permanent normal trade status with the United States in December 2006, which paved the way for its acceptance as the 150th member of the WTO on January 11, 2007. When considering IRF policy across the world, this snapshot regularly surfaces as a policy success. Even so, as the next section shows, progress in Vietnam was not linear.

International Religious Freedom Efforts During the Obama Administration

In the first few years of Obama's term, religious freedom conditions within Vietnam worsened. In 2009, Human Rights Watch (HRW) released a damning report, citing "sharp backsliding on religious freedom."[55] Years earlier, as the binding agreement was being formulated, Vietnam welcomed Buddhist monk and activist Thích Nhất Hạnh back home after almost forty years of exile. But, in September 2009, the Vietnamese government cracked down on Thích Nhất Hạnh's followers and extracted 150 monks from Bát Nhã monastery.[56] Much like the reaction to the explosive growth of Protestant groups in the early 2000s, the Vietnamese government feared the momentum of Thích Nhất Hạnh's followers. Elaine Pearson, the deputy director of the Asia division at HRW, said that "the government views many religious groups, particularly popular ones that it fears it can't control, as a challenge to the Communist Party's authority."[57] In response to the allegations of worsening persecution, USCIRF reiterated its stance, arguing that Vietnam deserved to be designated a CPC. Its 2010 annual report to Congress cited Vietnam's human rights deterioration since joining the WTO.[58] Importantly, as evidence of Vietnam's worsening religious freedom conditions snowballed, the IRF office did not have new leadership. It took over two years from the end of Hanford's tenure in January 2009 for Ambassador Suzan Johnson Cook to take over.

Within the halls of Congress, the pervasiveness of the religious freedom challenges in Vietnam remained contested. Some argued that the deterioration warranted the reinstatement of the CPC designation. Others claimed that the data used to criticize Vietnam was outdated and failed to account for the genuine progress being made.[59] Secretary of State Hillary Clinton acknowledged the tension in a speech marking the fifteenth anniversary of normalized relations between the United States and Vietnam: "It is true that profound differences exist . . . and the United States will continue to urge Vietnam to strengthen its commitment to human rights, and give its people even greater say over the direction of their own lives. But this is not a relationship that is fixed upon our differences. We have learned to see each other, not as former enemies, but as actual and potential partners, colleagues, and friends."[60] Before Clinton's visit, the CPV jailed several prominent dissidents, prompting protests throughout the United States and increased pressure from human rights groups.

Tension mounted in 2011 as Representative Edward Royce (R-CA) introduced H.R. 16, calling the State Department to redesignate Vietnam a CPC. The resolution cited continued abuse against the Unified Buddhist Church of Vietnam (UBCV), the Hòa Hảo Buddhists, Protestant Montagnards, and Catholics in Gia Lai Province as justification for the redesignation. At the release of the 2011 IRF report, Assistant Secretary of State for DRL Michael Posner acknowledged the discrepancies in religious freedom conditions throughout the country, noting that, while many new houses of worship were being built, some local provinces, particularly in the north and northwest highlands, actively prevented new churches from registering. Posner also lamented that the CPV rearrested Father Lý, who was previously released to receive medical attention after experiencing several strokes while imprisoned. Despite the setbacks, the State Department did not recommend redesignating Vietnam.

A new trade agreement, which became known as the "Trans-Pacific Partnership," was an integral part of the Obama administration's "pivot to Asia" and heavily influenced the U.S.-Vietnam relationship between 2009 and 2016. The TPP was a free trade agreement that brought together a dozen countries in the region.[61] Of the agreement, Secretary Clinton noted: "Our goal is to create not just more growth, but better growth."[62] The partnership included environmental and labor protections and explicit provisions to protect intellectual property and increase transparency in the market. Clinton continued: "Our hope is that a TPP agreement with high standards can serve as a benchmark for future agreements."[63] Per the agreement, Vietnam needed to reform its system—ending child labor, improving environmental conditions, and allowing workers to unionize. But Vietnam, which had the lowest per capita GDP of all the member countries, was poised to benefit the most from the agreement and determined the reforms were worth it. Much like Vietnam's response to the CPC designation during the Bush administration, where foreign officials cited China's aggression as reasoning for making change, security concerns and increased aggression in the South China Sea led the CPV to deepen its relationship with the United States during the Obama years. The TPP provided a prime opportunity.

Still, as Vietnam sought increased economic integration, its religious freedom conditions drew concern. Problems with Vietnam's registration system persisted even as the Vietnamese government issued Decree 92, yet another directive supposedly aimed at simplifying the registration process. But, overall, Decree 92 highlighted how the government intentionally prohibited churches from registering. Effective January 1, 2013, the decree required a twenty-year monitoring period before churches could complete the registration process. Here, they had to "operate stably and not violate the law." But, as scholar Reginald Reimer points out, this is impossible, as unregistered religious operations are, by definition, illegal.[64]

In a hearing before the Committee on Foreign Affairs in April 2013, Representative Chris Smith called on the United States to raise human rights concerns in its diplomatic efforts: "They need to know that we mean it, that we have not put this in a compartment, hermetically sealed from all other aspects of our bilateral relationship, that human rights matter to this country and matters to the American public." Smith also called out the IRF office specifically when he argued that the "State Department decided to allow political considerations to trump the facts." At the hearing, advocates and victims gave ample evidence of the worsening conditions. Representative Edward Royce noted that Vietnam was "backsliding" and "walking in the wrong direction."[65] Much to the dismay of these hard-liners in Congress, President Obama moved forward with the Comprehensive Partnership, an agreement formed with President Trương Tấn Sang in July 2013.

The agreement covered a range of issues ranging from security, economics, and human rights. President Obama explicitly supported Vietnam's integration into the global economy in the agreement. President Trương Tấn Sang "welcomed the United States' enhanced cooperation in the Asia-Pacific, which contributes to the peace, stability, and prosperity of the region."[66] With increased Chinese aggression and turmoil in the South China Sea, the agreement reaffirmed existing regulations like the Declaration of Conduct of Parties in the South China Sea. It reiterated the mutual commitment to solving maritime disputes peacefully.

Later that year, Representative Smith introduced the Vietnam Human Rights Act, which passed the House in August 2013. The act limited non-humanitarian aid to Vietnam, barring certification to Congress by the president that human rights conditions have improved.[67] Additionally, the act expressed Congress's belief that the United States should protect Radio Free Asia programming in Vietnam, oppose Vietnam's candidacy for membership in the U.N.'s Human Rights Council (UNHRC), and designate Vietnam as a CPC for its religious freedom violations. While the act signaled congressional frustration, it had little impact. After its passage, Vietnam's Foreign Ministry spokesperson Lương Thanh Nghị bristled, repeating the familiar party line: "The erroneous and prejudiced information on the human rights practices and religious freedom in Vietnam has raised in H.R. 1897 in no way draws a true picture of Vietnam or serves the development of bilateral relations."[68]

Secretary of State John Kerry called on Vietnam to improve its human rights protections as the United States and Vietnam moved forward with the comprehensive agreement. In a speech in December 2013, Kerry was more up front than he had been previously: "To realize our potential as a partner and for Vietnam to realize its potential as a thriving economy—and this is something we talked about openly and frankly— Vietnam needs to show continued progress on human rights and freedoms, including the freedom of religion, the freedom of expression, and the freedom of association."[69] In the months after Kerry's visit, Vietnam welcomed the U.N.'s special rapporteur for religious freedom. The report following the summer 2014 visit was mixed, noting "positive developments" alongside "serious problems." Most significantly, the report details that religious activities from unregistered churches are "restricted and unsafe," and that "the rights to freedom of religion or belief of such communities [were] grossly violated in the face of constant surveillance, intimidation, harassment, and persecution."[70]

Another blow to religious freedom occurred in 2015, as Vietnam released an early draft of what would become the primary legal document governing religion in Vietnam, the "Law on Belief and Religion." Despite reciting the same Articles 1 and 2, which protect religious freedom, the rest of the legislation "whittles away at the plain-language freedom guarantees they contained."[71] When the National Assembly published the law's final version in February 2017, the religious freedom community was saddened to learn of a small but meaningful shift in its Article 34. Where earlier, the government had to approve clergy after their congregations elected them, the new law required preapproval—yet another crackdown on denominational autonomy.[72]

Still, developments on other strategic priorities continued. Trade with Vietnam increased exponentially throughout Obama's tenure, growing from just over $10 billion to over $40 billion between 2009 and 2016. And the TPP, signed on February 4, 2016, promised further integration in the years to come. In May 2016, President Obama traveled back to Hanoi. Ahead of his visit, the Vietnamese government released Father Lý. By that time, the CPV had imprisoned Father Lý several times. Cumulatively, he spent over two decades in prison and fifteen years under house arrest.

During this visit, Obama lifted the ban on lethal weapons sales to Vietnam. In a speech in Hanoi, Obama claimed the move would remove "a lingering vestige of the Cold War" and ensure that Vietnam had the necessary "equipment it needs to defend itself."[73] Obama denied allegations that the decision was predicated upon China's growing aggression but reiterated his commitment to developing "strong defense ties with Vietnam in the region for the long term." Critics balked at the shift, arguing that the United States should require more definitive progress on human rights before removing the ban. Some feared that Vietnam might use American weapons to violate human rights. Obama acknowledged the criticism and stated: "As with all of our defense partners, sales will need to still meet strict requirements, including those related to human rights."[74]

Religious freedom violations continued by the end of Obama's term, but many expected the TPP would lead to extensive human rights reforms in Vietnam. In 2017, President Donald Trump withdrew from the TPP, citing concerns about the potential loss of American manufacturing jobs. Without the enforcement mechanism provided by the TPP, Vietnam jettisoned many of these new reforms and cracked down on dissidents.[75] Instead, Vietnam and the other TPP member countries signed the Comprehensive and Progressive Agreement for Trans-Pacific Partnership (CPTPP).

The story of international religious freedom efforts between 1993 and 2017 is at once hopeful and daunting. The progress realized under John Hanford's leadership shows how the IRFA, when creatively applied, can go beyond denouncing persecution to create change, even in one of the world's most hostile regimes. Undoubtedly, Vietnam's desire to integrate into the world economy and deepen its security relationship with the United States influenced its decision to change. Moreover, the IRF office was able to convince the Vietnamese government that religious freedom would enhance their security at home. As Seiple put it, the task was to "demonstrate why it was in their naked self-interest to embrace the concept of religious freedom."[76]

Up to this point, the Vietnam case marks the only time the IRF office has successfully negotiated a binding agreement. Still, it set an important precedent for other countries. This case also highlights the value of long-term vision and persistence. Seiple and Hanford were both fiercely committed to progress in Vietnam and gave it an outsized share of attention. This sustained pressure dissipated some throughout the Obama years. An important note, however, is that the time spent in Vietnam to monitor conditions and negotiate the agreement was immense—and difficult to sustain given the global mandate of the IRFA. But while the efforts of the binding agreement were successful, they were impermanent.

6

International Religious Freedom in the Birthplace of Islam

The directions were clear: wear any religious symbols, a cross or a Star of David, under the uniform. Observe religious holidays in secrecy, away from the public. Use nonreligious terminology to conceal the true nature of religious services. These directions and the emphasis on private displays of religious practice may not seem surprising from the Kingdom of Saudi Arabia (KSA). However, in the early 1990s, the intended audience was not Saudi citizens or even foreign workers. It was American soldiers.[1]

In the lead-up to the Gulf War, the United States sent troops to Saudi Arabia to counter Iraq's aggression and stabilize the region. The United States led coalition forces to expel Saddam Hussein's military from Kuwait and defend Saudi Arabia and Israel from Iraqi attacks. Despite the U.S.-Saudi unity in the Gulf War, deep cleavages remained, particularly concerning Saudi Arabia's human rights record and its intense control of religious expression. Saudi officials prohibited family and friends from sending Bibles to American soldiers on Saudi soil.[2] Officers ordered troops to call their chaplains "morale officers" instead.[3] Soldiers attended "fellowship meetings" instead of mass. This tension that surfaced during the Gulf War represents a much larger dilemma that has plagued U.S. foreign policy concerning Saudi Arabia for several decades: How can the U.S. balance its commitment to human rights and religious freedom and its dependency on Saudi Arabia as a major security partner?

But, in the case of Saudi Arabia, security and human rights were not easily disentangled. Religious intolerance in Saudi Arabia cost American lives—in the 1996 attacks on Khobar Towers, the attacks on foreign workers, including Americans, in Riyadh in 2003, and, of course, in the devastating attacks on 9/11. Fifteen of the nineteen perpetrators of the 9/11 attacks were Saudi citizens.

Of the KSA, scholar William Inboden states plainly: "Their entire existence is predicated on a religious narrative that is coercive, exclusive, and deeply hostile to any manner of religious dissent or diversity—and that often justifies, even mandates, violence."[4] However, as this chapter illustrates, it was often the threat of extremism and even violence that Saudi Arabia fomented that pushed international religious freedom efforts forward. This case considers the difficulties of promoting religious freedom within a staunchly theocratic system. It examines the delicate tensions involved in delineating religious expression and religious extremism. Does religious freedom allow for monitoring Friday prayers to prevent the mass transmission of intolerant ideas? What about the removal of imams who espouse extreme theologies? Where is the line between promoting diversity and pluralism while stopping religiously motivated violence?

The case of Saudi Arabia illustrates how the United States attempts to balance human rights concerns with urgent economic and security priorities. Besides Israel, Saudi Arabia is the most significant U.S. ally in the Middle East. The two nations share close economic ties because of the heavy participation of U.S. companies in the Saudi oil industry, beginning with partnerships between Standard Oil and Texaco in the 1930s and the establishment of the Arabian American Oil Company, or Aramco, in the 1940s. The security relationship between the two nations also spans decades. During the Cold War, the countries worked together to oppose the Soviet occupation of Afghanistan from 1979 to 1989. The United States relied heavily on Saudi Arabia during the 1991 Gulf War as the United States worked to remove Iraqi forces from Kuwait. It based many of its military operations in Saudi Arabia.

Not that U.S.-Saudi relations have existed without tension. Amid outrage during the Yom Kippur War in 1973, Saudi Arabia contributed to the oil embargo—penalizing countries perceived as supporting Israel, including the United States—eventually leading to an energy crisis. And, throughout the past few decades, the State Department repeatedly denounced Saudi Arabia's human rights practices and its exportation of fundamentalist ideologies worldwide. The most significant source of tension between the two nations throughout the late 1990s and early 2000s concerned the threat of terrorism. Ironically, this tension point provided the IRF office with leverage to push for reform, especially during the Bush administration. When Saudi Arabia faced the deadly effects of extremism within its borders, as Al-Qaeda attacked three compounds in Riyadh in 2003, the IRF office found its opening.

In his book *Weapon of Peace*, Nilay Saiya argues that repressive environments, like Saudi Arabia, "choke religious liberty and independent thinking and serve as a natural breeding ground for terrorism."[5] From Saiya's perspective, a lack of religious diversity foments violence as it silences moderate thinkers who could balance extremism. In effect, "attempts by states and societies to repress assertive religion produce the very fanaticism and terrorism that they seek to avoid."[6] Such is the case with Saudi Arabia. Throughout all three administrations under study, it found itself torn between wanting to uphold an ultraconservative view of Sunni Islam and wanting to quell terrorist violence in the country. This chapter shows this back and forth, with Saudi Arabia vacillating between modest modernization attempts and intense crackdowns on dissent. It also shows how the IRF office pushed its agenda forward despite numerous economic and security concerns demanding the State Department's focus. Further, it delves into the complex religious history of the Saudi regime and the competing priorities within the U.S.-Saudi Arabia relationship. Finally, it examines the IRF office's efforts to advance religious freedom amid the growing threat of extremism.

Historical Context

As the birthplace of Islam, Saudi Arabia is home to the two holiest sites of the faith: Mecca and Medina. The Qur'an and the Sunna (or traditions of the Prophet Muhammed) serve together as the nation's constitution, embedding political power and control within Islam. Without a binding legal code or national elections, the royal family retains total authority.

Tensions that plague the religious landscape in Saudi Arabia today have deep historical roots. The official religion of Saudi Arabia is Sunni Islam, and the majority of Muslims in the country are also Sunni. However, there is a sizable Shi'a population of approximately 10–15 percent. Most Shi'a in Saudi Arabia are "Twelvers," meaning they acknowledge and follow the Twelfth Imam, Muhammad ibn Hasan al-Mahdi. Most Twelvers are in the Eastern Province, where most of the persecution and abuse by the religious police occurs. The second largest Shi'a population in Saudi Arabia is the Sulaimani Ismailis, who live in the Najran Province. There are also small percentages of Bohra Ismailis and Zaydis in Saudi Arabia. While Shi'a Muslims enjoy some level of religious freedom within the Eastern Province, those who live in other regions of Saudi Arabia face less favorable conditions. The depth of the Shi'a and Sunni divide is acute within Saudi Arabia, and the monarchy assumes there is loyalty to Iran within the Shi'a communities. As a result, the government restricts the establishment of Shi'a mosques, cemeteries, and memorials and arbitrarily detains those it suspects of dissent.

The Saudi government persecutes individuals who belong to non-Muslim faiths and treats noncitizens with particular suspicion. Of Saudi Arabia's some 34 million people, approximately 10 million are foreign workers.[7] Often, they lack basic religious rights. Despite international pressure, apostasy and blasphemy remain capital offenses. The government targets former Muslims who convert to other faiths; executions and indefinite prison sentences occur regularly. The Committee for the Promotion of Virtue and Prevention of Vice (CPVPV), the agency that monitors religious activity, relies upon extensive surveillance systems by which the government successfully criminalizes dissent and prosecutes apostates. Saudi Arabia employs unrelated laws to persecute religious minorities and suspected dissidents. For example, the Saudi government often cites prohibitions on dress, gender mixing, noise disturbances, and zoning requirements to halt religious expression and detain religious dissidents.

Navigating the legal system in Saudi Arabia is doubly frustrating. On the one hand, its codes are rigid, explicitly preventing religious expression that deviates from the state-sanctioned form of Sunni Islam. Equally constraining, however, is the laws' often intentional vagueness. Rhetorically, the legal code may protect religious minorities, but broader mandates like "censoring objectionable content," "ensuring compatibility with Islam," or "maintaining public order" often supersede any religious protections.[8] The application of the laws is inconsistent. Furthermore, those charged with enforcing the law rarely follow it themselves, regularly acting outside of their formal jurisdictional authority. The combination of these factors forms a complex and burdensome system to navigate, especially for the nation's most vulnerable.

Legal Discrimination

From a legal perspective, the Saudi government is transparent on the bounds of religious freedom in the country: it does not exist. Despite rhetorical nods to securing non-Muslims' right to private worship, this protection proves elusive in practice. The lines between private and public worship remain undefined, making almost any practice subject to scrutiny or, worse, indictment.[9] In addition, the Saudi government severely contains religious practice within Islam. As the Qur'an and the Sunna jointly comprise the constitution of Saudi Arabia, religious leaders and regulators wield extensive political power.[10]

Only Muslims can be full citizens of Saudi Arabia.[11] Proselytizing is illegal, and the Saudi government prevents clergy from non-Muslim faiths from entering the country, though, sometimes, they gain access by claiming nonreligious aims. With this said, the Saudi government engages in large-scale efforts aimed at converting foreigners to Islam.[12] It is illegal for members of non-Muslim clergy to enter the country, as is the distribution of unsanctioned religious materials. While all forms of apostasy are grievous offenses in Saudi Arabia, "sorcery" or "black magic" is considered the worst form of polytheism and carries the penalty of death.[13]

The celebration of holidays is strictly limited, typically only to Eid al-Fitr at the end of Ramadan and Eid al-Adha after the Hajj. In some Shi'a-dominated areas, such as Qatif, the solemn celebration of Ashura is allowed.[14] Other holidays, particularly pagan holidays like Valentine's Day, are strictly forbidden. Those found buying or selling materials or celebrating unsanctioned holidays are routinely arrested.

The Ministry of Islamic Affairs (MOIA) oversees the construction and proper administration of mosques throughout the country, and the mutawwa'in police religious behavior and enforce the legal codes, however vague they may be. These include but are not limited to enforcing daily prayers, regulating men's and women's dress, breaking up illegal gatherings, and ensuring that associations between men and women remain confined to family members.

Motivations for Persecution

Unlike the China and Vietnam case studies, the motivations underlying Saudi Arabia's persecution are religious. This commitment is derived from an eighteenth-century agreement between Islamic leader Muhammad ibn Abd al-Wahhab and Muhammed bin Saud. The alliance ensured that the Al Saud dynasty would rule, and that it would promote and defend a strict form of Wahhabi Islamism. The agreement was reaffirmed in 1932, when modern-day Saudi Arabia was founded.

The Saudi regime views itself as protector of the faith and opposes anything that may weaken its fidelity. They want their society, in all ways and at all times, to align with their strict interpretation of Islam. This protection of their own religious devotion and purity means that they reject attempts at diluting the message. One Saudi judge, for example, maintained that "Saudi Arabia leads the world in the protection of human rights because it protects them according to the sharia of God."[15]

Often, this hard-line approach translates into skepticism of perceived foreign intervention. Throughout the period under study, the Saudi government imposed a "Saudization" plan that replaced foreign workers with citizens. Relatedly, the government reserves the most well-attended prayer services for citizens to lead and strictly limits the opportunities for foreign imams. For the IRF office, these motivations presented a distinct set of challenges. Instead of working to convince a regime not to fear religious activity, in Saudi Arabia, the IRF office needed to assure the Saudi regime that religious freedom could coexist with sincere religious devotion.

As Ani Sarkissian notes, Sunnis in Saudi Arabia still face repression because "the state in control over the institutions that interpret and enforce religious doctrine, making it impossible for the majority religion to govern itself."[16] Sarkissian argues that this system robs an individual's right to freely choose one's religious beliefs or practice. And, because Saudi Arabia controls the practice of religious faith, including, for example, the appointment of imams or the construction of mosques, "religion becomes a tool of the state, ready to be wielded to advance its interests."[17]

The Clinton Administration and Religious Freedom in Saudi Arabia

When Bill Clinton became president in January 1993, he already had strong connections to the Saudi regime. As governor of Arkansas, Clinton worked with Saudi Ambassador Prince Bandar bin Sultan to facilitate a large-scale donation from Saudi Arabia to create a new

Middle Eastern studies program at the state's flagship university.[18] Clinton promised economic revitalization throughout his campaign, and foreign policy often took a backseat. The U.S. relationship with Saudi Arabia was a notable exception, due largely to the economic interdependencies created by the oil industry and arms sales.

Home to expansive oil reserves, security and stabilization in the Gulf region became a primary strategic priority in the latter half of the twentieth century. After the Iraqi invasion of Kuwait in August 1990, the U.S. led a coalition of forces in Operations Desert Shield and Desert Storm. Here, the United States called upon Saudi Arabia to support its efforts. Despite a decisive victory, Saddam Hussein's rule in Iraq continued, as did threats to American interests and regional stability.

Throughout Clinton's first term, the U.S. military presence in the Middle East increased.[19] During this time, Clinton worked diligently to support Israeli and Palestinian leaders as they negotiated a peace settlement. In September 1993, Israeli Foreign Minister Shimon Peres and Palestinian foreign policy official Mahmoud Abbas signed the "Declaration of Principles on Interim Self-Government Arrangements." A hopeful step forward toward a more permanent peace settlement, the declaration included provisions to extend more control to the Palestinians in the West Bank and Gaza. Less than a year later, Yitzhak Rabin and Yasser Arafat signed the accord for Palestinian self-rule. Importantly, this agreement marked the first time that Palestinian leaders recognized Israel's right to exist. This peace process was particularly important for Saudi Arabia, as most Palestinians are Sunni Muslims. The negotiations for a long-term agreement recommenced during an extensive, weeks-long summit at Camp David. While the summit did not lead to a formalized agreement, the parties agreed to a set of principles to govern future negotiations.

This brief overview of foreign policy priorities shared by Saudi Arabia and the United States points to the depth of the relationship. Throughout this time, religious freedom conditions in Saudi Arabia were abysmal. Until the late 1990s, these issues were largely compartmentalized, and President Clinton avoided discussing Saudi Arabia's treatment of its citizens. But two forces combined to bring religious freedom to the forefront. First, as described in chapter 1, advocacy groups and congressional leaders urged the executive branch to prioritize international religious freedom and passed the IRFA. At the same time, the United States was forced to confront religious extremism emanating from Saudi Arabia.

The Extremist Threat

In June 1996, a terrorist attack on the Khobar Towers in Dhahran rocked Saudi Arabia and the United States. The building served as a housing complex for U.S. air forces stationed in Saudi Arabia. When a tanker truck destroyed the eight-story building, it left nineteen American airmen dead, and hundreds wounded. While questions surrounding the attack's perpetrators still exist, the intelligence community eventually attributed the attack to the Iranian-backed militant group Hezbollah. In a rousing speech in Pérouges, France, after the bombings, Bill Clinton proclaimed, "We will not rest in our efforts to discover who is responsible, to track them down, and to bring them to justice. My friends, we must rally the forces of tolerance and freedom everywhere to work against terrorism."[20]

The incident directly connected the need for religious tolerance with U.S. security priorities. Secretary of Defense William Perry noted that the attacks "were not only attacks on American citizens and forces, they were also an assault on our security strategy in the region."[21] Perry explained how extremists used terrorism because they could not defeat the United States militarily; they relied on methods of terror to weaken domestic and regional support for a strong U.S. presence in the Middle East. He concluded: "Terrorism hangs over this bright future like a dark cloud, threatening our hope for a future of freedom, democracy and cooperation among all nations. It is the antithesis of everything America stands for. It is an enemy of the fundamental principles of human rights—freedom of movement, freedom of expression, and freedom of religion."[22]

"Ongoing, Systemic, and Egregious"

When Bob Seiple became the first ambassador-at-large for international religious freedom, he knew he needed a strategy. With few resources and many nations demanding attention, a colleague at the State Department advised him to choose a few cases to focus on. Seiple recalled the advice:

Figure 6.1. Saudi security personnel inspect the aftermath of the devastating Khobar Towers bombing on June 25, 1996. Source: Records of the Office of the Secretary of Defense.

"Don't pick one hundred. You'll never get anything done." With this in mind, Seiple first prioritized the most egregious cases of persecution. Saudi Arabia made the shortlist.[23]

When the IRF office released its first annual report in October 1999, Representative Chris Smith praised the reports transparency and boldness: "I am impressed with the extent to which the report states hard facts even about governments with which the United States enjoys friendly relations." He listed several examples, including France, Austria, Belgium and, importantly, Saudi Arabia. Indeed, the inaugural report plainly stated that "freedom of religion does not exist" in Saudi Arabia. But Smith's commendation ended there. He joined a chorus of activists and policymakers in expressing frustration that the State Department did not designate Saudi Arabia as a Country of Particular Concern (CPC). In a hearing before the Committee on International Relations, Smith asked, pointedly: "Does the administration really believe these governments have not engaged in or tolerated particularly severe violations of religious freedom? Or were the President and his advisers more worried about injuring the relationship or interfering with ongoing efforts to improve the relationship than with giving the honest assessment required by the plain language of the statute?"[24] USCIRF Commissioners shared the concern.

In fairness, given the delicate context, Ambassador Seiple found himself in a difficult position. Under the advisement of the legal department at the State Department, he interpreted the CPC designation criteria laid out in the IRFA narrowly. The language in the law stipulated that, to merit designation, a nation must engage in "systematic, ongoing, and egregious" violations of religious freedom during the reporting period. In this view, while Saudi Arabia's treatment of religious minorities was at times brutal, it was sporadic and thus did not qualify as "systematic" or "ongoing."[25]

Seiple thought that designating Saudi Arabia as a CPC at this juncture might be counterproductive. In keeping with his pragmatic approach, he focused on incremental steps forward. Seiple described a meeting with Prince Saud Al-Faisal, the Saudi foreign minister. After listening to Seiple's description of the newly passed IRFA, the foreign minister countered: "Now let me tell you about divine legislation." Al-Faisal then described Saudi Arabia's unique role in the Islamic tradition, particularly as the home to two of the faith's holiest sites: Mecca and Medina. Throughout the discussions, Seiple realized they were "exchanging existential realities: it is not whether the other was right or wrong, but what the other believed to be true."[26] These conversations, grounded in mutual respect and cultural sensitivity, led to modest progress. Because of those discussions, Saudi Arabia publicly declared that individuals, including non-Muslims, had the right to worship privately.

Confronting Extremism: The Bush Administration and Religious Freedom in Saudi Arabia

During the early days of the Bush administration, then–Crown Prince Abdullah expressed frustration at the United States and George W. Bush himself for not playing a more active role in the Middle East peace process. In August 2001, these building tensions came to a head, with Crown Prince Abdullah threatening to halt military cooperation with the United States. The U.S. responded by amending its stance, advocating instead for creating a separate Palestinian state, one of Saudi Arabia's central goals. Secretary of State Colin Powell announced the change in November of that year.

The following year, in advance of the 2002 Arab League summit, and while Israelis and Palestinians were in the middle of negotiations, a Hamas suicide bomb killed thirty Israelis and wounded many others. In response, Israel launched a sweeping attack on the West Bank, obliterating the working peace plan. President Bush sent Secretary Powell, against Donald Rumsfeld's advice, on an emergency mission to Israel. With violence continuing, Powell was boxed in, with no room to make progress. Then, in front of reporters at a White House meeting, President Bush stated, "Ariel Sharon is a man of peace." In a conversation with Condoleezza Rice afterward, Powell responded angrily, "Do you have any idea how this plays on Arab TV? . . . Why is he giving Sharon a pass?"[27]

Abdullah was infuriated. In his memoir years later, President Bush recalled the precariousness of the U.S.-Saudi relationship during this time.[28] When Abdullah visited Bush at his ranch in Crawford, Texas—an attempt to strengthen personal ties between the leaders—he asked angrily, "When will the pig leave Ramallah?," referring to Israeli Prime Minister Ariel Sharon. Abdullah expected that, with pressure from the United States, Sharon would have already agreed to leave Ramallah ahead of his visit. With the Saudi contingency threatening to leave, Bush made a last-ditch effort to salvage the visit. He asked Abdullah to tour his ranch, and perhaps, through divine intervention, their relationship deepened. Bush recalls seeing a lone hen turkey on the property. Abdullah said, "It is a sign from Allah. This is a good omen." After this encounter, the tension dissipated, and the talks continued. As Peter Baker noted, "Bush never understood why a turkey hen would be taken as such an important sign, but its appearance avoided a foreign policy debacle."[29] And Condoleezza Rice stated after President Bush relayed the event that evening: "Whatever works."[30]

In the meantime, however, the relationship between the United States and Saudi Arabia changed forever. After decades of strategic partnership, the terror attacks of 9/11 altered U.S.-Saudi relations overnight. In the words of scholar David Ottaway, "That 'special' relationship was buried in the ashes of the World Trade Center and the Pentagon."[31] Indeed, efforts by the United States to promote religious freedom in Saudi

Arabia throughout the Bush administration can only be understood in recognition of the tensions that surfaced with 9/11.

The Implications of 9/11 and the War on Terror

Government-backed extremism is endemic to Saudi culture. But the state also suppresses the liberties of groups that do not fully align with its aims, fomenting extremism from disenfranchised groups. The combination can have deadly consequences. The attacks of 9/11 exposed the harsh reality that strategic partnership at the national level does not insulate the United States from the deadly reverberations of religious intolerance and terrorism. If there were ever an example showing the direct connections between international religious freedom and U.S. security, Saudi Arabia is it. William Inboden puts it bluntly: "The wonder is not that so many Saudi citizens raised in this environment took up the mantle of terrorism, but that so few did."[32] Of the nineteen hijackers who committed the attacks against the United States on that fateful day, fifteen were Saudi citizens. Since 9/11, debate regarding the Saudi government's direct involvement in the attacks has continued furiously. Many questions remain unanswered among redacted reports, the extensive 9/11 Commission process, and a delicate bilateral relationship. Perhaps most salient: What was considered "state-sponsored"? The line between individual responsibility and state sponsorship blurred, as many individuals with known connections to the terror attacks worked for the government.

The infamous "28 pages," a portion of the 2002 Congressional Joint Inquiry Report detailing Saudi ties to the terror attacks, was originally classified. When finally made public in July 2016, Saudi officials boldly claimed that "several government agencies, including the CIA and the FBI, have investigated the contents . . . and have confirmed that neither the Saudi government, nor senior Saudi officials, nor any person acting on behalf of the Saudi government provided any support or encouragement for these attacks."[33] Despite their insistence on innocence, the evidence released in the report says otherwise. It plainly states, "While in the United States, some of the 9/11 hijackers were in contact with, and received support or assistance from, individuals who may be connected to the Saudi Government."[34]

Much of the religious freedom progress during the Bush administration was only possible because of the sustained pressure now devoted to curbing extremism in the region and preventing another attack. And while the IRF office pursued many initiatives in Saudi Arabia under Ambassador John Hanford's leadership, it prioritized efforts to combat religious extremism. It is difficult to overstate the impact of the Iraq War on Middle East power dynamics, especially from a Saudi perspective. As Saddam Hussein's reign ended, so did Sunni rule in Iraq. Instead, the United States installed a new interim government led by Shi'a activist and politician Ayad Allawi. Though Iraq is one of the few countries with more Shi'a than Sunni Muslims, the Shi'a population had long been subjugated by the powerful Sunni minority. With the U.S. invasion of 2003, the post–World War I power dynamic collapsed.

Terrorism at Home Turns up the Pressure

The first few IRFA reports issued during the Bush administration detail the terrible abuses faced by believers of many types in Saudi Arabia. Government officials closed a Shi'a mosque in Hofuf in March 2001, claiming it was built without proper permission from the government. In January 2002, the mutawwa'in arrested Sheikh Ahmed Turki al-Saab after he publicly criticized the Saudi government. In April 2002, the mutawwa'in conducted multiple raids on Christian house-church services in Riyadh, which led to the arrest and detention of twenty-six people. In May 2002, the Saudi government arrested Christians from Ethiopia and Eritrea for worshipping publicly. In the years after the unrest in Najran, the mutawwa'in arrested over one hundred Ismaili Muslims.

Throughout this period, the international community, specifically the United States, pushed against extremism in Saudi Arabia, knowing its deadly consequences. But, in 2003, Saudi Arabia felt these consequences at home. On May 12, 2003, Al-Qaeda committed a terror attack on three compounds in Riyadh, resulting in the deaths of thirty-nine people and leaving many more wounded. Al-Qaeda targeted foreign workers in their campaign against Western influences in the Middle East. The attacks in Riyadh raised an important question: How might a proud and fundamentalist theocracy prevent violent extremism? Indeed, the attacks prompted new government initiatives to reign in violence. They fired hundreds of imams for preaching radicalized messages and increased oversight and training within the clerical ranks. These terror attacks also prompted public criticism against the mutawwa'in in newspapers and political cartoons. Jamal Khashoggi, the editor of a prominent newspaper in Saudi Arabia, *al-Watan*, lost his job after running such critiques. (Khashoggi would later be murdered by Saudi forces in Istanbul in 2018.) However, these terror attacks at home made the Saudi government more open to reform. Ambassador John Hanford noted, "The Saudis were as much or more attuned to this issue than we were because the Saudi royal family is well aware of their vulnerability to extremists."[35] Over the next several years, the international religious freedom community played an essential role in developing solutions to curb extremism, with varying degrees of success.

Saudi Arabia Finally Designated a CPC

In the wake of the terror attacks in Riyadh in 2003, the Saudi government took several important steps to counter violent extremism. In August 2003, some of the most high-ranking religious officials in Saudi Arabia shared a message of tolerance, calling on Muslims "to turn away from extremism and unjustified jihad." Also that month, Crown Prince Abdullah held the first session of the King Abdulaziz Center for National Dialogue to confront extremism and debate the merit of reformation. The second session, held in December 2003, resulted in a series of recommendations to modernize the education system. Then, in February 2005, Saudi Arabia hosted the Counter-Terrorism International Conference. In addition, the Saudi government deployed a large-scale public relations campaign to combat terrorism, and the Ministry of Education educated students on the dangers of extremism at a nationwide "security day." In March 2004, the government established the National Human Rights Association (NHRA), an organization charged with ensuring Saudi Arabia's cooperation with international human rights treaties and norms and Islamic Law.

Despite these public initiatives to support moderation, conditions on the ground did not improve. While reports of harassment and discrimination by the mutawwa'in decreased immediately after the terror attacks in 2003, these increased again in 2004. There was a marked increase in the number of arrests against non-Muslims. Among many other instances, the mutawwa'in detained Indian Christian Brian O'Connor, beating him mercilessly and confiscating his property. The religious police raided private worship services, often detaining or deporting religious believers. Mansur al-Nogaidan, a prominent writer in Saudi Arabia and longtime contributor to *al-Riyadh*, a government-run newspaper, published an editorial in *The New York Times* that was critical of the government's response to increasing religious extremism in the wake of the 2003 terrorist attacks. After the editorial ran in November 2003, the CPVPV arrested him and sentenced him to lashes.

No disagreements regarding CPC designation received as much attention as the Saudi Arabia case. The tension was plain. Just like the inaugural IRF report in 1999, the annual reports from 2000 to 2006 claimed simply: "Freedom of religion does not exist." And between 2000 and 2003, the State Department acknowledged the egregious persecution but did not designate Saudi Arabia as a CPC.

Policymakers and advocates alike had recognized the tension for years, but criticism reached a fever pitch in 2004. Why 2004? International religious freedom concerns, on their own, were rarely powerful enough to get on the political agenda. But, in the years after 9/11, amid ongoing allegations and unanswered questions about the Saudi role in funding terrorism, congressional leaders and advocates spoke out. In addition to USCIRF calling on Secretary of State Colin Powell to make the CPC designation, as they had for the previous three years, senators like Susan Collins, John McCain, and Chuck Schumer pushed for action to hold Saudi Arabia accountable.[36] In a statement released in August 2004, Chuck Schumer highlighted the perceived hypocrisy:

> It boggles the mind that even though our own government has concluded that religious freedom does not exist in Saudi Arabia, the State Department still refuses to put any muscle into its relationship with Saudi Arabia. We know that Saudi funded madrassas promote religious intolerance and violence in schools. We know that Saudi Arabia brutally prohibits the public expression of religion that is not the Wahhabi interpretation of Islam. And we know that Saudi efforts to export militant ideology inflame anti-Western sentiments throughout the world. If that isn't enough to land a country on a list of religiously intolerant nations, I don't know what is.[37]

During 2002–4, the IRF office prioritized Saudi Arabia, especially in the wake of the attacks of 9/11. Of witnessing persecution in Saudi Arabia, Hanford stated, "It's one thing to read about it; it's another thing to get on the ground and talk to people." Tom Farr, the director of the IRF office, described his point of conversion on the Saudi case. After previously assenting to the narrow legal definition, as espoused by Seiple and others during the Clinton administration, he reconsidered. He recalled the story of Professor Kazemzadeh, a Baha'i, standing up at a USCIRF meeting just after Farr had completed his legal analysis to defend not putting Saudi Arabia on the CPC list. Kazemzadeh asked: "In Saudi Arabia, I may not exist. Is that or is it not a systematic, ongoing, and egregious denial of life, liberty and security?" Farr agreed it was.[38]

Finally, in 2004, Secretary of State Colin Powell designated Saudi Arabia as a CPC. The designation itself was a heavy lift for Powell and the Bush administration. One staffer at the IRF office at the time recalled "the howls of protest among the Near Eastern Affairs bureau and other regional experts that adding the Kingdom to the CPC list . . . would cause irrevocable rupture in the U.S.-Saudi relations."[39] But Bob Jordan, the U.S. ambassador to Saudi Arabia and a long-time friend of George W. Bush, broke with his NEA colleagues and supported the designation. Eventually, Ambassador Hanford and NEA Assistant Secretary Bill Burns sent a "split memo," each arguing the case for and against the designation.[40] Powell sided with Hanford. But, given the complexities of the bilateral relationship, Powell sought President Bush's approval. After considering the case, Bush approved the designation. Before announcing the 2004 CPC list, Bush called Abdullah so he would not be blindsided by the decision. Here, Bush reiterated his own personal commitment to religious freedom but assured Abdullah that he did not want the designation to interfere with the strategic cooperation between the United States and Saudi Arabia.[41] Bush hoped the designation might prompt new initiatives and reforms. The following year, at his State of the Union Address on February 3, 2005, President Bush noted, "The government of Saudi Arabia can demonstrate its leadership in the region by expanding the role of its people in determining their future."[42]

Critics who believed IRFA's implementation to be unfairly selective and inconsistent welcomed the designation. Legal scholar Eugenia Relaño Pastor writes, "Perhaps the inclusion of Saudi Arabia as a CPC—

despite its continuing value to the United States as an ally in the War on Terror—indicates a step towards the inclusion of extreme violators of religious liberty as CPCs despite economic or strategic interests the United States may otherwise have in those violating countries."[43] As the War on Terror raged on, relationships in the Middle East were delicate. However, the designation itself prompted new initiatives and reforms. As expected, the CPC designation outraged Saudi officials. But this anger, combined with Saudi Arabia's fears of violent extremism and terrorism, provided an opportunity to push for change. Using the designation as leverage, Hanford and the IRF office got to work.

Discussions on Religious Practice and Tolerance

In 2005–6, the IRF office led a series of extensive discussions surrounding religious rights and tolerance in Saudi Arabia. Saudi Arabia released the official results of the discussions in July 2006. Full of specific details and expansive in scope, the results fell within four broad categories: 1) halting the dissemination of intolerant literature and extremist ideology; 2) protecting the right to private worship and to possess and use personal religious materials; 3) curbing harassment of religious practice, and; 4) empowering the Human Rights Commission. See Table 6.1 on the following page for the results of this discussion.

These are remarkable results given the context. The prescriptions were at once specific and practical, sweeping and aspirational. The document included small but meaningful changes, like ensuring that CPVPV officials wear public badges, denoting their proper authority. However, it also included large-scale goals to "bring the Kingdom's rules and regulations into compliance with human rights standards" and to "create a culture of human rights" throughout the government. Relatedly, the discussions focused on short-term and long-term goals; they called for pulling intolerant texts from classrooms immediately but also included provisions to retrain teachers and imams, hoping to interrupt the cycle of intolerance. Third, the results contained mechanisms to hold individuals accountable when they inevitably did not follow the new standards.

As an IRF Pragmatist, John Hanford considered where he might make progress and where further pushing would only damage the relationship. In this vein, Hanford devoted little time or resources to chang-

TABLE 6.1 Summarized Results of 2006 U.S.-Saudi Arabia Discussions on Religious Practice and Tolerance

Goal	Actions
Halting intolerant literature and extremist ideology	• Revise and update textbooks and literature across the country • Review revised material and remove any instances of intolerance still included • Review literature sent abroad and remove any instances of intolerance • Attempt to retrieve previously distributed intolerant materials • Retrain teachers in religious tolerance and hold them accountable to new standards • Retrain and, when necessary, reassign imams who continue to espouse intolerance
Protecting the rights to worship privately and possess personal religious materials	• Guarantee the right to private worship for all, including non-Muslims who gather in homes • Address grievances when this right is violated • Ensure that customs inspectors at the border will not confiscate personal religious materials • Make foreign workers aware of their rights to private religious activities
Curbing harassment of religious practice	• Ensure that the CPVPV (or mutawwa'in) does not detain or conduct investigations of suspects. • Permit only authorized individuals to work for the CPVPV • Require CPVPV authorities to identify themselves and wear public badges • If CPVPV officials overstep their role, hold them accountable • Require all future members of the CPVPV to be trained at a special institute
Empower the human rights commission	• Address all complaints through the commission • Educate the public and government about human rights and international standards • Bring the kingdom's rules and regulations into compliance with human rights standards • Ensure compliance with international human rights treaties

ing the legal code. Instead, he focused on implementation. The IRF office worked within existing codes. For instance, the Saudi government claimed that individuals had the right to worship privately but often failed to protect this right. Rather than push to make public worship legal, a proposition that the Saudi government would never assent to, he focused on correct implementation of existing law, to afford individuals the right to worship privately. Notably, the Saudi government made these results public on their own accord.

In releasing the results of the discussions, USCIRF celebrated. However, the relations between the IRF office and USCIRF quickly worsened after the 2006 annual IRF report was released. Instead of using the oft-quoted "Freedom of religion does not exist" phrasing as it had since the inaugural report, the 2006 annual report read, "There is no legal recognition or protection of religious freedom, and it is severely restricted in practice."[44] It is easy to dismiss these shifts as meaningless semantics. However, language holds significant power, especially when dealing with a sensitive relationship. In response, IRF Purists at USCIRF blasted the IRF office. In a press release from September 2006, issued just after the publication of the annual IRF report, Felice Gaer, then-chair of USCIRF, said she was "simply shocked" by the rhetorical change.[45] The statement continued: "The U.S. government confirmed a variety of Saudi policies to improve 'religious practice and tolerance'-many of which were first recommended in Commission reports. However, the new State Department report shows that such policies have not yet been implemented."[46] Indeed, the reforms did not occur overnight. In the following pages, religious freedom violations occurred, even against believers worshiping within the confines of the strict Saudi codes. Still, the agreement held significant symbolic weight, and that these discussions happened at all, let alone that Saudi Arabia publicly assented to them, was worthy of celebration.[47]

Mixed Results

Despite the success of the dialogues and Saudi Arabia's commitments to increase tolerance, abuse continued. In December 2006, the mutawwa'in raided a gathering of foreign workers of the Ahmadiyya religious group. The police detained as many as fifty people who were eventually deported without trial after decades of living and working in Saudi Arabia. In separate instances, two individuals died while in custody.[48] The deaths of two young women in 2006 showed how intensely many feared the mutawwa'in: one jumped out of a four-story window to escape the religious police, and one died in a car accident that resulted from a car chase. Allegations during this time also included hit-and-runs (by the mutawwa'in), unexplained violence, and failure to follow protocol. And in May 2007, the religious police brutally killed Suleiman Al-Huraisi, causing an international outcry.[49]

The United States condemned these persecutory acts, but other strategic priorities demanded attention. As Tom Farr notes, the War in Iraq and increased threats of regional sectarian violence "made the Bush administration even more hesitant to push the Saudis over something so sensitive as religion in the kingdom."[50]

Still, the United States welcomed Saudi Arabia's modest reforms. After these events, the government fulfilled its commitment, requiring all mutawwa'in to wear photo identification badges—an essential step in the implementation process of the 2006 discussions.[51] This new decree had dual purposes: to serve as a check against the poor behavior of the religious police, and to differentiate the mutawwa'in from extremists attempting to carry out vigilante justice.[52] There were signs of improvement, including a new graduate program at Umm al-Qura University aimed at helping the religious police work more effectively with the public. Furthermore, amid the outrage against the mutawwa'in, the Saudi government extended greater freedom to the press. Some went as far as calling for its disbandment without threats or retaliation from the government. The Saudi government announced a plan to "balance development," which simplified the legal process to pursue infrastructure projects.[53] Moreover, in line with the results of the dialogues released in the summer of 2006, the government increased accountability for the religious police. It issued a decree removing authority from the mutawwa'in from handling allegations against it in-house. Instead, the Board of Investigation and Prosecution, which operated independently in each province, would process any allegations. The IRF office celebrated these reforms even as it pushed for more change.

Then, in 2008, King Abdullah garnered international attention when he announced his Interfaith Dialogue Initiative, which aimed to promote tolerance and curb terrorism. They held the conference in Madrid in November 2008.[54] King Abdullah attempted to separate sincere and devout faith from religious fanaticism, arguing that "tragedies that have occurred in history were not caused by religion but extremism adopted by some of the followers of each one of the religions, and political systems." The speech garnered international attention and praise from the United Nations.[55]

From 2001 to 2009, the Bush administration made impressive strides to increase religious freedom within Saudi Arabia. It secured the CPC designation, which it used as leverage in its negotiations. The successful dialogues from 2005 to 2006, and the resulting commitments from the Saudi government, set the stage for international religious freedom efforts in the years to come. Still, this period highlighted the intractability of the problem of religious intolerance in Saudi Arabia. When a society is predicated upon fundamentalism, and norms of bigotry are reinforced by the state's religious police, the religious community, and the education system, breaking the cycle of intolerance proves to be a formidable challenge. From a U.S. foreign policy perspective, this reality compounded with the difficulties accompanying presidential transitions. Given the expansive scope of the 2006 negotiations, long-term vision was required, and the IRF office lacked leadership to push Saudi Arabia on its implementation efforts. After Hanford's appointment concluded, the Ambassadorship remained vacant for 16 months.

The Obama Administration and Religious Freedom in Saudi Arabia

Confronting "Religious Terrorism"

From 2008 to 2010, religious freedom conditions in Saudi Arabia remained inconsistent. King Abdullah and Saudi leadership instated a few significant reforms at the highest levels. The Center for National Dialogue ran a series of public service announcements during primetime television and sporting events, all aimed at curbing religiously motivated violence.[56] The king also reformed the justice system in 2009 by allowing scholars of any school of Islamic jurisprudence to join the Council of Senior Scholars. They held the fourth Interfaith Dialogue Conference in Geneva in September 2009 as part of an international effort to combat religious extremism. However, these reforms did not change the behavior of the mutawwa'in. In 2010, Princess Basmah bint Saud bin Abdulaziz, a daughter of King Saud, spoke publicly against the draconian religious police, calling their behavior a form of "religious terrorism."[57] Her sentiments reflected a growing discontent and would frame much of her activism in the coming years.

The "religious terrorism" she referred to included new commitments to prevent "sorcery" from several regional groups within the CPVPV. Between 2008 and 2009, several individuals faced death sentences for engaging in witchcraft. The CPVPV singled out African immigrants. For instance, in November 2009, they arrested 118 individuals on such charges in the Makkah Province. One of the most controversial allegations of witchcraft involved Fawza Falih Muhammed Ali, who was sentenced to death during an illegitimate trial. Despite winning an appeal of the case, the Saudi government reinstated her sentence to "protect the souls and property of the country."[58]

The IRF reports during this period contained a litany of other abuses, including the 2009 arrest of Hamoud Saleh Al-Amri, who was charged with blasphemy for sharing his Christian faith on his blog.[59] Throughout 2010, the Ministry of Islamic Affairs also monitored online activity in Saudi Arabia to curb extremism, often providing counterarguments on extremists' blogs and forums.[60] Despite these efforts, calls for "the humiliation of polytheists and non-theists" persistently came from Saudi-funded imams, especially at the end of Friday prayers.[61] But the surge in popularity of platforms like Twitter also provided new opportunities for citizens to criticize the Saudi regime. Rather than focusing on a few traditional newspapers or academic publications, individuals shared their opinions with a wide audience, sometimes in only a few characters. In 2011, several cases of high-profile activists and bloggers received notoriety. The police arrested human rights activist Raif Badawi on charges of apostasy for posts on his website, Free Saudi Liberals. Others, like Turki al-Hamad and Hamza Kashgari, were arrested for "blasphemous" tweets.

Meanwhile, President Obama actively sought to redefine and, in some ways, repair the United States' relationship with the Muslim world. In his famous speech at Cairo University in June 2009, Obama called for "a new beginning between the United States and Muslims around the world, one based on mutual interest and mutual respect, one based upon the truth that America and Islam are not exclusive and need not be in competition. Instead, they overlap, and share common principles— principles of justice and progress; tolerance and the dignity of all human beings."[62] In his speech, Obama talked about the enduring pain of 9/11. The KSA remembered these effects well. Attacks from Al-Qaeda, which had plagued the country since the 1996 Khobar bombings, continued, threatening civilian lives and disturbing the public order. Nevertheless, even as Saudi Arabia cracked down on dissidents, it sought to reiterate that the power to defend Islam rested with the state, not with individuals.

In August 2009, Saudi leadership felt the threat more acutely when an Al-Qaeda operative threatened the life of Saudi prince and counter-intelligence chief Mohammed bin Nayef. In response to the violence,

Saudi leadership continued to call for moderation. In October 2010, the Saudi regime founded the King Abdullah International Center for Inter-religious and Intercultural Dialogue in Vienna. In September, the Saudi government supported a conference surrounding the Islamic concept of *takfir*.[63] Takfir means declaring other Muslims to be apostates, based on their stated beliefs or un-Islamic behaviors. Extremist groups, like Al-Qaeda, often use this concept as license to kill and encourage the killing of other Muslims. Scholar Thomas Hegghammer argues that the concept of takfir is "the key to revolutionary violence. . . . Arab governments fear it because that is what legitimizes violence against them."[64] Such is the case with Saudi Arabia. The conference, which attempted to curb violence, brought together hundreds of Muslim scholars to reclaim more moderate concepts of takfir, which involve formal evidence and court processes rather than vigilante justice. Again, the impetus for this moderation was the growing threat of extremism and terrorist violence within Saudi Arabia.[65]

The Implications of the Arab Spring

In the wake of the Arab Spring, ideas of uprising and revolution prolifer-ated throughout the Middle East. The connectedness provided by social media made this diffusion possible.[66] In Saudi Arabia, unrest expressed itself in massive protests across the country in 2011–12. Scholar Toby Matthiesen termed the protests the "Saudi Spring" and argued that these events were too often overlooked in analyses of the Arab Spring. The Saudi Spring consisted of widespread protests, primarily by Shi'a Mus-lims pushing for greater freedom.

The uprisings in Tunisia and Bahrain heavily influenced the Saudi Spring in 2011. On February 15, Bahraini protesters gathered on the Pearl Roundabout in Manama, the capital city. These events marked the be-ginning of the uprising, where protesters attempted to overthrow the government. In the Persian Gulf, Bahrain neighbors the Shi'a-dominated Eastern Province in Saudi Arabia, accessible by the King Fahd Cause-way. The connections between Shi'a Muslims in Bahrain and Saudi Arabia included shared political activism, ideological persuasion, and devout religious commitment. Given the proximity of the regions, many Saudi citizens in the Eastern Province had family members in Bahrain.

Perhaps expectedly, then, the protest movement extended beyond Bahrain's borders. Of the movement, Matthiesen wrote, "In the defense of the uprising in Bahrain, the Saudi Shi'a found a banner around which they could rally to address their own particular problems, and through which they could criticize their own government's policies toward Bahrain, particularly after the entry of Saudi troops."[67]

In early 2011, widespread Shi'a protests in Qatif left many detained without trial. These incidents prompted the government to ban public protests. Also in 2011, dissidents in Saudi Arabia staged the most comprehensive series of protests in modern history, using social media to gain momentum. The Saudi government met these efforts with fury, dispatching extensive security forces to quell the "Day of Rage" protests in Riyadh in March. Still, thousands of people gathered in Al-Ahsa and Awwamiya. Unable to break up Shi'a protests in Qatif, Saudi police fired indiscriminately into the crowd. Clashes in the Eastern Province in October left eleven police officers injured. While ultimately controlled by strong Saudi security forces, the protests sowed anxiety.

During this time, President Obama reiterated the U.S. commitment to human rights. In a speech on U.S. policy in the Middle East and North Africa, Obama maintained that the United States "will continue to insist that universal rights apply to women as well as men."[68] While there was no explicit mention of Saudi Arabia during the speech, it came at a pivotal moment as protests against the KSA's restrictions on women's rights reached a fever pitch.

In 2014, a new Saudi law purporting to curb terrorism introduced new penalties for criticizing Islam and "sowing discord in society," giving new legal validity to long-standing practices of crushing dissent. The new legislation, the Law for the Crimes of Terrorism and its Financing, used nebulous definitions of terrorism under blanket statements like "disturbing the public order of the state."[69] Kyle Ballard, former IRF staffer, viewed these efforts as counterproductive. Doubling down on the Shi'a population simply pushed the Shi'a minority closer to Iran.[70] With this view, Ballard and other IRF officials encouraged the Obama administration to treat the Shi'a in the Eastern Province on their own merits rather than view them only as Iranian proxies—a view regularly espoused by the Saudis.

Undoubtedly, the Arab Spring disrupted power dynamics in the Middle East and presented new challenges for U.S. foreign policy. The conflict in Syria inflamed sectarian tensions and added pressure between Riyadh and Washington. By 2013, several policy disagreements had compounded. Reports alleged that an exasperated Prince Bandar bin Sultan, then Saudi Arabia's intelligence chief, said that Saudi Arabia would make a "major shift" in its relationship with the United States.[71] The policy disagreements leading to the rift focused on Obama's deepening relationship with Tehran. Included in the complaints was the United States' failure to act in Syria as a large-scale humanitarian crisis unfolded, resulting in hundreds of thousands of deaths. Moreover, as Iran backed Bashar al-Assad's regime, the Saudi government resented inaction from the United States. Prince Bandar also cited the United States' failure to support the government of Bahrain during the uprisings of 2011. In 2013, Saudi Arabia turned down a rotating seat on the U.N. Security Council, claiming that "double standards on the Security Council prevent it from carrying out its duties and assuming its responsibilities in keeping world peace."[72] Unsurprisingly, Saudi Arabia's primary complaint revolved around the Syrian Civil War. Recognizing the gravity of the tensions and their potential impact on American interests, the Obama administration sought to restore its relationship with Saudi Arabia. Even still, Obama took several actions with symbolic power to convey his commitment to progress. In March 2014, Obama awarded Saudi doctor Maha Al Muneef a Women's Rights Award for her tireless efforts to expose and ultimately decrease rates of domestic violence across the country.

The Case of Raif Badawi

In January 2015, the world watched in horror as religious officials flogged Raif Badawi in front of the Al-Juffali Mosque. Badawi, charged with insulting Islam, founded the blog Free Saudi Liberals in 2008. After years of harassment, the CPVPV arrested Badawi in June 2012 for criticizing the regime and disparaging the faith. They found him guilty in December 2012. Initially, the Saudi courts also recommended charging Badawi with apostasy, reportedly for liking a Christian Facebook page and asserting the equality of persons regardless of their religious convictions. They dropped these charges after Badawi recited the Shahadah, an Islamic declaration of faith.[73] But, in a chilling blog post from August 2010, Badawi predicted his own fate. "As soon as a thinker starts to reveal his ideas," he wrote, "you will find hundreds of fatwas that accused him of being an infidel just because he had the courage to discuss some sacred topics."[74] After a lengthy appeal process, Badawi was sentenced to ten years in prison and one thousand lashes. Carried out in full public view, reports and videos of the flogging proliferated quickly, causing worldwide outrage.[75]

International media lambasted President Obama for his response—or, rather, for his lack of response—during his visit to Saudi Arabia at the end of January. Just hours earlier, in a bold speech in India, Obama stressed the need for the Indian government to do more to promote women's rights and respect religious minorities. But when he traveled to Saudi Arabia to affirm his relationship with the new King Salman, following the death of King Abdullah, he failed to raise human rights concerns or Badawi's case. *The Guardian* called the debacle a "stark display of U.S. foreign policy compromises."[76] Obama did not necessarily disagree. In a statement to CNN, Obama argued, "Sometimes we need to balance our need to speak to them about human rights issues with immediate concerns we have in terms of counterterrorism or dealing with regional stability."[77]

Indeed, as the leadership in Saudi Arabia shifted, Obama reiterated his commitment to the Saudi regime. In the delegation, Nancy Pelosi, John Kerry, John Brennan, John McCain, Lloyd Austin, James Baker, Condoleezza Rice, Brent Scowcroft, and Sandy Berger joined Obama. Such an impressive list, with foreign policy heavyweights spanning multiple administrations and both major political parties, Obama conveyed that the United States' long-standing relationship with Saudi Arabia would continue as it had for decades. Just the next month, Obama spoke at the Summit on Countering Violent Extremism. Here, he directly connected religious freedom to regional and international stability:

> We have to address the political grievances that terrorists exploit. Again, there is not a single perfect causal link, but the link is undeniable. When people are oppressed, and human rights are denied—particularly along sectarian lines or ethnic lines—when dissent is silenced, it feeds violent extremism. It creates an environment that is ripe for terrorists to exploit . . . and so we must recognize that lasting stability and real security require democracy . . . and it means freedom of religion—because when

Figure 6.2. Former Secretary of State Condoleezza Rice with a member of the Saudi royal family after welcoming the new King Salman of Saudi Arabia. Source: U.S. State Department Photo Archive.

people are free to practice their faith as they choose, it helps hold diverse societies together. . . . We have to ensure that our diverse societies truly welcome and respect people of all faiths and backgrounds, and leaders set the tone on this issue.[78]

Importantly, in Obama's visit to Saudi Arabia the following year, where he met with leaders of the Gulf Cooperation Council, Obama raised concerns about human rights. Human rights groups and the international freedom community welcomed his involvement.

Tragedy in Yemen

Perhaps one of the most controversial parts of Obama's foreign policy record during this time concerns arms sales to Saudi Arabia during Yemen's civil war. Mohammed bin Salman intervened in the civil war in 2015, taking a more aggressive posture and confronting Iranian-backed Houthi rebels. The move was in response to the ousting of Abdrabbuh

Mansur Hadi, a vocal supporter of the Saudi regime. The United States provided intelligence, logistical support, and aerial refueling. In addition, it ramped up arms sales, providing the Saudi government with billions of dollars of weapons. In its military operations, Saudi Arabia killed thousands of Yemeni civilians. Of the disaster, Sarah Margon, the Washington director at Human Rights Watch, argued:

> Human rights concerns have always competed with national security considerations. For too long, Washington has adopted policies in the name of protecting national security that come at the expense of human rights, forgetting the long-term costs of doing so. The Obama Administration's arms sales to Saudi Arabia, despite the Saudi-let coalition's unlawful air strikes against civilians in Yemen, is a prime example of the harm this approach can do, with thousands of civilians killed and anti-American sentiment on the rise in the country.[79]

By the end of Obama's term, his administration halted arms sales to the Saudi campaign in Yemen. In 2018, thirty senior officials from the Obama administration called on Trump to end all support to Saudi Arabia in the war. The letter read: "We did not intend U.S. support to the coalition to become a blank check. But today, as civilian casualties have continued to rise and there is no end to the conflict in sight, it is clear that is precisely what happened."[80] Human rights groups welcomed the call to end support of the war but viewed the reckoning as incomplete.

Deferred Progress

Much like the Bush administration, the IRF office in the Obama administration focused on education reform. But the process surfaced the intractability of intolerance in Saudi Arabia. While obtaining impressive commitments in 2006, negotiations and reforms were often deferred, ignored, or insufficiently instituted. For example, in 2010, Saudi Arabia overhauled its curriculum for first, fourth, and seventh grades. But even the new textbooks were littered with intolerance. Calls to hate infidels and kill apostates remained. Even the "reformed" textbooks painted some minority groups, especially Jews, as having immutable character flaws.

Though slated for completion in 2013, bureaucratic obstacles prevented progress from occurring on secondary education textbooks (including grades ten, eleven, and twelve). Instead, the Ministry of Education retained draconian depictions of minorities, specifically Jews and Christians. The textbooks taught conspiracy theories against non-Muslims as historical facts.

Kyle Ballard, an IRF staffer during the Obama administration, worked extensively on the textbook reform process. His insights revealed that even in the most difficult of circumstances and the most rigid of regimes, incremental progress was possible. Ballard noted that many State Department officials, especially in the regional bureaus, thought that issues seen as particularly sensitive, such as religious freedom or human trafficking, should be spoken about infrequently, as they might disturb existing agreements and weaken the relationship. In Ballard's view, however, normalizing the conversation around these "sensitive" issues encouraged moderating voices. To Ballard, repeated conversation and normalization mitigated the controversy embedded in these issues, both real and perceived. In so doing, particularly regarding education reform in Saudi Arabia, the United States showed that it could simultaneously push hard on human rights interests like religious freedom and pursue other priorities.

When meeting with the Foreign Ministry in Saudi Arabia, Kyle Ballard recalled ineffective initial meetings whereby the Saudi officials became angry and spent incredible amounts of time berating and accusing Americans of their own human rights abuses. Instead of talking about education reform and religious rights, they switched the conversation to U.S. drone policy in the Middle East or the plight of the Palestinians. Ballard welcomed this criticism. He stated: "The basis of our engagement on these issues isn't that we've figured it all out and that we are completely superior but rather that it is a process and our strength is in our willingness to address it." But he recognized this as an avoidance tactic: "They know that if they get through that hour, they won't have to talk about this issue for another six months."[81] In his view, frequency and normalization of discussion—even on the most difficult issues–was the best way forward.

Looking Forward

As this chapter shows, there was a tenuous balance involved as Saudi Arabia wanted to control religious practice and avoid the devastating effects of violent extremism at the same time. This case highlights the need for long-term vision when promoting religious freedom, especially in a regime like Saudi Arabia. Religious persecution is endemic, and progress takes time and sustained effort. Offending governments are more likely to take concerns seriously when they know they are not going away, and that the United States will apply sustained pressure. Times of presidential transitions, especially when the ambassadorship is vacant, are a significant vulnerability within IRF policy.

This case also shows the importance of integrating religious freedom concerns within the larger foreign policy calculus. The recognition of religious freedom's connection to security and stability, made painfully clear by the attacks of 9/11, led the United States to put pressure on Saudi Arabia. A significant upsurge in terrorist incidents within Saudi Arabia during the early 2000s compelled the regime to take pivotal steps toward modernization. A vital component of this effort involved persuading Saudi leadership of the interplay between religious freedom and other objectives on their policy agenda. Acknowledging that religious freedom cannot be neatly isolated or compartmentalized is essential.

Conclusion

As with any foreign policy priority, presidential actions matter. Whether it was President Bush's decision to meet with Chinese dissidents in the White House despite explicit threats from the CCP or President Obama's unequivocal speech on religious freedom in India, presidential attention and action gave the IRF office more leverage to push for change for religious believers on the ground. However, as these case studies show, religious freedom was not the only strategic priority. Academics and practitioners studying IRF policy should resist the urge of viewing international religious freedom in isolation, as this leads to reductive caricatures of presidential priorities and intentions. By examining international religious freedom efforts through a geopolitical lens, these simplifications become less convincing. In China and Saudi Arabia—and, to a somewhat lesser degree, Vietnam—numerous policy challenges were competing for attention simultaneously.

Each presidential administration approached international religious freedom differently. The Clinton administration represented a final holdout of a previous diplomatic approach that separated religion and diplomacy. However, due to religion's resurgence, growing public awareness of religious persecution abroad, and congressional pressure to act, international religious freedom became part of the foreign policy calculus. Even top members of the administration, like Madeleine Albright, changed their perspective. As this shift took place, Congress passed the IRFA, and the National Security Strategy formally included international religious freedom as a foreign policy priority.

President Bush's approach was much more public and personal. He regularly spoke about religious freedom, met with religious leaders and dissidents, and incorporated religious freedom into the Freedom Agenda. However, his predominant focus was the War on Terror, which highlighted the difficult tensions between religious freedom and religious extremism. Scholar and former IRF staffer Judd Birdsall noted two different approaches to international religious freedom: the "first freedom" camp, which relied on U.S. history to promote the religious freedom, and the "Article 18" proponents, who focused on international law. President Obama was decidedly in the second camp; he resisted unilateral action and focused on a new strategy of religious engagement.

Another important dimension is that even with multiple strategic priorities vying for attention, there were still often opportunities for progress on religious freedom issues. Examples include Knox Thames's work on preserving religious sites in Iraq and Syria, and the IRF office's efforts to push for textbook and police reform in Saudi Arabia, even while the wars in Iraq and Afghanistan rocked the Middle East.

International Religious Freedom and Geopolitics

Despite these moments of progress, throughout the Clinton, Bush, and Obama administrations, the changing geopolitical landscape often constrained the ability of the IRF office to do its work. For instance, the sensitive relationship between the United States and Saudi Arabia likely prevented the Clinton administration from designating it a CPC even as the IRF report flatly maintained that "freedom of religion does not exist." In China, Clinton initially tied human rights progress to the prospective granting of MFN status. But, as U.S. economic interests in China increased, Clinton walked back his hard-line position and granted China MFN status despite its troubling religious persecution.

Of course, the changing geopolitical context also mattered to other states, and it affected their responsiveness to IRF efforts. Vietnam explicitly acknowledged that it would meet U.S. demands to improve religious freedom conditions in part because of its security concerns, given China's increasing aggression, and Saudi Arabia was only willing to partner with the IRF office to combat religious extremism when it felt the effects of terrorism within its own borders. International religious freedom policy does not occur within a vacuum.

Bureaucratic Tensions

Across the three administrations, but particularly during the Clinton and Bush years, this study revealed intense and damaging tensions within the international religious freedom community. The IRF Purists and the IRF Pragmatists warred over the correct way to promote religious freedom. The sources of these tensions date back to the development of the IRFA itself. The Purists, like the original supporters of the Freedom from Persecution Act, wanted a forceful instrument to prioritize religious freedom over other priorities, automatically limiting exports and ending U.S. assistance to offending governments. This ardent commitment—or inflexibility, as critics claimed—left the Purists regularly dissatisfied with the IRF office's efforts and they were often unable to acknowledge success when it occurred. These internal fights consumed extensive amounts of time and emotional energy.

But the IRF office also had to deal with tension within the State Department. The positioning of the office within DRL gave it little clout. And, as a niche policy issue within an already isolated functional bureau, it regularly fought for access to and attention from top leadership. Again, these bureaucratic challenges diverted valuable resources from IRF's mandate. However, both sources of tension dissipated significantly during the Obama years, especially under Rabbi David Saperstein's tenure as IRF ambassador.

The overwhelming number of issues competing for presidential and bureaucratic attention necessitated policy entrepreneurship. Interviews with IRF staffers noted two primary characteristics needed for an IRF ambassador. First, they noted the importance of a thorough knowledge of Washington and the State Department machinery itself. When an ambassador lacked an intimate understanding of the politics, processes, and personalities involved, the office suffered. Second, an ambassador "needs an ability to leverage goodwill and connections to buy space to make the sell."[1] "Buying space" itself is the primary challenge, given limited attention and tremendous amounts of information to process. IRF ambassadors like Bob Seiple, John Hanford, and David Saperstein leveraged preexisting networks in their role. Seiple brought a diverse network of relationships from his work with Christian NGO World Vision; Hanford relied on years of experience working on international religious freedom issues on the Hill when he joined the State Department; and Rabbi Saperstein brought decades of bipartisan experience through his work with the Religious Action Center of Reform Judaism. But the IRF office suffered without strong leadership, especially when the ambassadorship was vacant. Between Seiple and Hanford, the position was vacant for almost twenty months; between Hanford and Johnson Cook, it was vacant for over two years; and between Johnson Cook and Saperstein, the IRF office lacked an ambassador for fourteen months. Each of these vacancies negatively affected the IRF office's ability to make change. Since the issue requires long-term and devoted attention, these breaks weakened the IRF office's strategic position. For example, Hanford was in the early stages of implementing the 2006 agreements in Saudi Arabia when his tenure expired.

IRF Policy Looking Ahead

This book considers the first two decades of IRFA's implementation. Throughout this period, several salient takeaways emerged. First, IRF efforts require an honest evaluation of the leverage involved. What is the balance of power between the United States and the target government? If the U.S.'s relative position is diminishing, it should temper its rhetorical commitments and seek strategies that involve the international community. For example, Clinton's policy shift on China's MFN status resulted from failing to adequately consider the shifting geopolitical context. Conversely, success in the Vietnam case occurred in part because policymakers were able to recognize Vietnam's geopolitical vulnerabilities and use them to encourage human rights progress. Here, U.S. officials could afford to use strong rhetoric, because they had the political leverage to back it up. It was the combination of strategic pressure and diplomatic engagement that made success possible.

Second, the IRF office should consider a president's agenda and think creatively about how to integrate international religious freedom within existing priorities. IRF remains a niche policy issue. Policymakers working niche issues that lack sufficient institutionalization will be more successful if they can attach international religious freedom to larger agenda items that already receive adequate attention and resources. The two most obvious arenas here include trade and security.

Third, IRF policymakers and advocates should keep a target government's geopolitical context top of mind. By convincing target governments that religious freedom is not in opposition to its other goals increases the likelihood of IRF's success. Here, it is useful to point to growing research that shows that increased religious freedom is associated with higher levels of political stability and economic growth, and lower levels of political violence.[2] Moreover, the geopolitical context signals where power is concentrated. As each of the case studies showed, power is rarely located within the religious affairs bureau. Instead, focusing efforts on a nation's security apparatus or interior ministry may prove more productive.

Of course, there are also policy considerations at the presidential level. Crucially, presidents should choose IRF ambassadors who enjoy bipartisan respect and who can leverage their existing networks within the often difficult State Department bureaucracy. But, even more important, the president should nominate IRF ambassadors as quickly as possible. For a relatively minor office in the State Department, but one with a massive mandate, vacancies in the ambassadorship damage the office's ability to do its job, and disrupt the long-term strategies often needed to make significant progress for religious believers on the ground. In as much as is strategically tenable, presidents should reiterate the U.S. commitment to religious freedom thereby empowering the IRF office to more effectively do its job.

Conclusion

Speaking to the U.N. General Assembly in 2019, President Donald Trump proclaimed that "America stands with believers in every country who ask only for the freedom to live according to the faith that is within their own hearts." The year prior, in July 2018, Secretary of State Mike Pompeo hosted the first ever Ministerial to Advance International Religious Freedom. A massive undertaking, the event brought together hundreds of faith leaders throughout the world. There, Pompeo announced an accelerator program aimed at bolstering public-private partnerships to defend religious freedom. Vice President Mike Pence announced the Potomac Plan of Action, a document that reiterated the U.S. commitment to international religious freedom and offered multinational strategies to improve conditions across the globe. Former Representative Frank Wolf, one of the pioneers of legislative action in the 1990s to promote international religious freedom, praised the administration's commitment, and USCIRF Commissioner Johnnie Moore called the Potomac Declaration "religious freedom's Magna Carta."[3]

Others were not so sure. Critics maintained that the Trump administration polarized the issue, using religious freedom to further its conservative agenda. Kori Schake noted that the Trump administration's Judeo-Christian bias distorted U.S. foreign policy and, ultimately, sowed resentment among religious groups.[4] In June 2020, President Trump signed an executive order aimed at strengthening international religious freedom efforts across the government, directing at least $50 million to be allocated to IRF promotion along with detailed instructions for how to better integrate the cause at USAID, the State Department, the Department of the Treasury, and the Department of Commerce. While widely heralded as an important step forward for international religious freedom, the timing of the order was shrouded in controversy. Trump signed it the very day after he notoriously posed for a photo holding up a Bible at St. John's Anglican Church. They took the shot after law enforcement officers forcibly cleared demonstrators protesting the murder of George Floyd. IRF supporters lamented the move, noting that the substance of the order was lost in the controversy. Scholar and former USCIRF Commissioner Elizabeth Prodromou stated: "This executive . . . disrespects human dignity, and unfortunately the perception of confessional bias undermines his impact. . . . Paradoxically, the President's statements weaken the possibility and great potential for these IRF measures to have lasting positive outcomes."[5]

That there were conflicting views about Trump's policies is, of course, not limited to international religious freedom efforts. Political polarization, bitter culture wars, and distrust in American institutions has reached levels unseen in modern times. Efforts to keep international religious freedom efforts as a bipartisan commitment is becoming more difficult, especially as domestic religious liberty cases enflame activists on both sides of the aisle.

Though political divisions in the United States during the Trump and Biden eras are, undoubtedly, deeper than they were in administrations past, in some ways the tensions represent another cyclical iteration of the tensions that have surrounded international religious freedom efforts since the beginning: evangelicals clashing with secular understandings of human rights, fears about an unfair prioritization of religious rights over other human rights, skepticism that international religious freedom is only to protect Christians and their missionary activities—all familiar refrains.

One thing is for certain: religious persecution and its effects on individuals, communities, and the geopolitical landscape remains as virulent as ever. It will require an honest and careful approach—one that assesses the foreign policy calculus with clear vision and resolve. And it will require bold policy entrepreneurs to creatively integrate religious freedom and carve out its spot on the foreign policy agenda. But the purpose remains the same. As Ambassador Seiple noted in the opening pages of the very first IRF report, the goal is "to signal unambiguously to persecutor and persecuted alike that they will not be forgotten."

ACKNOWLEDGMENTS

Before I started this journey, several well-meaning academics warned me that writing a book was a lonely endeavor. Indeed, the process proved to be deeply personal and included many solitary hours writing (or, often, trying to write). But it wasn't lonely. Looking back over the last several years, I am overwhelmed with gratitude at the number and quality of colleagues, mentors, family, and friends who have walked with me every step of the way.

I wish to thank the team at New York University Press for their dedication and insightful guidance throughout this publishing journey. Special thanks to Clara Platter, Brianna Jean, and Valerie Zaborski for your belief in this project and your support each step of the way.

I conducted most of the research for this book while at the University of Texas at Austin. I am grateful to Will Inboden, who helped inspire the idea for this project and helped shepherd it through the entire process. A brilliant scholar, Will has modeled how to be a kind and magnanimous colleague at every turn. I cannot imagine a better mentor, and I owe him a tremendous debt of gratitude. I also wish to thank Victoria Rodríguez, a professor and now dear friend whose confidence in me changed the course of my life. In the most literal sense, I would not have begun nor finished this project if it had not been for Victoria.

I will forever be grateful for the community of friends and colleagues I built in Austin at the LBJ School of Public Affairs and the Clements Center for National Security. I thank my many professors, mentors, and colleagues at UT whose teaching sharpened my thinking and whose kind encouragement spurred me on. Jeremi Suri championed this project and his keen insights improved it tremendously. Erin Lenz took me under her wing and taught me the ropes of academia. Peter Ward modeled how to be deeply committed to research and students. Bryan Jones ignited my curiosity and challenged me to be bold. I also thank Admiral Bobby Inman, Paul Pope, Lawrence Lynn, Bill Spelman, and the late Howard Prince. I learned so much from each of you.

The Clements Center provided a supportive environment—and much-appreciated resources—that sustained this project. In addition to the incredible faculty associated with the Center from across the University of Texas and beyond, I'd like to thank the Clements Graduate Fellows, thoughtfully led by Mark Lawrence, and the ever-supportive staff at the Center for their continual encouragement and help. From this network, I found excellent thought partners and lifelong friends. Cindy Ewing and Megan Reiss offered wise counsel that propelled me forward, and Paul Edgar, Bryan Frizzell, Rachel Hoff, Charlie Laderman, Jeremy Kasper, and Charles Zug made the research process much more fun. Special thanks are due to my pals and confidants Augusta Dell'Omo, Alexandra Evans, and Theo Milonopoulos for their enduring support and much-needed humor. Finally, the Clements Center introduced me to Emily Whalen—a caring friend and seamless writing partner—for which I will always be grateful.

Several other academic institutions have provided support along the way. I would like to thank the Kissinger Center at Johns Hopkins SAIS. While the pandemic prevented normal operations, I owe a special thanks to Hal Brands, Frank Gavin, Mary Barton, and Susie Colbourn for their (virtual) support and friendship during my fellowship year there. I also spent some time at the Program in American Grand Strategy at Duke University. Though I was only there for a short time, I found inspiration and forged deep friendships while in Durham. Many thanks to Peter Feaver, Susie Colbourn, Simon Miles, Rachel Myrick, Taylor Pardue, Andrew Kenealy, Rebecca Dudley, Chen Wang, and Paige Rotunda for your support and friendship. Likewise, the America in the World Consortium generously supported this project and introduced me to friends like Marino Auffant and Daniel Chardell. Through this research, I have also crossed paths with scholars like Claire Yorke, Henry Thomson, and Will James, each of whom has broadened my thinking.

Finally, I thank the Center for Presidential History at Southern Methodist University for helping get this book to print. A wonderfully uplifting and generative academic home, Jeff Engel, Ronna Spitz, and Brian Franklin have built something special. Friends and colleagues at SMU include Cecily Zander, Carolyn Levy, Jonathan Ng, Camille Davis, Sharron Conrad, LaiYee Leong, Hervey Priddy, Greta Swain, Zachary Conn, and Jonathan Angulo. And sharing an office with my dear friend and colleague Augusta Dell 'Omo as I made final edits on this book was an added gift. Though we study difficult and heart-wrenching subjects, somehow, the office was full of joy. Thank you, Gus.

Overall, I would like to thank my incredible community of friends, who let me drone on about this project, and, importantly, told me when to stop. And I owe a great deal of thanks to my family, who mean the world to me. My sisters, Sue Ellen and Hallie, and their families provided much-needed understanding and levity during the most stressful writing periods. Likewise, the Hand family, which I joined in 2018, has cheered me on throughout this course.

And, of course, there is my husband, Mark, whom I came to know and to love as I began this project. To augment Whitman's phrase, Mark contains the very best of multitudes—brilliant yet unassuming, irrepressible and still thoughtful, bold and deeply kind. This book benefited from each of these attributes and more. And then there is baby Vivian, who could not help much by way of editing but who has brought more delight to our lives than I thought possible.

Finally, I wish to thank my parents, Sue and John Webb, who set a foundation of love and support that has empowered me since I was little and continues to buoy me today. I am sad that my dad did not get to see the final product but I hope he'd be proud. I dedicate this book to my mom and in loving memory of Dad.

NOTES

INTRODUCTION

1 Examples include *CNN Evening News* with Bernard Shaw on May 29, 1997, www.cnn.com; *CBS Evening News* with Dan Rather on July 22, 1997, www.cbsnews.com; and *ABC Evening News* with Peter Jennings on July 22, 1997, www.abcnews.go.com.

2 Frank R. Wolf, International Religious Freedom Act of 1998 (Passed Congress Version), November 28, 2018, www.govtrack.us.

3 See Anna Su, *Exporting Freedom: Religious Liberty and American Power* (Harvard University Press, 2016), for an analysis of U.S. leadership in crafting these international agreements, and, specifically, its efforts to ensure that religious freedom was sufficiently considered and explicitly protected.

4 A. M. Rosenthal, "On My Mind; A Year of Awakening," *New York Times*, October 10, 1997. See his other columns, including "The Double Crime" and "Gutless in New York," both from *New York Times*, www.nytimes.com.

5 See Allen Hertzke, *Freeing God's Children: The Unlikely Alliance for Global Human Rights* (Rowman & Littlefield, 2004), 107–43, for more details, including congressional visits to Soviet Gulag Perm Camp 35 and Beijing Camp 1. These visits would be formative for many congressional advocates for international religious freedom.

6 Hertzke, *Freeing God's Children*.

7 In his seminal work *The Elementary Forms of Religious Life*, Émile Durkheim notes that "God is society, writ large." *The Elementary Forms of Religious Life* (Oxford University Press, 2008), 206–7.

8 Peter L. Berger, "Secularization Falsified," *First Things*, February 2008, www.firstthings.com.

9 Karen Armstrong, *A History of God: The 4000-Year Quest of Judaism, Christianity, and Islam* (Ballantine, 1998), 379.

10 C. Wright Mills, *The Sociological Imagination* (Oxford University Press, 1959), 32–33, as cited in Pippa Norris and Ronald Inglehart, *Sacred and Secular: Religion and Politics Worldwide* (Cambridge University Press, 2004), 3.

11 William H. Swatos and Kevin J. Christiano, "Secularization Theory: The Course of a Concept," *Sociology of Religion* 60, no. 3 (1999): 209–28.

12 Swatos and Christiano, "Secularization Theory."

13 "A Bleak Outlook Is Seen for Religion," *New York Times*, February 25, 1968; as cited in Monica Duffy Toft, Daniel Philpott, and Timothy Samuel Shah, *God's Century: Resurgent Religion and Global Politics* (W. W. Norton, 2011).

14 As cited in Madeleine Korbel Albright and William Woodward, 2006. *The Mighty and the Almighty: Reflections on America, God, and World Affairs* (HarperCollins, 2006).

15 Rodney Stark, "Secularization, R.I.P.," *Sociology of Religion* 60, no. 3 (1999): 249–73; Jeffrey K. Hadden, "Toward Desacralizing Secularization Theory," *Social Forces* 65, no. 3 (1987): 587–611.

16 Monica Toft, Daniel Philpott, and Timothy Samuel Shah, *God's Century: Resurgent Religion and Global Politics* (W. W. Norton, 2011). 7–8.

17 Toft, Philpott, and Shah, *God's Century*, 2.

18 "The Changing Global Religious Landscape," Pew Research Center, April 5, 2017, www.pewforum.org/.

19 Gilles Kepel, *The Revenge of God: The Resurgence of Islam, Christianity, and Judaism in the Modern World* (Penn State University Press, 1994).

20 Toft, Philpott, and Shah, *God's Century*.

21 See chaps. 5 and 6 of Toft, Philpott, and Shah, *God's Century*.

22 Nilay Saiya, *Weapon of Peace: How Religious Liberty Combats Terrorism* (Cambridge University Press, 2018).

23 See Saiya, *Weapon of Peace*; and Melanie Kolbe and Peter S. Henne, "The Effect of Religious Restrictions on Forced Migration," *Politics and Religion* 7, no. 4 (2014): 665–83.

24 See H. Con. Res. 336, sponsored by Rep. Benjamin Gilman (R-NY), "Condemning the Taliban Regime and Supporting a Broad Based Government in Afghanistan," 105th Cong., 2nd sess., October 9, 1998.

25 See H. Res. 332, sponsored by Rep. Rod Blagojevich (D-IL), "Expressing Concern for the Plight of Assyrians in the Near East," 105th Cong., 2nd sess., December 3, 1997.

26 See Senator Gordon H. Smith's (R-OR) Amendment (SP 396) to Senate Bill 903 (Foreign Affairs Reform and Restructuring Act of 1997), 105th Cong., 1st sess., June 17, 1997.

27 See S. Res. 238, sponsored by Sen. Paul Wellstone (D-MN), "A Resolution Expressing the Sense of the Senate Regarding Human Rights Conditions in China and Tibet," 105th Cong., 2nd sess., December 3, 1997.

28 Benjamin Gilman, "Persecution of Baha'i Continues in Iran," Hearing at the House of Representatives, 105th sess., February 26, 1998.

29 Susan Woodward, "Upside Down Policy: The U.S. Debate on the Use of Force and the Case of Bosnia," in *The Use of Force After the Cold War*, ed. H. W. Brands (Texas A&M University Press, 2003), 115, as cited in Elliott Abrams, *Realism and Democracy: American Foreign Policy After the Arab Spring* (Cambridge University Press, 2017).

30 Jimmy Carter, Presidential Directive/NSC 30, February 17, 1978. Washington, D.C., The White House.

31 Gerald F. Seib, "Clinton Is Squeezed in Middle on Religious Persecution," *Wall Street Journal*, July 7, 1997, www.wsj.com.

32 This would shift during the Trump administration, when, under the leadership of Ambassador Sam Brownback, IRF would ascend higher on the priority list.

33 For more on presidential preferences and foreign policymaking, see Jeffrey S. Peake, "Presidential Agenda Setting in Foreign Policy," *Political Research Quarterly* 54, no. 1 (2001): 69–86; and Paul E. Peterson, "The President's Dominance in Foreign Policy Making," *Political Science Quarterly* 109, no. 2 (1994): 215–34.

34 Senior State Department official, interview with author, 2020.

35 Elliott Abrams, *Realism and Democracy, 17.*

36 Here, see Thomas Farr's discussion of both the need for humanitarian advocacy on an individual bases and the need for structural reform as he considers the "Karimini case" in chapter 6 of his book *World of Faith and Freedom: Why International Religious Liberty Is Vital to National Security* (Oxford University Press, 2008).

37 John Hanford and Laura Bryant Hanford, interview with author.

1. SUSTAINED ADVOCACY AND THE INTERNATIONAL RELIGIOUS FREEDOM ACT

1 Billy Graham, "Satan's Religion," *American Mercury*, August 1954, 41–46.

2 Allen Hertzke, *Freeing God's Children: The Unlikely Alliance for Global Human Rights* (Rowman & Littlefield, 2004).

3 Evangelical prominence decreased in the early twentieth century amid the debate between modernization and conservatism, which led to the fractionation of Protestantism in the United States. These dynamics are encapsulated in the infamous Scopes trial of 1925, which alleged that John Thomas Scopes had violated the Butler Act by teaching evolution in a state-funded school. See David N. Livingstone, *Darwin's Forgotten Defenders: The Encounter Between Evangelical Theology and Evolutionary Thought* (Eerdmans, 1987).

4 Harold John Ockenga, "The Unvoiced Multitudes," *Evangelical Action!*, April 7, 1942.

5 In 1950, this organization was renamed the National Council of Churches (NCC).

6 Lauren Frances Turek, *To Bring the Good News to All Nations: Evangelical Influence on Human Rights and U.S. Foreign Relations* (Cornell University Press, 2020).

7 William Inboden, *Religion and American Foreign Policy, 1945–1960: The Soul of Containment* (Cambridge University Press, 2008), 170.

8 See Turek, *To Bring the Good News*, chap. 3.

9 See Allen Hertzke, *Freeing God's Children*, chaps. 1 and 5, for a more detailed description on the impact of demographic shifts in global Christianity on global human rights movements.

10 First International Congress on World Evangelization, Lausanne Covenant, 1974, lausanne.org/.

11 Turek, *To Bring the Good News*, 105.

12 Mary Ann Glendon, *A World Made New: Eleanor Roosevelt and the Universal Declaration of Human Rights* (Random House, 2002).

13 Glenn Mitoma, "Charles H. Malik and Human Rights," *Biography* 33, no. 1 (2010): 222–41. See also Glendon, *World Made New*; Susan Waltz, "Reclaiming and Re-

building the History of the Universal Declaration of Human Rights," *Third World Quarterly* 23, no. 3 (2002): 437–48.

14 Linde Lindkvist, *Religious Freedom and the Universal Declaration of Human Rights* (Cambridge University Press, 2017), 22.

15 See Lindkvist, *Religious Freedom*, chap. 1, which describes the ideological debates of the UN Commission on Human Rights. These debates centered around the concepts of personhood in the Christian tradition.

16 United Nations, "Universal Declaration of Human Rights," 1948.

17 Glendon, *World Made New*, 70.

18 Glendon.

19 Saudi Arabia also objected to Article 16, which gives equal rights to men and women within marriage.

20 Later, this contentious clause was removed from early versions of the 1981 UN Declaration on the Elimination of All Forms of Intolerance and of Discrimination Based on Religion or Belief. Even more explicitly, the Universal Islamic Declaration of Human Rights, also passed in 1981, makes clear that while individuals have the "right to express thoughts and beliefs," such expression is constrained by Sharia law. See Daniel Philpott, *Religious Freedom in Islam: The Fate of a Universal Human Right in the Muslim World Today* (Oxford University Press, 2019), 203–4, for a deeper analysis of the relationship between Islam and international religious freedom statutes.

21 See Anna Su, *Exporting Freedom: Religious Liberty and American Power* (Harvard University Press, 2016) for an analysis of U.S. leadership in crafting these international agreements, and specifically, its efforts to ensure that religious freedom is sufficiently considered and explicitly protected.

22 Henry Kissinger, "Testimony Before the Senate Committee on Finance, March 4, 1974," *Department of State Bulletin* 70, no. 1812 (April 1, 1974): 323.

23 Richard Nixon, Office of the Federal Register, *Public Papers of the President: Richard Nixon, January 1 to August 9, 1974* (Government Printing Office, 1974).

24 Adam Nagouney, "On Nixon Tapes, Disparaging Remarks About Ethnic Groups," *New York Times*, December 10, 2010, www.nytimes.com.

25 Michael Gerson, "The Sad Limits of Realism," *San Diego Union-Tribune*, December 21, 2010, www.sandiegouniontribune.com.

26 Henry Kissinger, "Putting the Nixon Tape in Context," *Washington Post*, December 26, 2010, www.washingtonpost.com.

27 Turek, *To Bring the Good News*, 111.

28 Founded in 1967, Voice of the Martyrs focuses on alleviating Christian persecution. Its founder, Richard Wurmbrand, a committed Christian, spent fourteen years imprisoned in Romania for preaching the incompatibility of communism and Christianity. In 1966, Wurmbrand testified in front of the Senate's Internal Security Subcommittee, famously removing his shirt to show the scars left by years of torture. He also wrote *Tortured for Christ*, which explains, in grim detail, the brutality he endured. His story and ongoing advocacy work through

VOM heavily influenced congressional leaders and Christian activism during this period.

29 Founded in 1955, Open Doors serves persecuted Christians around the globe. Its work began as an effort of Andrew van der Bijl, commonly known as "Brother Andrew," to smuggle Bibles into communist-occupied areas.

30 Sarah B. Snyder, *From Selma to Moscow: How Human Rights Activists Transformed U.S. Foreign Policy* (Columbia University Press, 2018), 148–64.

31 Gerald Ford, "The Second Carter-Ford Presidential Debate," Commission on Presidential Debates, October 6, 1976, www.debates.org.

32 For a discussion on this skepticism and criticisms in the early days after the Helsinki Final Act was signed, see Sidney Liskofsky, "Human Rights: From Helsinki to Belgrade," *American Jewish Year Book* 78 (1978): 121–45.

33 Daniel K. Williams, *The Election of the Evangelical: Jimmy Carter, Gerald Ford, and the Presidential Contest of 1976* (University Press of Kansas, 2020).

34 Falwell's initiative "I Love America" included rallies across the United States during 1975–76. It represented a departure from Falwell's early warnings that faith should stay above politics. While these rallies mostly focused on contentious social issues of the day, they also denounced communism and secular humanism.

35 Clair Apodaca, *Human Rights and U.S. Foreign Policy: Prevarications and Evasions* (Routledge, 2019), 35.

36 The establishment of the Bureau of Human Rights and Humanitarian Affairs was the result of a sequenced set of actions beginning in 1975. With congressional pressure to act on human rights, The State Department created the position of Coordinator for Humanitarian Affairs.

37 Jimmy Carter, "Presidential Directive/NSC 30," February 17, 1978. Washington, DC, The White House.

38 Turek, *To Bring the Good News*, 119.

39 For a clear articulation of this common critique, see Jeane Kirkpatrick, "Democracy and Double Standards," *Commentary Magazine*, November 1979; and "Establishing a Viable Human Rights Policy," *World Affairs*, April 1981.

40 See Elliott Abrams, *Realism and Democracy: American Foreign Policy After the Arab Spring* (Cambridge University Press, 2017), 35–36. Here, Abrams recalled a meeting of the Coalition for a Democratic Majority (which included Kirkpatrick and Abrams) with President Carter and Vice President Mondale at the White House to discuss foreign policy and try to get on the same page. Here, Austin Ranney spoke for the group and expressed the group's support for changes in Carter's policy post-1979 invasion in Afghanistan. Carter balked, indicating that he only ever had one foreign policy and wasn't planning on changing. What was hoped to be a unifying moment for leaders in the Democratic Party actually solidified the differences. In the end, many in the Coalition would be drawn in by Reagan's fierce anti-communist approach and would campaign as "Democrats for Reagan" and eventually become some of his top foreign policy leaders.

41 Andrew Preston, *Sword of the Spirit, Shield of Faith: Religion in American War and Diplomacy* (Anchor, 2012).

42 Inboden, *Soul of Containment*, 63.

43 Barbara J. Keys, *Reclaiming American Virtue: The Human Rights Revolution of the 1970s* (Harvard University Press, 2014).

44 Keys, *Reclaiming American Virtue*, 104.

45 As cited in Abrams, *Realism and Democracy*, 3.

46 Rasmus Sinding Søndergaard, *Reagan, Congress, and Human Rights: Contesting Morality in US Foreign Policy* (Cambridge University Press, 2020), 47.

47 Søndergaard draws upon the work of Ralph Carter and James Scott and their book *Choosing to Lead: Understanding Congressional Foreign Policy Entrepreneurs*. See Søndergaard, chap. 4, for a detailed exploration of foreign policy entrepreneurship and international religious freedom.

48 Sondergaard, *Reagan, Congress*, 114.

49 Mark R. Amstutz, *Evangelicals and American Foreign Policy* (Oxford University Press, 2014), 76.

50 Voice of the Martyrs (VOM) is an organization initially founded by Pastor Richard Wurmbrand, a dissident imprisoned for fourteen years in Romania, that serves the persecuted church across the globe.

51 James Baker, "James Baker on Post-Soviet Policy," Princeton University Archives, 1991, universityarchives.princeton.edu.

52 George H. W. Bush, "The President's News Conference," June 5, 1989, bush41library.tamu.edu.

53 Thomas L. Friedman, "Taking the Measure of a 'Measured Response,'" *New York Times*, July 2, 1989, www.nytimes.com.

54 Charles Colson, "If Communism Fails, Do We Win?," *Christianity Today*, October 6, 1989, www.christianitytoday.com.

55 "Remarks of Governor Bill Clinton," presented at the Los Angeles World Affairs Council, August 13, 1992.

56 Amstutz, *Evangelicals and American Foreign Policy*, 144.

57 Hertzke, *Freeing God's Children*, 27.

58 See introduction.

59 Domestic religious liberty concerns also featured prominently in the 1990s, culminating in the Religious Freedom Restoration Act of 1993.

60 The Center for Religious Freedom at Freedom House was formerly known as the Puebla Institute, a Catholic human rights organization focused on addressing religious persecution in Latin America. Nina Shea helped found the Puebla Institute and helped lead the transition to Freedom House.

61 A copy of the statement can be found in the online archives of the Presbyterian Church in America: www.pcahistory.org.

62 Horowitz recognized the inflammatory nature of his comment and the limits of his analogy. He specified that the circumstances facing Christians abroad amounted to the earlier atrocities suffered by European Jews. Further, he claimed

that indifference, especially of Western elites, plagued both issues. See Peter Stein-fels, "Evangelicals Lobby for Oppressed Christians," *New York Times*, September 15, 1996, www.nytimes.com.

63 Steinfels, "Evangelicals Lobby."

64 Steinfels.

65 John Shattuck, "Statement at Opening Session of the Advisory Committee on Religious Freedom Abroad," presented at the Advisory Committee on Religious Freedom Abroad, February 13, 1997, Department of State, Washington, DC.

66 Shattuck, "Statement."

67 Madeleine Korbel Albright, "Remarks Before Public Meeting of the Secretary's Advisory Committee on Religious Freedom Abroad," presented at the Advisory Committee on Religious Freedom Abroad, February 3, 1997, Department of State, Washington, DC.

68 Despite this rhetorical nod to the committee and its efforts, Albright vocally op-posed international religious freedom legislation. She argued that it might "create an artificial hierarchy of human rights." See Madeleine Korbel Albright, "Remarks at the Columbus School of Law," presented at the Catholic University, October 23, 1997, Washington, DC.

69 Albright, "Remarks Before Public Meeting."

70 Matthew Lorin to National Security Advisor, November 8, 1996, "Roll-Out of Religious Committee," email, OA/ID 10137, Stack S, Row 90, Section 2, Shelf 7, Position 1, National Security Council Files, William J. Clinton Library, Little Rock, Arkansas.

71 State Department, "Summary of February 13, 1997 Meeting: Advisory Com-mittee on Religious Freedom Abroad," February 13, 1997, Department of State, Washington, DC.

72 State Department, "Summary of February 13, 1997."

73 Lorin, "Roll-Out."

74 See H. Con. Res. 336, sponsored by Rep. Benjamin Gilman (R-NY), "Condemning the Taliban Regime and Supporting a Broad Based Government in Afghanistan"; H. Res. 332, sponsored by Rep. Rod Blagojevich (D-IL), "Expressing Concern for the Plight of Assyrians in the Near East"; and Senator Gordon H. Smith's (R-OR) Amendment (SP 396) to Senate Bill 903 (Foreign Affairs Reform and Restructur-ing Act of 1997).

75 See S. Res. 238, sponsored by Sen. Paul Wellstone (D-MN), "A Resolution Ex-pressing the Sense of the Senate Regarding Human Rights Conditions in China and Tibet," S. Res. 238, 105th Cong., 2nd sess., June 1, 1998. Benjamin Gilman, "Persecution of Baha'i Continues in Iran," House of Representatives, February 26, 1998.

76 Sam Brownback, remarks in "Religious Persecution in the Middle East: Faces of the Persecuted," Hearings Before the Subcommittee on Near Eastern and South Asian Affairs of the Committee on Foreign Relations, U.S. Senate, 105th Cong., 1st sess., May 1, 1997.

77 Frank R. Wolf, U.S. House of Representatives, *Freedom from Religious Persecution Act of 1997.*

78 Jonathan Agensky, "Evangelical Globalism and the Internationalization of Sudan's Second Civil War," *Cambridge Review of International Affairs* 33, no. 2 (2019): 274–93.

79 Hertzke, *Freeing God's Children*, 197.

80 John Shattuck, "John Shattuck on Freedom from Religious Persecution Act," U.S. Department of State, September 9, 1997, 1997-2001.state.gov.

81 "Memo on the Wolf–Specter Bills," *Mother Jones*, May 1998, www.motherjones.com.

82 USA*Engage hired popular Washington lobbying firm Anne Wexler to coordinate these lobbying efforts.

83 Hertzke, *Freeing God's Children*, 211.

84 As cited in Hertzke, 215.

85 The following section outlines the primary elements of the law as it was passed. It does not include modifications to the act after its original passage. Those will be discussed in greater depth in subsequent chapters.

86 These included: the Universal Declaration of Human Rights, the International Covenant on Civil and Political Rights, the Helsinki Accords, the Declaration on the Elimination of All Forms of Intolerance and Discrimination Based on Religion or Belief, the United Nations Charter, and the European Convention for the Protection of Human Rights and Fundamental Freedoms. See Anna Su's *Exporting Freedom* for an analysis of U.S. leadership in crafting these international agreements, and specifically, its efforts to ensure that religious freedom is sufficiently considered and explicitly protected.

87 Here, the law means all reports submitted by the State Department to Congress under Section 116 and 502B of the Foreign Assistance Act of 1961.

88 See section §6445 of the International Religious Freedom Act for complete descriptions of potential presidential actions.

89 James W. Fulbright, U.S. House of Representatives and U.S. Senate, *The Foreign Assistance Act of 1961, as Amended* (Washington, DC: U.S. Government Printing Office, 1961).

90 Matthew L. Fore, "Shall Weigh Your God and You: Assessing the Imperialistic Implications of the International Religious Freedom Act in Muslim Countries," *Duke Law Journal* 52, no. 2 (2002): 423–53.

91 See Su, *Exporting Freedom*, chap. 1.

92 "In U.S., Decline of Christianity Continues at Rapid Pace," Pew Research Center's Religion & Public Life Project, October 17, 2019, www.pewresearch.org.

93 Laurie Cozad, "The United States' Imposition of Religious Freedom: The International Religious Freedom Act and India," *India Review* 4, no. 1 (2005): 59–83.

94 Cozad, "Imposition of Religious Freedom."

95 Lee Marsden, *For God's Sake: The Christian Right and US Foreign Policy* (Zed, 2008).

96 T. Jeremy Gunn, "A Preliminary Response to Criticisms of the International Religious Freedom Act of 1998 International Law and Religion Symposium," *Brigham Young University Law Review* (2000): 841–66.

97   See Cozad, "Imposition of Religious Freedom," 75.

98   Albright, "Remarks at the Columbus School of Law."

99   See introduction to this volume for a discussion on the term "first freedom" and its implications for international religious freedom activism.

100 Jacob Mchangama, "Freedom of Religion Doesn't Cut It," *Foreign Policy*, May 1, 2019, www.foreignpolicy.com.

101 Eugenia Relaño Pastor, "The Flawed Implementation of the International Religious Freedom Act of 1998: A European Perspective International Law and Religion Symposium," *Brigham Young University Law Review* 2005, no. 3 (2005): 711–46.

102 Gunn, "Preliminary Response," 845.

103 Thomas F. Farr, *World of Faith and Freedom: Why International Religious Liberty Is Vital to American National Security* (Oxford University Press, 2008).

104 For another description of different approaches to international religious freedom, see Judd Birdsall, "Will Biden Demote Religious Freedom in US Foreign Policy?," *Christianity Today*, November 17, 2020, www.christianitytoday.com.

2. STRATEGY AND INTERNATIONAL RELIGIOUS FREEDOM

1   Bryan D. Jones and Frank R. Baumgartner, *The Politics of Attention: How Government Prioritizes Problems* (University of Chicago Press, 2005).

2   U.N. General Assembly, "Universal Declaration of Human Rights," December 10, 1948, www.un.org.

3   "The 2000 Campaign: Second Presidential Debate Between Gov. Bush and Vice President Gore," *New York Times*, October 12, 2000, www.nytimes.com.

4   Nilay Saiya, *Weapon of Peace: How Religious Liberty Combats Terrorism* (Cambridge University Press, 2018).

5   George W. Bush, "Remarks to the American Jewish Committee," American Presidency Project, May 3, 2001, www.presidency.ucsb.edu.

6   This would shift during the Trump administration, when under the leadership of Ambassador Sam Brownback, IRF would ascend higher on the priority list.

7   Lars Schoultz, *Human Rights and United States Policy Toward Latin America* (Princeton University Press, 1981).

8   U.S. Congress, Public Law 99-433, Goldwater-Nichols Department of Defense Reorganization Act of 1986, § 603, October 1, 1986.

9   On multiple occasions, Clinton referenced Stephen Carter's *Culture of Disbelief*. See his 1993 remarks at the White House interfaith prayer breakfast and his November 1993 remarks at the singing of the Restoration of Religious Freedom Act.

10 Bill Clinton, "Remarks at a White House Interfaith Breakfast," American Presidency Project, August 30, 1993, www.presidency.ucsb.edu.

11 Bill Clinton, "Remarks on Signing the Religious Freedom Restoration Act of 1993," American Presidency Project, November 16, 1993, www.presidency.ucsb.edu.

12 Allen D. Hertzke, "The Clinton Presidency and the Pivotal Era for Religious Freedom," Religious Freedom Institute, July 17, 2016, www.religiousfreedominstitute.org.

13 Bill Clinton, "Clinton Materials Project: Virtual Library Publications," clinton-whitehouse6.archives.gov.

14 Ira Rifkin and Adelle M Banks, "The Year in Review," *Washington Post*, December 26, 1998, www.washingtonpost.com.

15 The article wrongly attributes the passage of the IRFA directly to the death of John Joseph, a Catholic Bishop in Pakistan who committed suicide in protest of the persecution of Christians.

16 Joseph Lieberman, "Remarks on President Clinton's Misconduct." CNN, September 3, 1998, www.cnn.com.

17 Stephen Braun, "Lieberman's Rebuke of Clinton Set a Tone," *Los Angeles Times*, January 22, 2004, www.latimes.com.

18 Bill Clinton, *My Life* (Vintage, 2005).

19 "The Clinton Presidency: Timeline of Major Actions," The White House, Accessed February 19, 2025, clintonwhitehouse5.archives.gov.

20 Some of these strategies expanded on prior versions. For instance, there were three iterations of "A National Security Strategy of Enlargement and Engagement" and three iterations of "A National Security Strategy for a Global Age." Notably, the Bush and Obama administrations issued only one per term.

21 The White House, "A National Security Strategy for a New Century," May 1997. Washington, DC: The White House.

22 The White House, "A National Security Strategy for a New Century," December 1999. Washington, DC: The White House.

23 Thomas E. Mann, "Reflections on the 2000 U.S. Presidential Election," Brookings Institution, January 1, 2001, brookings.edu.

24 As cited in Wilfred M. McClay, "The God of Princes," *Touchstone: A Journal of Mere Christianity*, March 2001, www.touchstonemag.com.

25 Melinda Henneberger, "The 2000 Campaign: Spiritual Seeker Gore Has Explored a Range of Beliefs from Old Time to New Age," *New York Times*, October 22, 2000, www.nytimes.com.

26 Notably, vice presidential candidate Lieberman was formally asked by the Anti-Defamation League to tone down his religious rhetoric as they feared it would alienate non-religious Americans from the political discourse.

27 George W. Bush, "George W. Bush on Why He Admires Christ." C-SPAN, December 13, 1999, www.c-span.org.

28 See George W. Bush, "How Billy Graham Changed My Life," *Wall Street Journal*, February 23, 2018, www.wsj.com.

29 George W. Bush, *Decision Points* (Crown, 2010), 34.

30 Richard Holtzman, "George W. Bush's Rhetoric of Compassionate Conservatism and Its Value as a Tool of Presidential Politics," History and Social Sciences Faculty Journal Articles, Paper 19, 2010, digitalcommons.bryant.edu.

31 George W. Bush, "Remarks by the President to the American Jewish Committee." The White House Website Archive, May 3, 2001, georgewbush-whitehouse.archives.gov.

32 Interestingly, for some IRF critics, the significance of rhetoric is usually only mentioned when such rhetoric is absent. Presidential speeches (of all presidents under study) can be quickly dismissed as toothless and inadequate to create policy change. But, if it the rhetorical concern for religious freedom is deemed insufficient, critics are quick to note the missed opportunity for robust public diplomacy. For example, compare Farr's critiques in Thomas F. Farr and William L. Saunders, "The Bush Administration and America's International Religious Freedom Policy," *Harvard Journal of Law and Public Policy; Cambridge* 32, no. 3 (2009): 949–70; and Thomas F. Farr, "Our Failed Religious Freedom Policy." *First Things: A Monthly Journal of Religion & Public Life*, no. 237 (November 2013): 35–40.

33 William Inboden, "Presidential Promotion of International Religious Freedom," *Review of Faith & International Affairs* 6, no. 2 (2008): 41–45.

34 M. H. Swahn, R. R. Mahendra, L. J. Pauloozi, R. L. Winston, G. A. Shelley, J. Taliano, L. Frazier, and J. R. Saul, "Violent Attacks on Middle Easterners in the United States During the Month Following the September 11, 2001 Terrorist Attacks, " *Injury Prevention* 9, no. 2 (2003): 187–90.

35 As quoted in Dennis R. Hoover, "Is Evangelicalism Itching for a Civilization Fight?," *Brandywine Review of Faith & International Affairs* 2, no. 1 (2004): 11–16.

36 It should be noted that Robertson's views on Islam were controversial prior to 2001, but he doubled down on his attacks against the faith after 9/11. For more on earlier controversies, see Carlyle Murphy, "Remarks by Pat Robertson Insult Islam, Muslims Say," *Washington Post*, November 8, 1997, www.washingtonpost.com.

37 Associated Press, "A Nation Challenged: The Religious Right; Islam Is Violent in Nature, Pat Robertson Says," *New York Times*, February 23, 2002, www.nytimes.com.

38 Susan Sachs, "Baptist Pastor Attacks Islam, Inciting Cries of Intolerance," *New York Times*, June 15, 2002, www.nytimes.com.

39 As cited in Anna Pukas, "Iftar at the White House: Trump's Recipe for Reconciliation in Ramadan," Arab News, May 30, 2018, www.arabnews.com.

40 George Bush, "'Islam Is Peace' Says President: Remarks by the President at Islamic Center of Washington, DC," The White House Website Archive, September 17, 2001, georgewbush-whitehouse.archives.gov.

41 Bush, "Islam Is Peace."

42 George W. Bush, "Remarks by President George W. Bush in Meeting with U.N. Secretary General Kofi Annan," The White House Website Archive, November 13, 2002, georgewbush-whitehouse.archives.gov.

43 Samuel P. Huntington, *Who Are We? The Challenges to America's National Identity* (Simon & Schuster, 2004).

44 George W. Bush, "Address to the Joint Session of the 107th Congress," The White House, September 20, 2001, accessed February 19, 2025, https://georgewbush-whitehouse.archives.gov.

45 D. Jason Berggren and Nicol C. Rae, "Jimmy Carter and George W. Bush: Faith, Foreign Policy, and an Evangelical Presidential Style," *Presidential Studies Quarterly* 36, no. 4 (2006): 606–32.

46 George W. Bush, "Address to the Joint Session of the 107th Congress," The White House Website Archive, September 20, 2001, georgewbush-whitehouse.archives.gov.

47 John Lewis Gaddis, *Surprise, Security, and the American Experience* (Harvard University Press, 2005).

48 George W. Bush, "Remarks by President George W. Bush at the 20th Anniversary of the National Endowment for Democracy," National Endowment for Democracy, November 6, 2003, www.ned.org.

49 James B. Steinberg, Ivo H. Daalder, and James M. Lindsay, "The Bush National Security Strategy: An Evaluation," Brookings Institution, October 1, 2002, www.brookings.edu.

50 George W. Bush White House, "The National Security Strategy of the United States of America," September 17, 2002, accessed February 19, 2025, georgewbush-whitehouse.archives.gov.

51 This EO also created a similar center within the Department of Agriculture.

52 George W. Bush, "Executive Order 13280: Responsibilities of the Department of Agriculture and the Agency for International Development with Respect to Faith-Based and Community Initiatives," December 12, 2002, www.govinfo.gov.

53 Richard W. Stevenson, "In Order, President Eases Limits on U.S. Aid to Religious Groups," *New York Times*, December 13, 2002, www.nytimes.com.

54 George W. Bush, "Second Inaugural Address, January 20, 2005," in *Public Papers of the Presidents of the United States: George W. Bush, 2005*, book 1 (Washington, DC: U.S. Government Printing Office), 87–90.

55 George W. Bush White House, "The National Security Strategy of the United States of America," The White House, March 16, 2006, accessed February 19, 2025, georgewbush-whitehouse.archives.gov.

56 Bush White House, "National Security Strategy."

57 Derek Davis, "The Dark Side to a Just War: The USA Patriot Act and Counterterrorism's Potential Threat to Religious Freedom," *Journal of Church and State* 44, no. 1 (2002): 5–17.

58 Eugenia Relaño Pastor, "The Flawed Implementation of the International Religious Freedom Act of 1998: A European Perspective International Law and Religion Symposium," *Brigham Young University Law Review*, no. 3 (2005): 711–46.

59 As cited in Christina M. Kelly, "The United States and Turkmenistan: Striking a Balance between Promoting Religious Freedom and Fighting the War Against Terrorism," *Pace International Law Review* 15, no. 2 (September 2003): 482–512.

60 Steven Wales, "Remembering the Persecuted: An Analysis of the International Religious Freedom Act," *Houston Journal of International Law* 24, no. 3 (Spring 2002): 579–648.

61 As discussed further in chapter 4, the State Department countered these claims, noting that other States like China and Sudan were designated as CPCs despite their support of the War on Terror.

62 U.S. Commission for International Religious Freedom, "Commission to Hold Hearing on Religious Freedom and the Campaign Against Terrorism," November 19, 2001, www.uscirf.gov.

63 Joe Carter, "Foreign Policy and the First Freedom," *First Things*, October 11, 2011, www.firstthings.com.

64 U.S. Commission for International Religious Freedom, "Afghanistan: Constitution Threatens to Institutionalize 'Taliban-Lite,'" November 3, 2003, www.uscirf.gov.

65 Richard John Neuhaus, "Religious Freedom in a Time of War," *First Things*, January 2002, www.firstthings.com.

66 John Hanford, interview with author, 2021.

67 See Walter Russell Mead, *Special Providence: American Foreign Policy and How It Changed the World* (Routledge, 2009); and Paul A. Marshall and Lela Gilbert, *Their Blood Cries Out: The Untold Story of Persecution Against Christians in the Modern World* (Word, 1997).

68 Barack Obama, "Keynote Address at the 2004 Democratic National Convention," PBS, July 27, 2004, www.pbs.org.

69 Barbara Bradley Hagerty, "Has Obama Waged a War on Religion?," NPR, January 8, 2012, www.npr.org.

70 In the years that followed, these differences grew significantly. In 2019, 61 percent of Republicans said that the Democratic Party is unfriendly to religion. See Michael Lipka, "Republicans and Democrats Agree Religion's Influence Is Waning, but Differ in Their Reactions," Pew Research Center, 2019, www.pewresearch.org.

71 Associated Press. 2008. "Obama Strongly Denounces Former Pastor," *NBC News*, April 29, 2008, www.nbcnews.com.

72 Barack Obama, "Remarks by the President at Cairo University," The White House Website Archive, June 4, 2009, obamawhitehouse.archives.gov.

73 Judd Birdsall, "Keep the Faith: How American Diplomacy Got Religion, and How to Keep It," *Review of Faith & International Affairs* 14, no. 2 (2016): 110–15.

74 Maria Otero, "Remarks to the Religion and Foreign Policy Working Group," State Department, October 18, 2011, 2009-2017.state.gov.

75 Former USCIRF Commissioner, Vice Chair, interview with author, 2020.

76 John Kerry, "We Ignore the Global Impact of Religion at Our Peril," *America: The Jesuit Review*, September 2, 2015, www.americamagazine.org.

77 Barack Obama, "Remarks by the President at the Acceptance of the Nobel Peace Prize," December 10, 2009, obamawhitehouse.archives.gov.

78 Frank R. Wolf, "To Provide for the Establishment of the Special Envoy to Promote Religious Freedom of Religious Minorities in the Near East and South Central Asia," H.R.301—113th Congress, 2013–14, www.congress.gov.

79 Ashley E. Samelson, "Why 'Freedom of Worship' Is Not Enough," *First Things*, February 22, 2010, www.firstthings.com.

80 Barack Obama, "Remarks By President Obama to the Turkish Parliament," April 6, 2009, obamawhitehouse.archives.gov.

81 Barack Obama, "Remarks by President Obama in Address to the People of Vietnam," May 24, 2016, obamawhitehouse.archives.gov.

82 Barack Obama, "Remarks by President Obama in Address to the People of India," January 27, 2015, obamawhitehouse.archives.gov.

83 Knox Thames, interview with author, 2020.

3. NAVIGATING THE BUREAUCRACY

1 John Shattuck, "'The International Religious Freedom Act': Statement Before the Senate Committee on Foreign Relations," May 12, 1998, 1997-2001.state.gov.

2 Daniel W. Drezner, "Ideas, Bureaucratic Politics, and the Crafting of Foreign Policy." *American Journal of Political Science* 44, no. 4 (2000): 733–49.

3 Drawing upon the work of Bendor, Taylor, and Van Gaalen 1987, Drezner defines missionary institutions here as 1) having consensus re: ends and means and 2) purposefully limiting the introduction of new goals to avoid value conflicts or tradeoffs.

4 This Office of Humanitarian Affairs replaced the Office of the Special Assistant for Refugee and Migration Affairs.

5 In November 1976, the coordinator's position was elevated to be on par with assistant secretaries of state but was not given the formal title until 1977, when the number of secretaries of state expanded from eleven to thirteen.

6 Bureau of Democracy, Human Rights and Labor Affairs, *1999 Country Reports on Human Rights Practices*, 2000, 2009-2017.state.gov.

7 Passed in 1997.

8 Drezner, "Ideas, Bureaucratic Politics," 736.

9 As of February 2020.

10 Some of these bureaus report on certain matters directly to the secretary of state instead of being mediated by the undersecretary for civilian security, democracy, and human rights. These include: CSO, CT, and IRF as of February 2020.

11 Senior State Department official, interview with author, 2020.

12 Robert Seiple, "Commemorating the 20th Anniversary of the International Religious Freedom Act," Religious Freedom Institute, November 8, 2018, www.religiousfreedominstitute.org.

13 For example, Seiple signed a statement by Richard John Neuhaus and Charles W. Colson in October 1997 entitled "We Hold These Truths: A Statement of Christian Conscience and Citizenship" (www.firstthings.com).

14 Robert Seiple, interview with author, 2020.

15 For a more detailed discussion of the Advisory Committee's efforts, see chapter 2.

16 Robert Seiple and Berkley Center for Religion, Peace, and World Affairs, "A Discussion with Robert A. Seiple, First U.S. Ambassador for International Religious Freedom," October 29, 2009, berkleycenter.georgetown.edu.

17 Seiple, interview with author.

18 Seiple.

19 Seiple.

20 Seiple and Berkley Center, "Discussion."

21 T. Jeremy Gunn, "Full of Sound & Fury: Polemics at Home and Abroad Does Not Prevent Religious Persecution," *Christianity Today*, Janury 1, 2003, www.christianitytoday.com.

22 Michael Horowitz, "Cry Freedom," *Christianity Today*, March 1, 2003, www.christianitytoday.com.

23 Seiple, interview with author.

24 Seiple's successor, John Hanford, would later be excluded from these briefings.

25 Robert Seiple, "Religious Liberty: How Are We Doing?," *Christianity Today*, October 22, 2001, www.christianitytoday.com.

26 For the first six months of Amb. Seiple's tenure, the office staff consisted of temporary positions or "staff-on-loan" from DRL.

27 Thomas F. Farr, interview with author, 2020.

28 Rabbi Saperstein served as the first chair of the commission. Years later, he would serve as the ambassador-at-large for IRF under the Obama administration.

29 Bolton would serve as President George W. Bush's undersecretary of state for arms control and international security affairs and then as the U.S. ambassador to the U.N. Years later, he served as U.S. national security advisor under the Donald Trump Administration.

30 Abrams held a variety of positions in the Reagan, H. W. Bush, Bush and Trump administrations.

31 As quoted in Erin Rodewald and Lou Ann Sabatier, "A Retrospective: 20th Anniversary of the International Religious Freedom Act," 21Wilberforce, December 2018. www.21wilberforce.org.

32 Nina Shea, "Testimony Regarding the First Annual State Department Report on International Religious Freedom," U.S. House of Representatives, October 6, 1999, www.uscirf.gov.

33 U.S. Commission for International Religious Freedom, "The U.S. Commission on International Religious Freedom: First Annual Report," May 1, 2000, www.uscirf.gov.

34 Laila Al-Marayati, "The Biases of Elliot Abrams," Counter Punch, December 16, 2002, www.counterpunch.org.

35 Cardinal McCarrick was laicized in February 2019 for sexually abusing seminarians and boys since the 1990s.

36 U.S. Commission for International Religious Freedom, "Commission Regrets Chinese Naming of Bishops," January 12, 2000, www.uscirf.gov.

37 The Catholic Patriotic Association (CPA), founded in 1957, is the CCP's sanctioned Catholic Church in China. However, because the CPA is regulated by the CCP and does not recognize the authority of the Pope, it is not considered fully Catholic by the Vatican.

38 Nina Shea to Archbishop Theodore McCarrick, "Re: China and Ordination," January 10, 2000. This is an unpublished letter from Nina Shea, which I received as an e-mail attachment. It is not part of a publicly available collection.

39 Elliott Abrams, "Religious Freedom Is More Important Today," *Middle East Quarterly* Winter (2001): 88–94.

40 Lauren Woods, interview with author, 2020.

41 As quoted in Maryann Cusimano Love, "The Vietnam Dilemma," Georgetown University Institute for the Study of Democracy, September 2, 2020, www.uscirf.gov.

42 International Religious Freedom Act of 1998. Public Law 105-292. U.S. Statutes at Large 112 (1998): 2787. Enacted October 27, 1998. https://www.congress.gov/bill/105th-congress/house-bill/2431.

43 Robert Seiple, "Religious Liberty: How Are We Doing?," *Christianity Today*, October 22, 2001, www.christianitytoday.com.

44 Seiple, interview with author.

45 Robert Seiple, "Cursing Darkness, Lighting Candles," *Brandywine Review of Faith & International Affairs* 2, no. 1(2004): 1–2.

46 Seiple, interview with author.

47 Beginning in August 1998, Seiple served as the secretary of state's special representative on IRF, making his entire tenure at the State Department just over two years.

48 The official statement also makes note of the Milosevic regime and the Taliban as other severe violators of religious freedom.

49 As cited in Rodewald and Sabatier, "Retrospective."

50 See Representative Chris Smith's statement here: Chris Smith. "The First Annual State Department Report on International Religious Freedom." U.S. House of Representatives, October 6, 1999. Accessed February 19, 2025. https://chrissmith. house.gov.

51 Seiple, "Religious Liberty."

52 Hanford served under prominent Presbyterian minister Tim Keller and lived with the Keller family temporarily.

53 Knox Thames, interview with author, 2020.

54 Kyle Ballard, interview with author, 2020.

55 Thomas F. Farr, *World of Faith and Freedom: Why International Religious Liberty Is Vital to American National Security* (Oxford University Press, 2008), 11. See chapters 1 and 2 in this volume for more information about the State Department's allergy to discussing matters of religion in its diplomatic efforts.

56 Judd Birdsall, "Keep the Faith: How American Diplomacy Got Religion, and How to Keep It," *Review of Faith & International Affairs* 14, no. 2 (2016): 110–15.

57 The Qur'an refers to the Ummah as one universal community. For further detail, see OIC, "Organization of Islamic Cooperation," www.oic-oci.org.

58 U.S. State Department, Office of Electronic Information, Bureau of Public Affairs, "Special Envoy to the Organization of the Islamic Conference (OIC)," 2003, 2001-2009.state.gov.

59 See chapter 3 for more details.

60 Birdsall, "Keep the Faith."

61 State Department Official, interview with author, 2020.

62 As cited in Joseph Liu, *International Religious Freedom: Religion and International Diplomacy*, Pew Research Center, 2007, www.pewforum.org.

63 Chapter 2 discusses this concern from a domestic point of view in the context of legislative debates. But, this concern applied to other nations as well. Part 2 will discuss this tension in greater detail, especially in the China and Saudi Arabia chapters.

64 Frank R. Wolf, "International Religious Freedom Act of 1998," www.congress.gov.

65 U.S. State Department, "Authority, Responsibility and Organization," Foreign Affairs Manual, May 7, 2020, fam.state.gov.

66 The coordinator for counterterrorism has dual rankings of ambassador-at-large and assistant secretary.

67 For further discussion on the tension between Craner and Farr, see chapter 6 of Farr's *World of Faith and Freedom*.

68 John Hanford, interview with author, 2021.

69 U.S. State Department, Broadcasting Board of Governors, and Office of the Inspector General, *Report of Inspection: Bureau of Human Rights, Democracy, and Labor*, 2003, www.stateoig.gov.

70 Hanford, interview with author.

71 Farr, *World of Faith and Freedom*.

72 Love, *Vietnam Dilemma*.

73 As cited in Liu, *International Religious Freedom*.

74 As cited in Frederick Barton, Karin Von Hippel, and Center for Strategic and International Studies, eds., *Mixed Blessings: U.S. Government Engagement with Religion in Conflict-Prone Settings* (Center for Strategic and International Studies, 2007), 13.

75 Hanford, interview with author.

76 Other offices were similarly affected.

77 Seiple, "Religious Liberty."

78 Hanford, interview with author.

79 Farr, *World of Faith and Freedom*, 193–95.

80 Outside of the report development, Hanford methodically considered how to find new positions for the IRF office and to expand the staff.

81 As cited in Melani McAlister, *The Kingdom of God Has No Borders: A Global History of American Evangelicals* (Oxford University Press, 2018).

82 Birdsall, "Keep the Faith."

83 Thames, interview with author.

84 Judd Birdsall, "Obama and the Drama over International Religious Freedom Policy: An Insider's Perspective," *Review of Faith & International Affairs* 10, no. 3 (2012): 33–41.

85 Birdsall, "Obama and the Drama."

86 Berkley Center for Religion, Peace, and World Affairs, "A Discussion with Maryann Cusimano Love, Associate Professor of International Relations, Catholic University of America." July 6, 2010, berkleycenter.georgetown.edu.

87 As cited in Rodewald and Sabatier, "Retrospective."

88 Will Inboden, "What the Senate Should Ask the Rev. Suzan Johnson Cook," *Foreign Policy*, July 5, 2010, www.foreignpolicy.com.

89 U.S. Senate, Nominations of the 112th Congress—First Session, hearing before the Senate Committee on Foreign Relations, 112th Congress, 1st sess., March 16, 2011.

90 U.S. Senate, "Nominations."

91 Senior State Department Official, interview with author, 2020.

92 Senior State Department Official, interview with author.

93 Maria Otero, "Remarks to the Religion and Foreign Policy Working Group," October 18, 2011, 2009–2017.state.gov.

94 The subsequent Foreign Service Institute Course, titled Religion and Foreign Policy (PP225), focused on laying a theoretical foundation of the intersection of religion and foreign policy and giving the U.S. practical tools to leverage relationships with religious actors. Topics include promoting religious freedom, integrating religion and national security, engaging with religious leaders at post, confronting islamophobia and anti-Semitism. For more detail, see Bureau of Democracy, Human Rights and Labor Affairs, "Appendix E: Training at the Foreign Service Institute Related to the International Religious Freedom Act," 2011, 2009–2017.state.gov.

95 Religion and Foreign Policy Working Group of the Secretary of State's Strategic Dialogue with Civil Society, "Ensuring the Opportunity for Mutual Counsel and Collaboration," Institute for Global Engagement, October 16, 2012, Accessed February 19, 2025, https://globalengage.org.

96 The working group explicitly noted that the mandate of the IRFA was too narrow to handle all engagement efforts and noted that collaboration and integration is necessary.

97 Religion and Foreign Policy Working Group, "Ensuring the Opportunity."

98 John Kerry, "We Ignore the Global Impact of Religion at Our Peril," America: The Jesuit Review, September 2, 2015, www.americamagazine.org.

99 Shaun Casey, "Remarks at the Launch of the Office of Faith-Based Community Initiatives," U.S. Department of State, August 7, 2013, 2009-2017.state.gov/.

100 Shaun Casey, "Global Dynamics of Faith." Reflections Journal, Spring 2016, reflections.yale.edu.

101 For an in-depth discussion of the IRFA and its scope, see chapter 1.

102 After her resignation, she cited the ability to give her kids a debt-free college education as the reason for her departure. See Lauren Markoe, "Suzan Johnson Cook Defends Her Work on Religious Freedom and Explains Why She Left," Religion News Service, October 28, 2013, www.religionnews.com.

103 His extensive résumé also includes a long tenure of teaching courses on the separation of church and state at Georgetown University Law Center. In addition, he held leadership positions with the Coalition to Preserve Religious Liberty, the Leadership Conference on Civil and Human Rights, and the World Development Dialogue.

104 David Saperstein, "Testimony of Rabbi David Saperstein," U.S. Senate Committee on Foreign Relations, September 11, Accessed February 19, 2025. https://www.foreign.senate.gov.

105 Frank R. Wolf, "H.R.301—113th Congress (2013–2014): To Provide for the Establishment of the Special Envoy to Promote Religious Freedom of Religious Minorities in the Near East and South Central Asia," September 19, 2013, www.congress.gov.

106 James Lankford, "Senator Lankford Questions Obama Administration Commitment to International Religious Freedom," October 9, 2015, www.lankford.senate.gov.

107 Thames, interview with author.

108 Sharon Alvarez and Jay Barney, "Discovery and Creation: Alternative Theories of Entrepreneurial Action," *Revista Organizações em Contexto* 3, no. 6 (2007): 123–52.

109 Chiara De Cesari, "Post-Colonial Ruins: Archaeologies of Political Violence and IS," *Anthropology Today* 31, no. 6 (2015): 22–26.

110 Christopher W. Jones, "Understanding ISIS's Destruction of Antiquities as a Rejection of Nationalism," *Journal of Eastern Mediterranean Archaeology and Heritage Studies* 6, nos. 1–2 (2018): 31–58.

111 Thames, interview with author.

112 Eliot L. Engel, "H.R.1493—114th Congress (2015–2016): Protect and Preserve International Cultural Property Act," May 9, 2016, www.congress.gov.

113 Quoted in Nikita Lalwani, "State of the Art: How Cultural Property Became a National Security Priority," *Yale Law Journal* 130 (July 19, 2020), www.yalelawjournal.org.

114 In May 2018, these items were finally repatriated to Iraq. See U.S. Immigration and Customs Enforcement, "ICE Returns Thousands of Ancient Artifacts Seized from Hobby Lobby to Iraq," May 2, 2018, www.ice.gov.

115 Knox Thames, "Today's Struggle to Protect and Preserve the Cultural Heritage of Religious Minorities," paper presented at the Metropolitan Museum of Art, New York, September 20, 2016.

116 U.S. Department of State, Office of the Spokesperson, "U.S. Department of State Announces New Cultural Heritage Initiatives," U.S. Department of State, September 22, 2016, Accessed February 19, 2025, https://2009-2017.state.gov.

117 Shea, interview with author.

118 As cited in Markoe, "Suzan Johnson Cook."

119 Markoe.

120 Shea, interview with author.

121 Richard Durbin, "United States Commission on International Religious Freedom Reform and Reauthorization Act of 2011," U.S. Senate, December 15, 2011, www.govinfo.gov.

122 The appointment of Zuhdi Jasser, a reformed Muslim who was often criticized for contributed to islamophobia in the United States, caused significant controversy. In addition, USCIRF faced a lawsuit from former employee Saiya Ghori-Ahmad, who claimed that she had been discriminated against because of her Muslim faith and previous work with Muslim civil rights associations. See Tobin Grant, "One of the Most Ironic Religious Freedom Lawsuits Ever Filed," *Christianity Today*, www.christianitytoday.com/.

123 Grant, "One of the Most Ironic."

124 Using one of the chamber's rules, a single senator reportedly put a hold on the reauthorization legislation. While not made public, it is assumed that Senator Richard Durbin (D.-Ill.) held up the bill. As the bill was held, Congress approved three temporary agreements that kept USCIRF operational.

125 Former USCIRF Commissioner, Vice Chair, interview with author, 2020.

126 Former USCIRF Commissioner, Vice Chair, interview with author.

127 All Party Group on International Religious Freedom, "Article 18: An Orphaned Right," May 2013, appgfreedomofreligionorbelief.org.

128 International Panel of Parliamentarians for Freedom of Religion or Belief. *New York Resolution for Freedom of Religion or Belief.* British Council, September 19, 2015. Accessed February 19, 2025. https://www.britishcouncil.us.

129 Thames, interview with author.

4. INTERNATIONAL RELIGIOUS FREEDOM IN CHINA

1 Bill Clinton, "In Their Own Words; Transcript of Speech by Clinton Accepting Democratic Nomination," *New York Times*, July 17, 1992, www.nytimes.com.

2 James Mann, *About Face: A History of America's Curious Relationship with China, from Nixon to Clinton* (Vintage, 2000), 275.

3 Zhou Qi, "Conflicts over Human Rights Between China and the US," *Human Rights Quarterly* 27, no. 1 (2005): 105–24.

4 See archives of Amnesty International, Human Rights Watch (or Asia Watch), reports from the U.N.'s Office of the High Commissioner for Human Rights (OHCHR), U.S. State Department country reports, and International Red Cross and Red Crescent Movement.

5 For more on the CCP's view of religion and for an accounting of the sociological underpinnings of revival and crackdowns on dissent, see Fenggang Yang, *Religion in China: Survival and Revival Under Communist Rule* (Oxford University Press, 2011).

6 The Boxers were part of the Righteous and Harmonious Society Movement, which began in the Shandong Province of eastern China in the 1890s. For more on the origins of anti-missionary activity and the Boxer Uprising see Paul A. Cohen, *History in Three Keys: The Boxers as Event, Experience, and Myth* (Columbia University Press, 1997); and Joseph Esherick, *The Origins of the Boxer Uprising* (University of California Press, 1987).

7 Scholars Tatsuro Yamamoto and Sukimo Yamamoto trace the origins of the anti-Christian sentiment movement to the "New Thought Movement" that originated a decade prior. This movement prioritized science and democracy, lauding rationalism as the key to forward progress. While some in the movement decried religion explicitly, others found it to be useless, preferring instead to devote time and energy toward scientific advancement. Second, Yamamoto and Yamamoto note the nationalism of the Anti-Christian Federation. One of the primary criticisms from this perspective was that mission schools, built upon the texts and ideas of Westerners, sometimes neglected Chinese language and culture. Chinese

intellectuals rallied around the cause to prevent this type of interjection, fearing it might dilute national pride. Finally, the scholars consider the nascent effect of communism in China. Connecting Christianity to capitalism, the Anti-Christian Federation argued that "on the one hand a looting and oppressing class, and on the other a looted and oppressed class. Christianity and the Christian church of the present time are devils who support and help the former, and loot and oppress the latter." See Yamamoto, Tatsuro, and Sumiko Yamamoto. "The Anti-Christian Movement in China, 1922–1927." *The Far Eastern Quarterly* 12, no. 2 (February 1953): 144. Together these three strands coalesced to form a vigorous and violent movement against Christians.

8   The CCP forbids any party members from religious practice. As such, the formation of religious restrictions and the implementations of Chinese law is divorced from religious involvement or perspective.

9   The state-sanctioned versions of these congregations are known as the Buddhist Association of China, the Chinese Patriotic Catholic Association, the Chinese Taoist Association, the Islamic Association of China, and the Three-Self Patriotic Movement, respectively. The Protestant network of churches in China follows the three self-principles of self-governance, self-support, and self-propagation. This concept originated in the late 1800s when Christian missionaries recognized the need for indigenous leadership and the necessity for culturally dependent forms of worship. Under the CCP, however, the Three-Self Patriotic Movement is subordinate to the will of the state.

10 The true political aims of the Uyghur people are many, ranging from securing the rights to cultural and religious expression within China to the formation of a separate Uyghur state. Neither of these aims is acceptable to the CCP, the power of which hinges on nationalism and unity.

11 The CPC views eschatology as a dangerous part of religiosity, as it ascribes ultimate punishment and thus ultimate fear in something other than the state. Similar fears exist surrounding the salvationist teachings of the Falun Gong.

12 Central Committee of the Chinese Communist Party and the State Council, "Circular on Some Problems Concerning the Further Improvement of Work on Religion, Document No. 6," February 5, 1991, tandfonline.com.

13 This typically concerns the East Turkestan Islamic Movement (ETIM) and Tibetan activists.

14 See Asia Watch. *Religious Intolerance in China.* New York: Human Rights Watch, January 1995. For more on the razing of the Jesus Family church and the imprisonment of its leader, Zheng Yunsu.

15 While the exact cause of death remains unknown, extensive scarring on his body showed signs of torture. See Human Rights Watch (Organization), and Asia Watch Committee (U.S.), eds., *Continuing Religious Repression in China* (Asia Watch, 1993). This incident was especially gruesome. The CCP forced fellow community members to take active roles in the torture. If they refused, they too were tortured and then detained.

16 Asia Watch, *Religious Intolerance in China.*

17 See Human Rights Watch, "China, Organ Procurement, and Judicial Execution in China," August 1994, www.justice.gov. The report describes the strategic approach to their transplant initiatives: "The use of corpses or organs of executed criminals must be kept strictly secret. . . . A surgical vehicle from the health department may be permitted to drive onto the execution grounds to remove the organs, but it is not permissible to use a vehicle bearing health department insignia or to wear white clothing."

18 Warren Christopher, "Asylum Claims by Chinese—Country Conditions Paper, Part II," U.S. Department of State, February 25, 1994, foia.state.gov.

19 Chris Yeung, "Persecution Claims Denied; Religion 'Should Serve Economic Progress,'" *South China Morning Post*, September 8, 1993, www.scmp.com.

20 Bill Clinton and Jiang Zemin, "The President's News Conference with President Jiang Zemin of China in Beijing," June 17, 1998, www.govinfo.gov.

21 With specific regard to religious restrictions, the new articles singled out "superstitious sects and secret societies" or religious activities that could adversely affect the health of the people. True to form, the articles gave no more detail. What constitutes a "superstitious sect"? What types of religious activities could negatively affect people's health? Another instance of language left intentionally vague appears in Regulation No. 145, "On the Management of Places for Religious Activities," issued by the State Council and signed by Premier Li Peng, the regulation claims to "protect normal religious activities." But the regulation does not define "normal."

22 Regulation No. 145, "On the Management of Places."

23 Initially, the amendment focused on curtailing emigration restrictions and, in particular, discouraging the Soviet Union from levying prohibitive taxes on Soviet Jews trying to flee.

24 U.S. Congress. Senate. Committee on Foreign Relations. Nomination of Warren M. Christopher to Be Secretary of State. 103rd Cong., 1st sess., January 13, 1993.

25 Legislation calling for the disapproval of China's MFN waiver was introduced in each congressional session since 1980.

26 For a full discussion on this process, see Ka Zeng, *Trade Threats, Trade Wars: Bargaining, Retaliation, and American Coercive Diplomacy* (University of Michigan Press, 2004), 106–10.

27 Bill Clinton, "Executive Order 12850: Conditions for Renewal of Most-Favored-Nation Status for the People's Republic of China in 1994," Federal Register 58, no. 103 (June 1, 1993), Accessed February 19, 2025. www.archives.gov.

28 Anthony Lake, "From Containment to Enlargement," paper presented at the Johns Hopkins School of Advanced International Studies, Washington, DC, September 21, 1993.

29 Lake, "From Containment to Enlargement."

30 Michael J. Green, *By More than Providence: Grand Strategy and American Power in the Asia Pacific Since 1783* (Columbia University Press, 2017), 463.

31 James Mann, *About Face: A History of America's Curious Relationship with China, from Nixon to Clinton* (Vintage, 2000), 295.

32 Green, *By More than Providence*, 463.

33 Wei Jingsheng was arrested for his pro-democracy activities and his manifesto "The Fifth Modernization" in 1979. He was released briefly in 1993 before being rearrested in 1994. He was finally released in 1997 and deported to the United States. His ardent pro-democracy activism continues today.

34 Green, *By More than Providence*, 463.

35 Green, 153.

36 As cited in Zeng, *Trade Threats, Trade Wars*, 108.

37 Scholars have sometimes used the phrases "intensive engagement" or "expansive engagement" to describe the strategic approach. Notably, the Clinton administration was careful not to use the term "constructive engagement" lest it conjure memories from Reagan's foreign policy toward South Africa years earlier. See P.M. Kamath, "US-China Relations Under the Clinton Administration: Comprehensive Engagement or the Cold War Again?," *Strategic Analysis* 22, no. 5 (1998): 691–709.

38 It should be noted here that the terminology was altered in 1998. What was MFN status is now, less controversially, termed "permanent normal trade relations" (PNTR).

39 Bill Clinton, "President Clinton Press Conference on Human Rights in China, 1994 | US-China Institute," May 26, 1994, china.usc.edu.

40 Warren Christopher, "America and the Asia-Pacific Future," address presented at the Asia Society Conference, New York City, May 27, 1994.

41 John Broder and Jim Mann, "Clinton Reverses His Policy, Renews China Trade Status: Commerce: President 'de-Links' Most-Favored-Nation Privilege from Human Rights. He Admits Failure of Earlier Course and Says Broader Strategic Interests Justify Switch," *Los Angeles Times*, May 5, 1994, www.latimes.com.

42 Barton Gellman, "U.S. and China Nearly Came To Blows in 1996," *Washington Post*, June 21, 1998, www.washingtonpost.com.

43 Madeleine Korbel Albright and William Woodward, *The Mighty and the Almighty: Reflections on America, God, and World Affairs* (HarperCollins, 2006).

44 Advisory Committee on Religious Freedom Abroad, "Interim Report to the Secretary of State and to the President of the United States." U.S. State Department, Bureau of Democracy, Human Rights, and Labor, January 23, 1998, 1997-2001. state.gov.

45 Hari M. Osofsky, "Understanding 'Hostage-Diplomacy': The Release of Wei Jingsheng and Wang Dan," *Yale Human Rights & Development Law Journal* 1, no. 1 (1999): 143–47.

46 A. E. Kent, *China, the United Nations, and Human Rights: The Limits of Compliance* (University of Pennsylvania Press, 1999), 247.

47 Bill Clinton and Jiang Zemin, "The President's News Conference with President Jiang Zemin of China in Beijing," June 27, 1998, www.govinfo.gov.

48 Darin W. Carlson, "Understanding Chinese-U.S. Conflict over Freedom of Religion: The Wolf-Specter Freedom from Religious Persecution Acts of 1997 and 1998," *Brigham Young University Law Review*, no. 8 (2001): 46.

49 U.S. State Department, "1999 Annual Report for International Religious Freedom: China," Bureau of Democracy, Human Rights, and Labor, 1999, 1997-2001.state.gov.

50 The official statement also makes note of the Milosevic regime and the Taliban as other severe violators of religious freedom.

51 Robert Seiple, interview with author, 2020. Despite confidence of its religious freedom violations, without access to North Korea, it was impossible to monitor conditions and subsequently, impossible to levy the designation.

52 Information Office of the State Council of the People's Republic of China, "White Paper: Freedom of Religious Belief in China," Information Office of the State Council of the People's Republic of China, October 14, 1997, www.china-un.org.

53 Freedom House, "Report Analyzing Seven Secret Chinese Government Documents on Religious Freedom," February 11, 2002, www.hudson.org.

54 Freedom House, "Report," 10–21.

55 Timothy C. Morgan. "A Tale of China's Two Churches," *Christianity Today*, July 13, 1998, www.christianitytoday.com.

56 The Patriotic Association was founded in 1957 as Mao Zedong expelled the remaining bishops associated with the Vatican. The Patriotic Association was created to supervise and control Catholicism in mainland China.

57 "Bishop James Su Zhimin," Tom Lantos Human Rights Commission, 2015, humanrightscommission.house.gov.

58 Human Rights Watch, "China Tightens Control on Religion," October 21, 1997, Human Rights Watch, www.hrw.org.

59 "Vatican Accuses China of Subjecting Priests to Sexual Blackmail," Religion News Service, January 1, 1999, religionnews.com.

60 Erik Eckholm, "China Is Said to Rearrest Bishop Released for Clinton's '98 Visit," *New York Times*, September 18, 2000, www.nytimes.com.

61 U.S. State Department, "2000 Annual Report for International Religious Freedom: China," Bureau of Democracy, Human Rights, and Labor, September 5, 2000, 1997-2001.state.gov.

62 A potential reason for this toleration is that the threat of foreign influence is lessened (or removed). In contrast, Islam and Christianity are often viewed as mechanisms for nefarious intervention by other world powers.

63 Human Rights Watch, *Dangerous Meditation: China's Campaign Against Falun Gong* (Human Rights Watch, 2002).

64 Associated Press, "Chinese Demand U.N. Meeting After Belgrade Embassy Attacked," May 7, 1999, web.archive.org.

65 Bill Clinton, "Speech on China Trade Bill," paper presented at the Johns Hopkins School of Advanced International Studies, Washington, DC, March 9, 2000.

66 USCIRF, "Accession of China to the WTO," May 3, 2000, www.uscirf.gov.

67 Richard Boucher, "Response to International Religious Freedom Annual Report," U.S. Department of State, May 1, 2000, 1997-2001.state.gov.

68 Ned Graham, "US-China Trade Relations and Its Impact on Religious Activity in the PRC," CATO, July 13, 1999, www.cato.org.

69 Eric Schmitt and Joseph Kahn, "The China Trade Vote: A Clinton Triumph," *New York Times*, May 25, 2000, www.nytimes.com.

70 See Richard Baum, "'Strategic Partners' to 'Strategic Competitors': George W. Bush and the Politics of U.S. China Policy," *Journal of East Asian Studies* 1, no. 2 (2001): 191–220.

71 Condoleezza Rice, "Leadership in a Changing World," C-SPAN, January 28, 2000, www.c-span.org.

72 George W. Bush, "Excerpts of George W. Bush's Speech in Washington State," *New York Times*, May 18, 2000, www.nytimes.com.

73 Embassy of the People's Republic of China in the United States of America, "Bush's Visit to China Reaffirms Constructive Ties," February 28, 2002, www.china-embassy.org.

74 Hanford and Hanford, interview with author.

75 Thomas F. Farr, *World of Faith and Freedom: Why International Religious Liberty Is Vital to American National Security* (Oxford University Press, 2008), 273–74.

76 U.S. State Department, "2001 Annual Report for International Religious Freedom: China," Bureau of Democracy, Human Rights, and Labor," December 2001, 2009-2017.state.gov.

77 Henry Chu, "'Illegal' Houses of Worship Targeted in China Crackdown," *Los Angeles Times*, December 15, 2000, www.latimes.com.

78 Human Rights Watch, "China: White Paper a 'Whitewash,'" 2001, www.hrw.org.

79 Attilio Pisanò, "Human Rights and Social Development in the Chinese White Papers on Human Rights," *Peace Human Rights Governance* 2, no. 11 (2018): 301–30.

80 George W. Bush, "Bush Vows Taiwan Support," *ABC News*, November 10, 2003, abcnews.go.com.

81 "Chinese Jets Intercept U.S. Navy Plane," *ABC News*, January 6, 2006, abcnews.go.com.

82 James Mann, *The Great Rift: Dick Cheney, Colin Powell, and the Broken Friendship That Defined an Era* (Henry Holt, 2020).

83 George W. Bush, *Decision Points* (Crown, 2010), 426.

84 U.S. State Department, "2002 Annual Report for International Religious Freedom: China," October 7, 2002, 2009-2017.state.gov.

85 Freedom House, "Report Analyzing Seven Secret Chinese Government Documents on Religious Freedom," February 11, 2002, www.hudson.org.

86 Congressional Research Service, "President Bush's 2002 State Visits in Asia: Implications," March 11, 2002, crsreports.congress.gov.

87 George W. Bush, "President Bush Speaks at Tsinghua University," presented at Tsinghua University, February 22, 2002, georgewbush-whitehouse.archives.gov.

88 Jiang Zemin and George W. Bush, "Speech Transcript: President Bush Meets with Chinese President Jiang Zemin," February 21, 2002, georgewbush-whitehouse. archives.gov.

89 Michael K. Young, "Administration, Congress, Must Press Religious-Freedom Cases with China," U.S. Commission for International Religious Freedom, January 16, 2002, www.uscirf.gov.

90 John Hanford and Laura Bryant Hanford, interview with author, 2021.

91 Hanford and Hanford, interview with author.

92 Department of State, Office of Electronic Information, Bureau of Public Affairs, "U.S.-China Human Rights Dialogue," December 20, 2002, 2001-2009.state.gov.

93 Department Of State, "U.S.-China Human Rights Dialogue."

94 Michael Dillon, *Xinjiang: China's Muslim Far Northwest* (Routledge, 2003), 82–84.

95 Hanford and Hanford, interview with author.

96 U.S. Commission for International Religious Freedom, "China: Commission Trip to China Postponed," August 8, 2003, www.uscirf.gov.

97 U.S. Commission for International Religious Freedom, "China."

98 U.S. State Department, "2003 Annual Report for International Religious Freedom: China," December 18, 2003, 2009–2017.state.gov/j/drl/rls/irf/2003/23826.htm.

99 Some exceptions are made for the state-sponsored religious schools but even still, the curriculum is developed and administered by the CPC.

100 U.S. State Department, "2004 Annual Report for International Religious Freedom: China," September 15, 2004, 2009–2017.state.gov.

101 Xiaobing Li, *Civil Liberties in China* (ABC-CLIO, 2010), 59–61.

102 Robert B. Zoellick, "Whither China: From Membership to Responsibility?," September 21, 2005, 2001-2009.state.gov.

103 Zoellick, "Whither China."

104 The term "responsible stakeholder" does not translate to Chinese easily. Executive Vice Foreign Minister Dai Bingguo initially questioned why the term strategic partnership could not be used to which Zoellick cited a lack of shared norms as the reasoning. Even still, Dai appreciated the elevated position implied in the speech and welcomed further strategic discussions in Beijing. See Green, *By More than Providence*, 497–98.

105 The "old ways" of thinking included military expansion shrouded in secrecy, unfair trade practices, and support of oil-rich regimes regardless of their "misrule at home or misbehavior abroad." George W. Bush White House, "The National Security Strategy of the United States of America," March 16, 2006, history.defense. gov.

106 George W. Bush, "President Attends Church Service as Gangwashi Church in Beijing, China," November 20, 2005, accessed March 20, 2020, https://georgewbush-whitehouse.archives.

107 Michael J. Gerson, *Heroic Conservatism: Why Republicans Need to Embrace America's Ideals* (HarperOne, 2008).

108 Gerson, *Heroic Conservatism*, 98. Yu Jie was arrested in 2010 and placed on house arrest for over a year before emigrating to the United States with his family in 2012. Li Baiguang died in a military hospital in Nanjing in February 2018 under suspicious circumstances. A prominent human rights attorney, Li was under fire from the Chinese government for his religious activism and his defense of farmers whose land was seized by the government. Wang Yi, a Protestant pastor, was sentenced to nine years in prison in January 2020 for his work with the Early Rain Covenant Church.

109 Andrew Jacobs, "Olympic Official Calls Protests a 'Crisis,'" *New York Times*, April 11, 2008, www.nytimes.com.

110 Sheryl Gay Stolberg, "Bush Meets 5 Dissidents From China Before Games," *New York Times*, July 30, 2008, www.nytimes.com.

111 Bush, *Decision Points*, 429.

112 Zbigniew Brzezinski, "The Group of Two That Could Change the World," *Financial Times*, January 13, 2009, www.FT.com.

113 Embassy of the People's Republic of China in the United States of America, "Wen Jiabao Meets with U.S. President Obama," November 24, 2009, www.china-embassy.org.

114 Embassy of the People's Republic of China, "Wen Jiabao."

115 Green, *By More than Providence*, 534.

116 Hillary Clinton, "America's Pacific Century," *Foreign Policy*, October 11, 2011, foreignpolicy.com.

117 Barack Obama, "Remarks by President Barack Obama at Suntory Hall," November 14, 2009, obamawhitehouse.archives.gov.

118 Tom Donilon, "The United States and the Asia-Pacific in 2013," March 11, 2013 obamawhitehouse.archives.gov.

119 Janine Davidson, "The U.S. 'Pivot to Asia,'" *American Journal of Chinese Studies* 21 (2014): 77–82.

120 Davidson, "U.S. 'Pivot to Asia.'"

121 As cited in Daniel W. Drezner, "Bad Debts: Assessing China's Financial Influence in Great Power Politics," International Security, 2009, www.belfercenter.org.

122 See Drezner, "Bad Debts"; and John Maynard Keynes, "Keynes v. Hayek in China." *Economist*, November 17, 2011, www.economist.com.

123 Ana Palacio, "What's Obama's European Legacy?" Politico, April 21, 2016, www.politico.eu.

124 Green, *By More than Providence*, 521.

125 Sophia Richardson, "Hillary Clinton's Beijing Gaffe," February 26, 2009, Human Rights Watch, www.hrw.org.

126 State Department Official, interview with author, 2020.

127 U.S. State Department, "Annual International Religious Freedom Report: China (Includes Tibet, Hong Kong, Macau)," 2009, 2009–2017.state.gov.

128 Hanford and Hanford, interview with author.

129 U.S. State Department, "Report on International Religious Freedom: China (Tibet, Hong Kong, and Macau)," July 30, 2012, 2009-2017.state.gov.

130 While Cao was released shortly thereafter, he was rearrested and held for another thirteen days when he returned back to the park to preach.

131 U.S. State Department, "2009 Annual International Religious Freedom Report: China (Includes Tibet, Hong Kong, Macau)," October 26, 2009, 2009–2017.state.gov.

132 U.S. State Department, "International Religious Freedom Report: China (Tibet, Hong Kong, Macau)," November 17, 2010, 2009-2017.state.gov.

133 U.S. State Department, "Report on International Religious Freedom: China (Tibet, Hong Kong, and Macau)," July 30, 2012, 2009-2017.state.gov.

134 Korla is the second largest city in Xinjiang Province.

135 U.S. State Department. 2012. 2011 Report on International Religious Freedom: China (Tibet, Hong Kong, and Macau), 2009-2017.state.gov.

136 The genocide was first acknowledged by the Trump administration and was reaffirmed by President Biden.

137 U.S. State Department, "Background Briefing with Senior State Department Officials on Chen Guangcheng," May 2, 2012, www.2009-2017.state.gov/.

138 Green, *By More than Providence*, 534.

139 Mark Memmott, "White House Launching Trade Complaints Against China." NPR, September 17, 2012, www.npr.org.

140 "Report by Chen Quanguo at the Ninth Congress of the Xinjiang Uyghur Autonomous Region of the Communist Party of China," *People's Daily Online*, October 29, 2016, cpc.people.com.cn.

141 Sheena Chestnut Greitens, Myunghee Lee, and Emir Yazici, "Counterterrorism and Preventive Repression: China's Changing Strategy in Xinjiang." *International Security* 44, no. 3 (2020): 9–47.

5. INTERNATIONAL RELIGIOUS FREEDOM IN VIETNAM

1 When Vietnamese converted to Catholicism, many physically extracted themselves from villages to create new Catholic communities. Moreover, the newly converted found some common rituals to be incompatible with their faith, causing rifts and separation between the converted and the unconverted. See Mark W. McLeod, "Nationalism and Religion in Vietnam: Phan Bội Châu and the Catholic Question," *International History Review* 14, no. 4 (1992): 661–80.

2 Bruce Matthews, "The Place of Religion in Vietnam Today," *Buddhist-Christian Studies* 12 (1992): 65–74.

3 Ani Sarkissian, *The Varieties of Religious Repression: Why Governments Restrict Religion* (Oxford University Press, 2015), 79.

4 John Gillespie, "Human Rights as a Larger Loyalty: The Evolution of Religious Freedom in Vietnam," *Harvard Human Rights Journal* 27, no. 1 (2014): 107–49.

5 As cited in Gillespie, "Human Rights as a Larger Loyalty."

6 Reginald E. Reimer, "Christian Responses to Persecution in Communist Vietnam and Laos," in *Under Caesar's Sword: How Christians Respond to Persecution*, ed.

Daniel Philpott and Timothy Samuel Shah (Cambridge University Press, 2018), 298–333.

7   See Reimer, "Christian Responses to Persecution."

8   Bill Clinton, "Remarks on Lifting the Trade Embargo on Vietnam and an Exchange with Reporters," February 3, 1994, www.govinfo.gov.

9   Clinton, "Remarks on Lifting the Trade Embargo."

10 Bill Clinton, 1995. "Remarks Announcing the Normalization of Diplomatic Relations with Vietnam," July 11, 1995, www.govinfo.gov.

11 Minh-Đức T. Lê, "ROVR: Resettlement Opportunities for Vietnamese Returnees or Refoulement of Vietnamese Refugees Note," *Georgetown Immigration Law Journal* 12, no. 1 (1997): 125–44.

12 Stanley O. Roth, "Waiver of Jackson–Vanik for Vietnam," U.S. Senate, July 7, 1998, 1997-2001.state.gov.

13 It was renewed in 1999 and 2000.

14 Robert Seiple and Berkley Center for Religion, Peace, and World Affairs, "A Discussion with Robert A. Seiple, First U.S. Ambassador for International Religious Freedom," October 29, 2009, berkleycenter.georgetown.edu.

15 Robert Seiple and Connie McDougall, "Blessed Are the Peacemakers: An Interview on Reconciliation," November 7, 2001, spu.edu.

16 Seiple also regularly talks about faithfulness and obedience rather than performance. Seiple and Berkley Center, "Discussion."

17 Robert Seiple, interview with author, 2020.

18 Christopher Smith, "The First Annual State Department Report on International Religious Freedom," U.S. House of Representatives, October 6, 1999, 2009–2017. state.gov.

19 Benjamin Gilman, "The First Annual State Department Report on International Religious Freedom," U.S. House of Representatives, October 6, 1999, 2009–2017. state.gov.

20 Chris Smith, "State Department Annual Report on International Religious Freedom for 2000," Hearing before the Subcommittee on International Operations and Human Rights on International Relations, U.S. House of Representatives, 106th Cong., 2nd sess., September 7, 2000, Washington: U.S. Government Printing Office, https://chrissmith.house.gov.

21 Seiple was careful to note USCIRF Commissioner Firuz Kazemzadeh disagreed with USCIRF's recommendation.

22 Seiple, interview with author.

23 Robert Seiple and Elizabeth Taylor, "Brown Vietnam Veterans Oral History Project," May 9, 2011, Brown University Library, University Archives and Manuscripts, Box A.

24 This release included prominent dissidents Thích Quảng Độ, Thích Tuệ Sỹ, Reverend Nguyễn Châu, and Trần Hữu Duyên Đạt, among others.

25 Seiple and Berkley Center, "Discussion."

26 U.S. Congress, Senate Committee on Foreign Relations, Subcommittee on East Asian and Pacific Affairs. Trade and Human Rights: The Future of U.S.-

Vietnamese Relationships. 108th Cong., 2nd sess., February 12, 2004, Washington: U.S. Government Printing Office, 2004. Accessed September 2, 2020, https:// www.congress.gov.

27 Stephen Liston, interview with author, 2020.

28 Vietnam Committee on Human Rights, *Violations of the Rights of Ethnic and Religious Minorities in the Socialist Republic of Vietnam* (International Federation for Human Rights, 2012).

29 John Hanford and Laura Bryant Hanford, interview with author, 2021.

30 John Hanford, "Vietnam Stands at a Crossroads on Religious Freedom," testimony before the Subcommittee on East Asian and Pacific Affairs of the Committee on Foreign Relations, United States Senate, 108th Cong., 2nd sess., February 12, 2004. Accessed February 23, 2023. https://www.govinfo.gov.

31 The ordinance was more friendly to religious practice than the previous Order n°234/S.L. which was passed in 1955 but still prioritized national unity above individual rights.

32 Government Committee for Religious Affairs: Vietnam, "Ordinance on Religion and Belief: Vietnamese Legal Documents on Belief and Religion," June 18, 2004, religion.vn.

33 As cited in Maryann Cusimano Love, "The Vietnam Dilemma," Georgetown University Institute for the Study of Democracy, PEW Case Study Center, Washington, DC, September 2, 2020, www.uscirf.gov.

34 As cited in Love, "Vietnam Dilemma."

35 As cited in Love.

36 Hanford and Hanford, interview with author.

37 Hanford and Hanford.

38 Kenneth Chan, "Vietnam, China, Myanmar Reject U.S. Religious-Freedom Report," *Christian Post*, September 17, 2004, www.christianpost.com.

39 Previous CPCs included Burma, China, Iran, North Korea, and Sudan, all of which had preexisting sanctions that were also used to satisfy IRFA requirements. Saudi Arabia and Eritrea, also designated in 2004, did not.

40 The legal battle within the State Department regarding the binding agreement proved another formidable challenge. In the end, the IRF office agreed to call the binding agreement an "exchange of letters." An official binding agreement would have to go through the same process as U.S. treaties. Needing to move more quickly, Hanford and his team compromised.

41 Love, "Vietnam Dilemma."

42 As cited in Love.

43 Hanford and Hanford, interview with author.

44 Richard Boucher, "Press Statement: United States-Vietnam Religious Freedom Agreement," U.S. Department of State, May 2, 2005, 2001-2009.state.gov.

45 Vietnam released a decree in March 2005 alleviating implementation problems with the Ordinance.

46 Boucher, "Press Statement."

47   U.S. State Department, "2005 Annual Report for International Religious Freedom: Vietnam," November 8, 2005, 2009-2017.state.gov.

48   Nina Shea, "Human Rights in Vietnam," June 20, 2005, www.uscirf.gov.

49   Shea, "Human Rights in Vietnam."

50   As cited in Keith Roshanger, "Religious Freedom Violators Noted," Religion News Service, November 17, 2006, religionnews.com.

51   John Hanford, "On-the-Record Briefing on the Release of the Department of State's Annual Report on International Religious Freedom," September 15, 2006, 2001-2009.state.gov.

52   Hanford and Hanford, interview with author.

53   Hanford and Hanford.

54   Office of the Press Secretary, The White House, "President Bush Attends Church Service in Vietnam," November 19, 2006, georgewbush-whitehouse.archives.gov/.

55   "Vietnam: Sharp Backsliding on Religious Freedom," Human Rights Watch, October 18, 2009, www.hrw.org.

56   Earlier, the Vietnamese government cut off the monastery's access to essential services like water, electricity, and telephone lines in an effort to evict the monks but the efforts were ultimately unsuccessful.

57   "Vietnam."

58   U.S. Commission for International Religious Freedom, "United States Commission on International Religious Freedom: Annual Report 2010," May 2010, www.uscirf.gov.

59   See the congressional hearing debates here: U.S. House of Representatives, "Calling on the State Department to List Vietnam as a Religious Freedom Violator," December 17, 2010, www.govinfo.gov.

60   Hillary Clinton, "Celebration of the 15th Anniversary of United States-Vietnam Relations," presented in Hanoi, Vietnam, July 22, 2010. 2009–2017.state.gov.

61   Other TPP countries included Australia, Brunei, Canada, Chile, Japan, Malaysia, Mexico, New Zealand, Peru, Singapore, and the United States.

62   Hillary Clinton, "America's Pacific Century." *Foreign Policy* 189 (2011): 56–63.

63   Clinton, "America's Pacific Century."

64   Reginald E. Reimer, "Vietnam's Religion Law," World Watch Monitor, May 8, 2015, www.worldwatchmonitor.org.

65   U.S. Congress, House, Committee on Foreign Affairs, Subcommittee on Africa, Global Health, Global Human Rights, and International Organizations, Highlighting Vietnamese Government Human Rights Violations in Advance of the U.S.-Vietnam Dialogue, 113th Cong., 1st sess., April 11, 2013, Washington, U.S. Government Printing Office, accessed February 19, 2025, https://www.govinfo.gov.

66   Embassy of the Socialist Republic of Vietnam in the United States of America. "President Truong Tan Sang Visits the United States in July 2013," Embassy of Vietnam, July 26, 2013, accessed January 3, 2025, https://vietnamembassy-usa.org.

67   Christopher H. Smith, "H.R.1897—Vietnam Human Rights Act of 2013," U.S. House of Representatives) 113th Congress, 1st sess., September 9, 2013, www.congress.gov.

68 Lương Thanh Nghị, "Remarks by Foreign Ministry Spokesman Lương Thanh Nghị on the Passage of the Vietnam Human Rights Act of 2013," August 23, 2013, accessed April 19, 2021, https://presscenter.org.vn/.

69 John Kerry, "Joint Press Availability with Vietnamese Deputy Prime Minister and Foreign Minister Phạm Bình Minh," December 16, 2013 2009–2017.state.gov/.

70 U.N. Human Rights Council, "Report of the Special Rapporteur on Freedom of Religion or Belief, Heiner Bielefeldt: Mission to Viet Nam," January 30, 2015, www.ohchr.org/.

71 Reimer, "Vietnam's Religion Law." 2015.

72 Reimer, "Christian Responses to Persecution."

73 "Remarks by President Obama and President Quang of Vietnam in Joint Press Conference," May 23, 2016, obamawhitehouse.archives.gov.

74 "Remarks by President Obama."

75 See Simon Denyer and David Nakamura, "How a Trump Decision on Trade Became a Setback for Democracy in Vietnam," *Washington Post*, October 11, 2018, www.washingtonpost.com.

76 Love, "Vietnam Dilemma."

6. INTERNATIONAL RELIGIOUS FREEDOM IN THE BIRTHPLACE OF ISLAM

1 Philip Shenon, "Standoff in the Gulf: Out of Saudi View, U.S. Force Allows Religious Their Rites," *New York Times*, December 22, 1990, www.nytimes.com.

2 "HRW: Freedom of Expression and the War: Press and Speech Restrictions in the Gulf and F.B.I. Activity in U.S. Raise First Amendment Issues," Human Rights Watch, January 28, 1991, www.hrw.org.

3 Shenon, "Standoff in the Gulf."

4 William Inboden, "Religious Freedom and National Security," Hoover Institution, Washington Policy Review, October 2012. www.hoover.org.

5 Nilay Saiya, *Weapon of Peace: How Religious Liberty Combats Terrorism* (Cambridge University Press, 2018).

6 Saiya, *Weapon of Peace.*

7 This figure is from December 2020. For most of the period under study, this figure was much higher. Over the last decade, Saudi Arabia has engaged in its "Saudization Plan"—a large-scale attempt to replace foreign workers with Saudi nationals. See "Saudi Arabia: Migrants Held in Inhuman, Degrading Conditions," Human Rights Watch, December 15, 2020, www.hrw.org.

8 Saudi Arabia: Communications and Information Technology Commission (CITC), "General Information on Filtering Service," accessed December 30, 2024, filter.sa/en.

9 As the next section illustrates, IRF Ambassador Bob Seiple was able to make progress on this front.

10 The Sunna involves the words and actions of the prophet Muhammad. The Sunna is comprised of all the hadiths which record specific teachings and actions of Muhammed.

11 In order to maximize control, however, even noncitizens are required to carry resident identification cards, or iqamas, that explicitly list an individual's religious designation. There are only two choices: Muslim and non-Muslim.

12 The efforts are part of the Ministry of Islamic Affairs' (MOIA) "Call and Guidance" centers. These centers employee hundreds of citizens and clerics around the country. When successful conversions occur, the Saudi government readily highlights them.

13 The definition of "sorcery" remains murky, and many are accused of occult practices without sufficient evidence.

14 This holiday commemorates the martyrdom of Muhammed's grandson, Husayn ibn Ali, in 680 CE. This commemoration is important for Shi'a Muslims, as they held Husayn ibn Ali to be the rightful successor. The right to celebrate Ashura is inconsistent, both in geography and time. Freedom to celebrate changed significantly from year to year in other areas with a significant Shi'a minority, including Al-Ahsa, Damman and the southwestern province of Najran.

15 As quoted in Van Gorder, "Christian Reponses to Persecution."

16 Ani Sarkissian, *The Varieties of Religious Repression: Why Governments Restrict Religion* (Oxford University Press, 2015), 87.

17 Sarkissian, *Varieties of Religious Repression*, 87.

18 The first installment, totaling $3.5 million, was received in the summer of 1992. In the weeks following Clinton's inauguration, the University of Arkansas received another $20 million. Tim Weiner, "Clinton and His Ties to the Influential Saudis," *New York Times*, August 23, 1993, www.nytimes.com.

19 In 1993, the intelligence community uncovered an Iraqi plot to assassinate former president George H. W. Bush. The United States responded with a series of targeted missile strikes against Iraq's intelligence headquarters. The following year, Iraq threatened to invade Kuwait, and in 1996, Iraqi forces attacked the Kurdish city of Irbil. In response to Iraq's aggression, the United States increased its footprint in the region, an effort supported by the Saudi regime.

20 Bill Clinton, "Remarks to the Citizens of Pérouges, France," June 27, 1996, www.govinfo.gov.

21 William J. Perry, "Report to the President: The Protection of U.S. Forces Deployed Abroad," September 15, 1996, fas.org.

22 Perry, "Report to the President."

23 Seiple, interview with author.

24 Smith, "First Annual State Department."

25 Farr, *World of Faith and Freedom*, 223–24.

26 Robert Seiple, "Respecting Existential Reality," *Liberty Magazine*, July–August 2014, www.libertymagazine.org.

27 Peter Baker, *Days of Fire* (Anchor, 2014), 197.

28 For the full account, see Bush, *Decision Points*, 401–3.

29 Baker, *Days of Fire*, 198.

30 Condoleezza Rice, *No Higher Honor: A Memoir of My Years in Washington* (Crown, 2011), 141.

31 David Ottaway, "The King and Us: U.S.-Saudi Relations in the Wake of 9/11," *Foreign Affairs* 88, no. 3 (2009): 121–31.

32 William Inboden, "Religious Freedom and National Security," Hoover Institution, June 17, 2020, www.hoover.org.

33 Jim Sciutto, Ryan Browne, and Deirdre Walsh, "Congress Releases Secret '28 Pages' on Alleged Saudi 9/11 Ties," CNN, July 15, 2016, www.cnn.com.

34 U.S. Select Committee on Intelligence and U.S. House Permanent Select Committee on Intelligence, "Joint Inquiry into Intelligence Community Activities Before and After the Terrorist Attacks of September 11, 2001," December 2002, intelligence.house.gov/.

35 Hanford and Hanford, interview with author.

36 See Charles Schumer, S.Con.Res.131, U.S. Senate, July 22, 2004, www.congress.gov.

37 Charles Schumer, "Schumer, Collins Urge State Dept to Add Saudi Arabia to List of Religiously Intolerant Nations," August 8, 2004, www.schumer.senate.gov.

38 Farr, *World of Faith and Freedom*, 224–26.

39 William C. Inboden, "Saudi Arabia's Religious Intolerance and the Execution of Sheikh Nimr al-Nimr," *Foreign Policy*, January 4, 2016, foreignpolicy.com.

40 William Inboden, interview with author, 2021.

41 Inboden, interview with author.

42 For full quotation and the response in Middle East, see Hassan M. Fattah, "Arabs Bristle at Bush's Agenda for Region," *New York Times*, February 25, 2005, www.nytimes.com.

43 Eugenia Relaño Pastor, "The Flawed Implementation of the International Religious Freedom Act of 1998: A European Perspective," *Brigham Young University Law Review*, no. 3 (2005): 711–46.

44 In 2007, after a discussion of the country's basic laws and theocratic system, the annual report notes that "under the Government's interpretation of Islam, there is no legal recognition or protection of religious freedom, which is severely restricted in practice."

45 U.S. Commission for International Religious Freedom, "USCIRF 'Simply Shocked' At State Department's Unwarranted Softening of Assessment of Saudi Arabia in Annual Report on International Religious Freedom," September 15, 2006, www.uscirf.gov.

46 U.S. Commission for International Religious Freedom, "USCIRF 'Simply Shocked.'"

47 A useful comparison here is the Helsinki Commission. Refer to chapter 1 for more detail on the symbolic power of the commission, its inconsistent implementation, and accountability challenges.

48 These deaths included Ahmad al-Bulawi, a fifty-year-old driver who was detained for having an unrelated female in his car. Allegedly, al-Bulawi died of a heart attack, but a trial ensued in the years following.

49 The mutawwa'in beat to death Suleiman al-Huraisi, a twenty-eight-year-old accused of making and selling alcohol, at CPVPV offices. One official went to trial for his role in killing al-Huraisi after protests from friends and family members.

50 Farr, *World of Faith and Freedom*, 241.

51 Another step forward occurred in 2007, when the Saudi government made special provisions to ensure that the mutawwa'in had access to radio equipment so that they could rightfully involve the police, when necessary, instead of taking matters into their own hands.

52 An ongoing challenge that affected IRF policy in all three administrations under study was the reality that the Saudi people were often more intolerant than the government. Thus, changes at the top did not always translate to improved conditions for believers on the ground.

53 This allowed for Shi'a and Ismailis to improve their education facilities, roads, and dams.

54 Somewhat ironically, it couldn't happen in Saudi Arabia because of the religious pushback against engaging with non-Muslims.

55 Juan Medina Reuters, "Saudi King Opens Interfaith Conference in Spain," MSNBC, July 16, 2008, www.nbcnews.com; U.N. General Assembly, "Interfaith Initiatives Can Ensure Rich Cultural Diversity Made World More Secure, Not Less, Secretary-General Tells Assembly Debate on Culture of Peace," November 12, 2008, www.un.org.

56 U.S. State Department. 2010. "International Religious Freedom Report 2010: Saudi Arabia," November 17, 2010, 2009–2017.state.gov.

57 "International Religious Freedom Report 2010: Saudi Arabia."

58 "International Religious Freedom Report 2010: Saudi Arabia."

59 "International Religious Freedom Report 2010: Saudi Arabia."

60 U.S. State Department, "International Religious Freedom Report 2011: Saudi Arabia," July 30, 2012, 2009-2017.state.gov.

61 "International Religious Freedom Report 2011: Saudi Arabia."

62 Barack Obama, "Remarks by the President at Cairo University," June 4, 2009, obamawhitehouse.archives.gov.

63 Caryle Murphy, "House at War: Saudi's Struggle to Reclaim Islam," The World from PRX, June 24, 2010, www.pri.org.

64 As cited in Murphy, "House at War."

65 This conference, while small in scale, speaks to one of the "seeds of freedom" in Islam as identified by political scientist Daniel Philpott. He argues, "The point is not to demand that the Qur'an contain the content of modern human rights conventions. None of the world religions' holy books could meet such a standard. It is rather to show what sorts of developments are needed if this seed is to grow into the full human right of religious freedom." See Daniel Philpott, *Religious Freedom in Islam: The Fate of a Universal Human Right in the Muslim World Today* (Oxford University Press, 2019).

66 Halim Rane and Sumra Salem, "Social Media, Social Movements, and the Diffusion of Ideas in the Arab Uprisings," *Journal of International Communication* 18, no. 1 (2012): 97–111.

67 Toby Matthiesen, "A 'Saudi Spring?': The Shi'a Protest Movement in the Eastern Province 2011–2012," *Middle East Journal* 66, no. 4 (2012): 628–59.

68 Barack Obama, "Remarks by the President on the Middle East and North Africa," The White House: Office of the Press Secretary, May 19, 2011, obamawhitehouse. archives.gov.

69 Amnesty International, "Saudi Arabia: New Terrorism Law Is Latest Tool to Crush Peaceful Expression," February 3, 2014, www.amnesty.org.

70 Kyle Ballard, interview with author, 2020.

71 "Saudi to Reassess Relations with US: Report," Al Jazeera, October 23, 2013, www. aljazeera.com.

72 "Saudi Arabia Turns Down UN Security Council Seat," BBC News, October 18, 2013, bbc.com.

73 U.S. Commission for International Religious Freedom, "Raif Badawi," March 15, 2017, www.uscirf.gov.

74 Ian Black, "A Look at the Writings of Saudi Blogger Raif Badawi—Sentenced to 1,000 Lashes," *Guardian*, January 14, 2015, www.theguardian.com.

75 Conscious of their reputation in the international community, several interviewees attributed Saudi Arabia's abolition of flogging in April 2020 to the Badawi case. Still, as of September 2020, Badawi remains in prison. He is scheduled to be released in 2022, but he will be unable to leave Saudi Arabia for ten years after his release.

76 Dan Roberts and Jason Burke, "Obama Forced to Defend Saudi Arabia Cosiness After India Tolerance Speech," *Guardian*, January 27, 2015, www.theguardian.com.

77 Jeremy Diamond, "Obama Defends Saudi Relationship: 'Sometimes We Have to Balance,'" CNN, January 27, 2015, www.cnn.com.

78 Barack Obama, "Obama at Summit on Countering Violent Extremism," February 19. 2015, no.usembassy.gov.

79 Sarah Margon, "Giving Up the High Ground—America's Retreat on Human Rights," Human Rights Watch, March–April 2018, www.hrw.org.

80 Missy Ryan, "Top Obama-Era Officials Urge Immediate End to U.S. Involvement in Yemen War," *Washington Post*, November 11, 2018, www.washingtonpost.com.

81 Kyle Ballard, interview with author, July 15, 2020.

CONCLUSION

1 Senior State Department Official, interview with author, 2020.

2 See Jason Klocek and Scott Bledsoe, "Global Trends and Challenges to Protecting and Promoting Freedom of Religion or Belief," United States Institute of Peace, June 21, 2022, www.usip.org; and Saiya, *Weapon of Peace*.

3 Jayson Casper, "Will International Religious Freedom Survive the Trump Administration?," *Christianity Today*, 2020, www.christianitytoday.com.

4 Kori Schake, "Religious Bias Is Distorting American Foreign Policy," *Atlantic*, 2017, www.theatlantic.com.

5 As cited in Casper, "Will International Religious Freedom Survive?"

INDEX

Page numbers in italics indicate Photos

ABOUT THE AUTHOR

ASHLYN W. HAND is a Postdoctoral Fellow at the Center for Presidential History at Southern Methodist University. Her research focuses on U.S. foreign policy and human rights. She received her PhD from the LBJ School of Public Affairs at the University of Texas at Austin. Her work has been featured in *Journal of Church and State, Journal of Conflict Resolution,* and *Foreign Policy.*